Praise for
"BLACK PEOPLE ARE MY BUSINESS"

"Lewis intervenes by re-establishing the boundaries and intergenerational building blocks of the Black Arts Movement by situating Bambara as a midwife for the creative legacy of the moment. He also reorients his readers to Bambara's role as foremother to some of the most acclaimed and well-read works by black women. This is essential for recognizing and placing Bambara within a more sustained discourse on the Black Arts Movement and Black women's evolution from that moment into their own creative renaissance. A necessary and overdue study."

—Kameelah L. Martin, professor of African American
studies and English, College of Charleston

"Lewis captures the significance of one of the most important figures in black and women's liberation struggles of the 60s and 70s in the U.S. Though Bambara has been undervalued as a revolutionary writer/activist/theorist of the Black Arts Movement, Lewis articulates in new ways, through an examination of her short stories and novels, the nature of her Black nationalist/feminist commitments and her 'spiritual wholeness aesthetic.' Lewis also underscores how Bambara practices 'nation building in her art' in unapologetic, creative, and brilliant ways."

—Beverly Guy-Sheftall is founding director of the Women's Research
and Resource Center and Anna Julia Cooper Professor of
Women's Studies at Spelman College

"Lewis does a superb job of defending a unique and overdue analysis of Toni Cade Bambara's fiction. The technique of viewing Bambara's fiction through the lens of the spiritual wholeness aesthetic with its most frequent source in the Black Aesthetic Movement moves readers' attention from the dominant paradigm of viewing Bambara's fiction from a heavily womanist perspective to an interrogation of how Bambara's spiritual, political aesthetic reflects an interweaving of self and ethnic identity, community engagement and responsibility, a balancing of black male and black female identity and of how self-awareness or lack of it influences interactions within and outside the black community."

—Joyce A. Joyce, professor of English, Temple University

"*Black People Are My Business*' offers an insightful and empathetic analysis of Bambara's complete corpus—her popular short stories, her novels, and her nonfiction prose. Thabiti Lewis is an astute reader who illuminates the many ways in which Bambara was and is an indispensable writer."

—Cheryl A. Wall, Zora Neale Hurston
Professor of English, Rutgers University

"There can't be enough good books on Toni Cade Bambara, so Thabiti Lewis's *Black People Are My Business*' is a real gift. His close readings of Bambara's fiction adds an important layer to the conversation about Bambara and, as importantly, about reading/writing as a practice of liberation in African American literary studies."

—Dana Williams, professor of African
American literature, Howard University

"Black People
Are My Business"

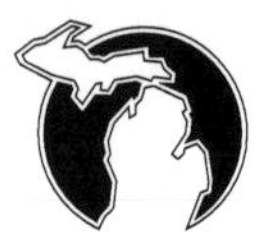

African American Life Series

A complete listing of the books in this series can
be found online at wsupress.wayne.edu

Series Editor

Melba Joyce Boyd
Department of Africana Studies, Wayne State University

"Black People Are My Business"

Toni Cade Bambara's Practices of Liberation

Thabiti Lewis

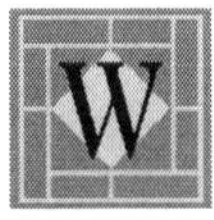

WAYNE STATE UNIVERSITY PRESS

DETROIT

ISBN 978-0-8143-4429-3 (paperback); ISBN 978-0-8143-4607-5 (case); ISBN 978-0-8143-4431-6 (ebook)

Library of Congress Control Number: 2020935129

Published with support from the Arthur L. Johnson Fund for African American Studies.

Wayne State University Press
Leonard N. Simons Building
4809 Woodward Avenue
Detroit, Michigan 48201-1309

Visit us online at wsupress.wayne.edu

Contents

Acknowledgments

No book comes to fruition without the help, input, and support of many entities. This book is no different. *"Black People Are My Business"* has its genesis in my dissertation work at Saint Louis University under the direction and support of Joyce Uraizee, Don Matthews, and Stephen Casmier. It was an important topic then and remains important. They provided the encouragement and space to explore Bambara and Black culture, feminism, and nationalism in ways that led to the final product here before the reader. I also want to thank the many people who, at different points over the past four or five years, either gave me lodging in their home, challenged my conceptual framework, or helped to tease out ideas with me—some of them did all three things. It is only fitting that a study of Bambara would be published by Wayne State University Press, because she served on one of the early editorial boards of the African American Life Series. It is an honor, and I honor her spirit and intellectual legacy with this book.

Earlier I mentioned that many people provided support in multiple ways. Over the years I have traveled to Atlanta, where my brother, Lawrence Jackson, often opened his home to me when I visited the Spelman and Emory archives to work on the book. During those trips Larry often modeled for me discipline and commitment. Each morning, during a visit, he would cut short any conversation by 9 a.m. and tell me to have a productive workday, and at the end of the day we would meet back at his house to run and go to dinner. I am also grateful to my good friend Dana Williams who ventured out to the Pacific Northwest to discuss the project and also made space for me at her home and linked me up with Eleanor Traylor, who blessed me with insights into Bambara, her own genius, no-nonsense perspectives, and even gave me lodging.

My good friend and mentor Donald Matthews never left my side. Although we long ago finished the dissertation, he took me to the Las Vegas desert to reconstruct a couple of key chapters for the book and, for that, I am forever grateful. I am equally appreciative of John and Maria Jackson who offered the quiet of their home at one point. I would be remiss if I did not acknowledge my cousin who suggested the idea of writing about Bambara as a dissertation topic and Marie-Paule, Carolyn, and Stephanie who helped juggle childcare in the early days of parenting so I could write.

In addition, I am appreciative of the extensive intellectual community that helped shape this text, allowing me to share ideas at key moments. Among those who aided me in finding the right words to describe what it is I think Bambara is doing are people such as Dana and Don, Jerry Ward Jr., Davarian Baldwin (my "brother from another" and king of frameworks), Kalamu Ya Salaam, Linda Holmes, Kameelah Martin (African spirituality guru), Scot Brown, Pavithra Narayanan (who encouraged me to speed things up), Lisa Alexander, Beauty Bragg, Joyce Ann Joyce, Bakari Kitwana (thirty-three years and counting), Haki Madhubuti, Eugene Redmond, and Tony Bolden (who, without knowing it, pushed me in the right direction and gave me the idea for one of my chapters). I think Bambara would love the village that has supported the journey of this book, because she was known to open her home to folk or lodge with folk to work on projects.

I also want to thank other supporters such as the Washington State University ADVANCE Grant, the Timeul Black Fellowship, Black Metropolis Fellowship, the Washington State University English

Department Buchanan Summer Grant, and the Emory University Marble library short-term fellowship. A very special thanks to Melba Boyd for her immense support of this project and for convincing me to bring the book to the African American Life Series. I want to thank Sandra Judd for her editorial assistance and also Annie Martin. Finally, I want to thank my biggest supporters: my daughters Safina Theard-Lewis and Ayodele Theard-Lewis and my wonderful wife, Angele Theard, all of whom have endured my fluctuating mood and uselessness at different points during the writing process.

INTRODUCTION

Playing it safe doesn't make you safe; being quiet doesn't make you safe. Trying to play it safe makes you crazy.

Toni Cade Bambara

Black people are my business, sugar.

Toni Cade Bambara

In 1974, thirty-five-year-old Toni Cade Bambara decided to walk away from what many of her peers would have killed for: a tenured professorship at Rutgers University (Livingston College). Sidestepping "friends ready to commit [her]" to a mental institution (Holmes 2014, 59), Bambara packed her four-year-old daughter, Karma, and her household belongings and moved to Atlanta, where she did not even have a definite job. Many were baffled why Bambara chose to abandon the certainty of a tenured job where she was beloved by faculty (they elected her speaker of the faculty chamber) and had become an advisor and mentor to countless students to live in Atlanta where employment was uncertain. One answer was that Bambara was governed by a different set of principles that impacted her artistic and life choices—she was not, in her own words, a "playing it safe" type of person. Another answer was that she had lost faith that mainstream educational institutions could be transformed in any radical way.[1] However, as Bambara herself contends, her

1

relocation to Atlanta was mostly fueled by her need to be "committed" to writing, which she saw as a legitimate way to practice liberation.[2] Her writing is one aspect of what I am calling a spiritual wholeness aesthetic. This aesthetic comes out of her practices of liberation that entail family, faith, feeling, and freedom. Indeed, she had a unique idea about liberation and the manifestation of liberation that I term spiritual wholeness, which can be seen in her life, her writing, and her films. At this point her immense impact has not been fully acknowledged. Her philosophy and aesthetic was tied to a lived social and political context that allowed her to reorient feminism and Black Nationalism. She embraced the raw realness of Black people and Black culture to construct new narrative possibilities (spiritual wholeness) in Black literature that are pluralistic, complex, and rich.[3]

In making this commitment she "packed up the kid and the household [goods] and moved to Atlanta . . . and sat down and . . . wrote."[4] In Atlanta Bambara contributed to the growth of the southern Black Arts Movement and she also held out faint hope that historically Black colleges and universities (HBCU) might be different from mainstream institutions.[5] Bambara, who understood the power of art and culture, set her sights on Atlanta's Cultural Arts Center, where, as writer in residence, she executed what I will call the yeowoman's work of making the community the base of her radical educational cultural work of liberation. She completed one collection of fiction and two novels during her Atlanta residency.

Toni Cade Bambara is an important and understudied figure of the Black Arts/Black aesthetic/Black feminist moment.[6] She was unafraid to take unpopular paths in her life or art, and there is nothing "safe" about being a self-described writer, feminist, and cultural worker. Bambara's aversion to playing it safe produced space for her to create art that truly personified the ideals of Black Nationalism and feminism. In fact, one cannot discuss Bambara separate from the Black Arts Movement (BAM). She is among the early activists whose fiction should be viewed as a principal voice in organizing and cultural work that sought to be holistic, to unify men and women, and to advocate doing *people work* to achieve liberation. Bambara's art privileges practices that integrated the ideals of community, family, gender, and transnationalism that were the foundation of the traditional conception of Black Studies. To be sure, her lived social and political art reflected these ideals, which placed her on the cutting edge of Black life. Bambara's art and life personified what Black intellectualism and Black studies were conceived to do: give voice to the people and change the quality of life in Black communities. Deeper examination of her work is necessary as more scholars begin to reassess the value of this era.[7] This study seeks to illuminate this pioneering and brilliant writer's unique ideas about liberation. Indeed, *"Black People Are My Business": Toni Cade Bambara's Practices of Liberation* explores Bambara's articulation in her fiction of a transformative impulse that intersects race, gender, and the nature of Black women's roles in Black communities.[8] My analysis of Bambara's fiction delineates her holistic discourse that successfully negotiates and reorients and dissolves the dichotomy between earlier feminist and Black Nationalist aesthetics.[9] Another impetus of this study is to examine how her art embodies a revolutionary feminist approach and early transnational perspective that extended Black aesthetic and Black feminist tradition differently and in some ways more effectively than many of her contemporaries did. Her art practices the creation of alternative communities where liberation is possible through a focus on acts of revolution that produce energy from family, community, faith, feeling, and Black culture.

There has been a resurgence of interest in the BAM period and the writings of some of its authors. A handful of books have recently emerged on the Black Arts Movement and its importance, including *SOS–Calling All Black People: A BAM Reader* (Bracey, Sanchez, and Smethurst 2014); *New Thoughts on the Black Arts Movement* (Collins and Crawford 2006); *Renegade Poetics: Black Aesthetics and Formal Innovation in African American Poetry* (Shockley 2011); *The Black Arts Movement: Literary Nationalism in the 1960s and 1970s* (Smethurst

2005); *The Black Arts Enterprise and the Production of African American Poetry* (Ramsby 2011); *Writers of the Black Chicago Renaissance*; and *Black Arts West*. To date there have been several books, such as my own *Conversations with Toni Cade Bambara* (2012), Janet Holmes and Cheryl Wall's *Savoring the Salt: The Legacy of Toni Cade Bambara* (2008), and, of course, Janet Holmes's wonderful biography *A Joyous Revolt: Toni Cade Bambara, Writer and Activist* (2014), that are useful and necessary to Bambara studies. This resurgence along with recent articles about Bambara is an encouraging sign that her influence is growing. But no scholar has written a book that examines Bambara's unique approach and important literary contribution to one of the most important moments in American literature. Several good journal articles have emerged in the last decade or so, however none of these works engage her ethos as I have here.[10] I am intrigued with her unique ethos, which cleared space for the innovations that became central to Black women's fiction of the 1980s and 1990s. While useful for the Bambara critical canon, many studies of Bambara, especially most early essays and some recent studies, limit their focus to adults betraying children, women in conflict with men, the civil rights struggle and struggles with capitalism, or the role of dialect representation without paying closer attention to the role of dialect as a product of Black aesthetic.

However, there are several critics that capture the essence of what Bambara is doing. For example, Joyce A. Joyce's essay "Toni Cade Bambara's *Those Bones Are Not My Child* as a Model for Black Studies" (2006) correctly lauds Bambara's last novel as a continuum of the material value of the African American experience because it captures the psychological dynamics and phobias of Atlanta's Black community and a female character. Also, Kelly Wagner (2016) correctly examines the importance of giving testimony to racialized violence and Sheila Smith-McKoy (2011) offers a good discussion of the ontology of African American religious tradition in the African diaspora. Moreover, Salamishah Tillet's (2015) essay sheds important light on the cultural worker in twenty-first-century cultural production, and Courtney Thorsson's important study *Women's Work* (2014) does a fine job of drawing attention to Bambara's ideas in *The Black Woman* and situates Black women as cultural workers and doing women's work (although Bambara might argue she is doing *people* work and not solely women's work). While I broach similar issues, my argument is that Bambara's ability to position women doing the cultural work—leading or in collaboration with men—is an essential practice for successful Black nation-building. This is a shift from the dominant paradigm of viewing Bambara's fiction from a heavily womanist perspective. My examination of Bambara's fiction using spiritual wholeness reflects an interweaving of self and ethnic identity, politics, community engagement, and responsibility, with the impetus of balancing Black male and female identity influences and interactions within and outside the community. Thus, I situate Bambara's nationalist/feminist/Marxist/spiritualist liberation discourse in her fiction within an uncompromising Black aesthetic tradition and Bambara in a pivotal place as a precursor.

Bambara was at once, in her own words, a feminist, nationalist, and Marxist cultural worker. She was distinctive among her peers because she also premised a racial discourse of nationalism that negotiated ideological and formal priorities of Black feminism and Marxism. Bambara was uniquely committed to deep introspection, building self, and freeing self, community, and nation.[11] Her contemporaries such as Alice Walker (*Meridian* [1976]), Toni Morrison (*The Bluest Eye* [1970] and *Sula* [1973]), Gloria Naylor (*Mama Day* [1982]), Paule Marshall (*Praisesong for the Widow* [1983]), and Ntozake Shange (*Sassafrass, Cypress & Indigo* [1982]) also wrote fiction that tackled feminism, oppression, and liberation.[12] Also, Bambara's fiction is representative of the second wave 1970s BAM aesthetics. These authors were involved in self-critiques that energized the BAM focus on the future and were conscious about avoiding limbo and stasis and concentrated on Black consciousness raising. However, Bambara's nationalist/feminist/Marxist discourse practiced a distinctive notion of "nation." Not only is the notion of future often symbolized by the overwhelming presence of youth in her fiction but as a Black feminist she displayed solidarity around womanhood while rejecting an anti-male ideology that excluded Black men. She chose a reformist and coalitional ethos that produced a revolutionary Black praxis. In this way her liberation impulse privileged gathering and organizing the people to discover their internal consciousness to unite with one another to create a better nation.

Bambara's fiction employed a practiced cultural nationalism that addressed an expanded notion of nation during the 1970s and 1980s. Her iteration of liberation practiced an impulse that privileged faith in self, self-knowledge, family, feeling, and organizing community to create a humanist discourse. These practices comprise a discourse of spiritually holistic Black Nationalism, Marxism, and feminism for Black nation freedom that I term "spiritual wholeness." I am reading her work in conversation with the liberation impulse of her life and the Black aesthetic movement in order to understand how she used writing consciously in dialogue with the BAM to present feminist critiques that extended the BAM's lofty goals of creativity and expression.[13] Bambara's writing represents transformative, activist, and interventionist impulses. Furthermore, she used writing to enlarge and redirect discourses related to Black people. Viewed in this way, the ethos of her discourse expands the possibilities of Black aesthetics. Thus practices of liberation in her texts map the social struggle to envision alternative communities that do the work of liberation in myriad ways that produce spiritual wholeness. The spiritual wholeness aesthetic can be viewed as a practice of humanism that empowers the liberation impulse of her fiction to negotiate and enlighten the feminist, Black Nationalist, and Black aesthetic ethos of the 1960s to the early 1980s.[14]

A closer examination of Bambara's fiction reveals that it heeds and "practices" Larry Neal's call in *Black Fire* (Baraka and Neal, 1968) for the "New Breed" that is capable of defining "itself through actions, be they artistic or political."[15] She is consistently artistic and political. Toni Morrison remarked that Bambara's work is "absolutely crucial to twentieth century literature as it unveiled a voice and consciousness that has resonated throughout African American literature of the latter half of the twentieth century and continues today."[16] Thus, one goal of this study is to reposition Bambara through the lens of a spiritual wholeness aesthetic. Morrison is correct that Bambara was a leading second-wave BAM artist capable of complicating her art with a unique combination of women's work and Black aesthetic to produce some of the most evolved ideals and aspirations of BAM and Black feminism. She is indeed among the most influential thinkers, activists, and creative writers to emerge during the late 1960s and 1970s.

However, Bambara was not the only Black female writer trying to negotiate these dynamics. Several Black women fiction writers of the 1960s and 1970s displayed a multidimensional feminist thrust that was prominently influenced by Black aesthetic interest in community and nation. While not often studied, Bambara was among a select contingency of Black women writers whose approach to nation is practiced and multifocal. Unlike her contemporaries Bambara's feminism and liberation impulse privilege spiritual wholeness that extends to all the people. Beginning with her trailblazing anthology *The Black Woman* (1970) and her early collections of short fiction *Gorilla, My Love* (1972) and *The Sea Birds Are Still Alive* (1977) and her novel *The Salt Eaters* (1980a), the motif of practicing family, faith, feeling, and freedom equate to a spiritual wholeness aesthetic that reorients Black feminism and the Black Nationalist aesthetic. Bambara's nationalist/feminist/ liberation discourse in her fiction posits social workers and activists in stories like "The Lesson," "Gorilla, My Love," "The Apprentice," "The Organizer's Wife," and "The Seabirds," and her novels *The Salt Eaters* (1980a) and *Those Bones Are Not My Child* (1999) undertaking practices of liberation.

A close examination of her fiction reveals BAM-influenced ideals adroitly theorized by thinkers such as James T. Stewart ("The Development of the Black Revolutionary Artist"), Addison Gayle Jr., Amiri Baraka, and Larry Neal ("And Shine Swam On") in *Black Fire* (Baraka and Neal, 1968). The Black aesthetic freed Black artists from the proscriptive trap that conformed to particular definitions of other men that were irrelevant to Black artists' life and art. It allowed writers of the Black aesthetic to create outside of the White-imposed social and cultural symbols of Black inferiority and correct concepts of Black art and culture as inferior. Bambara expands this by including in all her fiction the spiritual wholeness motif of family, faith, feeling, and freedom. Indeed, Bambara builds a unique liberation impulse that artfully reflects a spiritual wholeness ethos that embraces Black feminism, the Black aesthetic, and elements of Marxism. She deploys a readable Black Nationalist, Black sociological, and psychological discourse that does not betray or contradict a feminist discourse but rather creates space for Black femininity to rise strong and proud to lead the Black community against oppressors. The strongest examples of this come across in stories like "Hammer Man" (*Gorilla, My Love*), "The Organizer's Wife" (*The Sea Birds Are Still Alive*), and "The Apprentice"[17] (*The Sea Birds Are Still Alive*).

Few artists of the 1960s and 1970s balance a revolutionary impulse that negotiates gender with the same adroit dialectics that Bambara consistently exhibited. While critics such as Joyce A. Joyce and Eleanor Traylor offer similar analyses, Margo Crawford's analysis aligns even closer to my reading of Bambara. Crawford explains that the end of the 1960s can be characterized as Black Post-Blackness. She posits that conceptions of revolution during this moment had a circular, unfinished nature that would exist until the finished, stable nature of global White supremacy was eradicated. I tend to agree with Crawford's analysis, which explains the open nature of the liberation impulse in much of Bambara's fiction. Thus, I am reading Bambara as among the most evolved representations of second-wave BAM liberation impulse. Indeed, what makes her unique is her ability to posit her work in a self-sufficient individuality that applies to women and men and youth in a manner that practices a complex and complicated communal sensibility whereby characters critique self, men, or women without boundaries. Her fiction is also distinctive because of its commitment to a multidimensional or multifocal political response. What also emerges from this is a balance of African cosmology that divulges the complexity and diversity of Blackness and community. Such practices of liberation emphasize the imperative of freedom for the outer nation if the self or inner nation expects to be spiritually whole. Thus the iteration of nation and Black aesthetic impulse that resonates in Bambara's fiction positioned Black struggle, women's struggle, and resistance perpetually in polyrhythmic sync. Therefore, the spiritual wholeness aesthetic that I articulate here negotiates and unites Black femininity and the ethos and spirit of Black cultural nationalism in a manner that differs from that of most critics. Bambara's fiction exposes the capacity for experimentation for not just Black women's literature but Black literature in general.

During an interview with Beverly Guy-Sheftall, Bambara unabashedly described herself as a feminist, "socialist," pan-Africanist, "black Nationalist," and cultural worker.[18] This made her unique among her peers and compelled her "business" to be women's and the people's struggle for liberation. The practices that make spiritual wholeness and the people's liberation viable are central to the business of crafting fiction that negotiates a feminist lens that revises without compromising or rejecting cultural nationalism. Bambara's fiction practices introspection, building self, community, and nation in the same way that Bambara did in her own life. Thus a constant thrust in her fiction is providing the people with interior political, social, and spiritual truths.

Another constant in Bambara's fiction is a liberation impulse that infuses a robust Black feminist thrust rooted in BAM principles such as change, dialectical ontology, fluidity of movement, and transcending double consciousness. I read her fiction as an intersectional blueprint for challenging patriarchy, eliminating gender hegemony, and building spiritually whole communities. She effectively practices what Larry Neal (who also happened to be her colleague at City College) theorized about the Black aesthetic in his anthology *Black Fire*

(Baraka and Neal, 1968).[19] As a result, her fiction embodies what Larry Neal terms: "literature primarily directed at the consciences of [all] black people" (Baraka and Neal 1968, 647–48). BAM principles and the spiritual wholeness aesthetic collaborate to reach high ideological aspirations and are exemplified in several of the stories in *The Sea Birds Are Still Alive (1977)*. Stories like "Xmas Eve at Johnson's Drug Store," "The Apprentice," and "The Organizer's Wife" are wonderful examples of this.[20] Her novel *Those Bones Are Not My Child* (1999) is also imbued with this impulse, which is capacious and at times mines the richness and power of spirituals to give voice to Black people partaking in practices of liberation that comprise spiritual wholeness.

Because her fiction also seeks to understand and calm the nature of gendered and generational fissures, and because it advocated that wrestling with internal problems was essential to Black people's quest for liberation, *"Black People Are My Business"* inspects Bambara's legacy as a pioneering voice for contemporary feminist struggles and the Black struggle for freedom. Bambara's art is in the tradition of abolitionist Maria Stewart, who deftly negotiated Christianity, Black Nationalism, and feminism. Indeed, this impulse gives her fiction its own distinct imprint of nation and liberation for the people. In this way her *business* is listening to the people in order to discern their needs and desires and gathering this information to help organize them to discover their internal consciousness and help them to unite with one another to create a better nation. Her legacy does not reflect the enormity of her literary contributions; not enough critics pay homage to how innovatively Bambara led the charge in creating new ways of imagining liberation textually or to the fact that her fiction was an adroit extension of BAM ideals that became central to negotiations of feminism and nationalism in women's fiction of the 1970s, 1980s, and beyond.

In addition, her fiction is infused with West African–based religions, which creates space for the spontaneous spiritual ethos that simultaneously embraces, expands, and negotiates with more ease than her contemporaries Black aesthetic and Black feminist tensions around power, structure and order, and hierarchy. Bambara privileges ancestors, and as Donald Matthews explains in *Honoring the Ancestors*, spirituals are "the strength and presence of the ancestors—stand[ing] ready to provide new generations of black Americans hope in the midst of despair" (1998, 64). Drawing on the paramount status of ancestors, Bambara's fiction builds on the spiritual search begun during the Black aesthetic movement that sought "a new spiritual quality, or recapture of an old one, lost, buried deep in our African past."[21] Her iteration honors spiritual values, mining the spirituals and the feminine without separating from males, but uses the feminine to entrench the struggle of the people for freedom. Bambara's Black aesthetic criterion includes women, the spirituals, and a direct relationship with the lives of African American people.

The initial evidence that her perspective and approach were unique can be found in her anthology of feminist resistance and agency, *The Black Woman* (1970). The ideas that surfaced in her anthology and first collection of fiction, *Gorilla, My Love* (1972), take full bloom in her second collection of short stories, *The Sea Birds Are Still Alive* (1977) and include a focus on transnational resistance. Her first novel, *The Salt Eaters* (1980a), which is about individual and communal civil rights recovery, and her posthumous novel, *Those Bones Are Not My Child* (1999), about the post–civil rights failures to stay true to the promise, confirm a unique liberation impulse that conjures gendered, individual, and community renewal that is holistic. Considered collectively, her fiction's characters represent a chorus of voices connected to the eradication of global White supremacy via family, African spirituality, and faith in freedom through practices of social work, organizing, and nation building. Bambara is mindful of the historical power of spirituals and African spirituality as a source of strength and rebellion. Moreover, not only do her impulse practices invite the reader to see cross-gender alliances but she also invokes cross-generational and, at times, transnational cross-ethnic alliances. This comes across clearly in *The Sea Birds Are Still Alive* (1977) and *The Salt Eaters* (1980a). Bambara's fiction reimagines strategies for revolution and liberation through a prism that deftly negotiates individual and community concerns. Her work as an artist is a practice of liberation because her conjuring bridges worlds where praxis and theory work together.

To be sure, Bambara's work as an artist conjures a unique ethos that produces fiction that promises the transformative process that powers sustained liberation. My close reading of her fiction situates Bambara's genius as an agent of change whose focus is building individual consciousness, then community consciousness one story at a time. The ethos in her stories is a manifestation of her work in Black studies and what she theorized in *The Black Woman*. Her insistence on producing art that practiced what she describes as: "an embrace of community and a hardheaded attempt to get basic with each other" (1) carved a framework that met and exceeded the radically imagined alternative spaces articulated by several Black aesthetic theorists.

I have chosen *"Black People Are My Business"* as the title of this book because these are Bambara's words. She recounts uttering these words to her daughter in her essay "Deep Sightings and Rescue Missions" in response to her daughter reprimanding her for being a busy body interfering in the business of members of the Black community. In response to her daughter she retorts: "Black people are my business, sugar." Hence the title of this book is derived from Bambara's stated business and the liberation impulse of the 1960s and 1970s Black literature. These core ideas drove the ethos of Bambara's fiction. The *people* are key to the spiritual wholeness aesthetic in her fiction. Bambara embraced and extended the liberation thrust of this era with her own unique twist that does not view Black Nationalism and feminism as in opposition. Indeed, the *people* are the focus of her work, and to better comprehend the relationship between her writing practices and these ideas I suggest her fiction be read through a spiritual wholeness lens. The characters in her fiction represent the people and are for the people. Bambara's fiction models the *people* engaged in aspects of family, faith, feeling, and freedom practices en route to spiritual wholeness. Her stories are lessons populated with regular people: teachers, organizers, wives, husbands, mothers, fathers, little girls, crazy men and boys, preachers, church women, domestic laborers, jazz and bluesmen, and social workers engaging in practices of liberation, always practicing some act of liberation. Undeniably, her *business* is the people in all their beauty and ugliness, trying to become spiritually whole by doing the work of engaging in practices that repair and sustain a shared sense of community.

Perhaps better than that of any of her contemporaries, her liberation impulse privileges the process and practice of the work of the people educating themselves to cultivate the critical consciousness she models in short stories like "The Lesson," "The Apprentice," and "Gorilla, My Love." The people in these stories divest themselves of capitalist paradigms, White supremacist assumptions and values, and male privilege. In this way her art teaches practices of liberation that clear space for revolution and liberation to grow freely and naturally. Her stories are internal narratives that reimagine strategies for effective revolution, feminism, and individual and community transformation and that focus on myriad representations of Black community.

As I articulated earlier, critics such as Margo Crawford, Joyce A. Joyce, Kelly Wagner, Sheila Smith McKoy, Salamishah Tillet, and Courtney Thorsson do a fine job of capturing aspects of Bambara's artistic significance, from seeing the value of Bambara's continuum of the material value of the African American experience to examining the importance of giving testimony to racialized violence and the ontology of African American religious tradition in the African diaspora. Several of them correctly situate Bambara's focus on Black women as cultural workers and on women's work. These are important contemporary contributions. I broach similar issues, but I primarily focus on Bambara's emphasis on the people's work and on spiritual wholeness and her fluid positioning of women as doing the cultural work—as leaders themselves or alongside men—that was essential to success in the Black nation-building that was being discussed at the time.[22] What also distinguishes this study is its hefty reliance on Bambara's words to shape literary analysis, while also emphasizing Bambara's alliance with Black aesthetic influences to shape an analysis of the power of Black cultural production (primarily jazz, gospel, and spirituals) to raise consciousness and heal the people.

Overview of the Chapters

Chapter 1, "Understanding Toni Cade Bambara," situates components of practices of liberation that Bambara articulates in her fiction to the life she lived. Here I extend a biographical lens to some of her lived liberation practices as a teacher, social worker, and cultural activist to amplify the importance of the salvation, introspection, and self-identity motifs prominent in her fiction. Her life experiences reflect her insistence on a feminist agenda that is inclusive of Black aesthetic ideals and goals. By outlining who she is and her interests and describing the impetus of the liberation impulse in her life that reflected a commitment to practices of family, faith, and freedom, I hope to help the reader better understand her fiction. These life practices are essential to the unique formation of a spiritual wholeness aesthetic that extended Black aesthetic ideals in a feminist context that privileges community and nation.

Chapter 2, "Slaying Gorillas to Empower Sisters and Community," is an examination of Bambara's first collection of short stories, *Gorilla, My Love* (1972). This chapter takes into consideration and contextualizes Bambara's understanding of the Black aesthetic in relation to leading Black aesthetic theories. Among the issues broached are feminine equity, female leadership, and honor and the necessity of respect for children and elders as revolutionary practices. Prominent in these stories is a focus on individual and communal liberation, ancestors, and the future. I pay particular attention to her negotiation of relationships between women and men in a manner that is critical of patriarchy but instructive for healing riffs and forging a united community.

Chapter 3, "Irresistible Love and Struggle in *The Sea Birds Are Still Alive*," explores Bambara's transnational and global approach to feminism and culture work. Her protagonists wage local and global war against the politics of capitalism, sexism, and racism in these stories. Female cultural workers abound in these stories, which were written at the height of her political organizing in Atlanta and at the time of her extensive travel to places like Vietnam and Cuba. On full display here is Bambara's understanding of the possibilities of activism for a writer. Her second collection of fiction displays a more mature liberation impulse that navigates the spiritual wholeness aesthetic on multiple levels. Bambara focuses on women of color entrenched in revolutionary activity or training for participation in revolutionary activity. *The Sea Birds Are Still Alive* (1977) is populated with characters who are cultural workers in the streets, working with the people, enmeshed in the business of helping people discover and create possibilities using Afrocentric, Marxist, and feminist models.

Chapter 4, "Spiritual Wholeness in *The Salt Eaters*," examines her first novel, *The Salt Eaters* (1980a), which conjures and features a multidimensional narrator and characters. I examine the role of spiritual wholeness via family, faith, and healing in renewing and transforming the protagonist, Velma, and the Claybourne (clay can be shaped and "bourne" suggests renewal) community members to make them spiritually and politically whole. Renewal and transformation are essential practice(s) of liberation in her work, especially in *The Salt Eaters*. Bambara's conjured women are not limited by the oppressiveness of patriarchal culture, and they disrupt ideologies of gender, religion, sexuality, and power. These women challenge hegemonic thought, and their presence in the literature and Bambara's engagement as a conjurer narrator help the community heal from past cultural traumas.

Chapter 5, "Remembering the Covenant: Summoning Choral Spirits in *Those Bones Are Not My Child*," examines how Bambara's posthumous novel shifts the liberation impulse focus to upholding the covenants with ancestors, children, and family for freedom. I examine the practices that are catalysts for action and the relentless self-critique that keeps community balanced and on the path to liberation. The power of the spirituals and the covenant of family, faith, feeling, and freedom are imperative to the community whose youth has been decimated in this novel about an Atlanta community that has forgotten the promise of sustained struggle for change and liberation in post–civil rights America. To correct the past a conversion or conjuring of individual and community perspective is necessary to change the present and future for her characters. Here my application of a spiritual wholeness aesthetic relies on African-influenced belief in renewal, or life after death. This renewal is literal in *Those Bones Are Not My Child (1999)*. The notion of spiritual death reflects lost cultural traditions and community responsibility and direction, which are important themes in this essay. Using the ethos of spirituals, I examine practices of liberation that promise salvation, conversion, or renewal in a way similar to how spiritual conversion renews a person's soul.

The conclusion, "Liberation Art for the People," echoes the importance of practices of liberation that shape a spiritual wholeness aesthetic and highlights the essence of Bambara's liberation impulse, which is about avoiding monoliths or intransigence that threatens change and progress. In addition, the essay pushes back against stagnant notions of "post-Blackness" and recaps Bambara's rich legacy as a writer whose artistic approach represented the paragon of the BAM's desire to express the capaciousness of Blackness. In the vein of scholars such as Steven Bracey, Sonia Sanchez, James Smethurst, Linda Holmes, Cheryl Wall, Howard Rambsy, Evie Shockley, Courtney Thorsson, Margo Crawford, and others, who have written books that help us see the value and creativity of Bambara and writers like Bambara and her Black aesthetic peers, this essay adds to the claim that this era was profoundly important and demands contemporary scholarly attention.

My contention throughout is that Bambara and her art embodied and modeled what the Black aesthetic encouraged: interdisciplinary, transnational, and community-oriented expression.[23] Moreover, because my spiritual wholeness analysis of Bambara's fiction is guided by her own words, it captures her unique trans-ideological, transnational, and intersectional approach that was unmatched by her peers. To be clear, the fiction of Paule Marshall, Alice Walker, and Toni Morrison collectively raises similar themes, but not to the extent that we see in Bambara's fiction. Given the current social and political climate, this study offers valuable insight into contemporary discussions of Blackness, identity, and the importance of the BAM in shaping these ideas.

Bambara's fiction is also significant because it is steeped in a Black aesthetic tradition of transaction between writer and reader and performer and audience. It serves three functional purposes for explorations of African American literature: (1) it unites the community; (2) it includes female voices in discussions of Black culture and life; and (3) it opens multiple approaches to reading African American literature and culture. What is also distinctive about Bambara's fiction is her ability to counteract the hostilities and debasements projected by White society and patriarchy, as well as to interpret the "entire range and spectrum of the experiences of black women" (Guy-Sheftall 1979, 236). Perhaps a reason her work stands out is because it digs beneath the "Black is beautiful" phrase. It touches and "unearths the treasure of [female] beauty lying deep in the untoured regions of the Black experience" (236).

Bambara's fiction embodies a changing, dynamic phenomenon that can "adapt itself to prevailing social situations or can transform itself" (Matthews 1998, 9). Undeniably, Bambara accomplishes the seemingly impossible feat of expressing herself in a Black idiom, foregrounding

African American discourse, individualism, and nation without sacrificing a Black feminist agenda. Her ingenious liberation ethos requires a partnership between Black women, men, youth, and elders and sets her apart from her contemporaries.[24] Thus the spiritual wholeness aesthetic I explore throughout this book confirms a message or ideology that corrals Black Nationalism and feminism into an ethos or aesthetic that privileges freedom of individual and the people in what Eleanor Traylor termed an "Afrofemme" context.[25] Bambara, in her own words, is concerned with women being "considered as cooperative partner with the black men in the struggle for liberation . . . to strengthen the family system because it's a strong political cell."[26] She models individuals and communities trying to figure out, according to Bambara, "where the hell we are going and why."[27]

This spiritual wholeness aesthetic is reliant on improvisational tones and experiential structures like jazz and spirituals, and on mediums and griots to propel a Black aesthetic forward without denouncing it, neglecting women's issues, or alienating Black men. Preceding Womanism, Bambara called for a new Black femininity that did not deconstruct the Black aesthetic but rather pushed it toward its highest ideological aspirations. Indeed, Bambara's fiction models spiritual wholeness via artful practices of liberation.[28] Her art practices Black (inter)nationalism that is in physical, intellectual, and spiritual solidarity with what she called "downpressed" people across the globe. The one constant in her art is presenting ways for *all* the *people* to obtain political and intellectual development, which is why Bambara's vision and work cast a broad net of accessible, capacious, and complex representations of "blackness" that did not betray feminism or Black Nationalism. Always community based, her art aligns with what and who the people really are and is a genuine celebration of the people.

1

UNDERSTANDING TONI CADE BAMBARA

She [Toni Cade Bambara] read the world in the way
I tend to do also, but she really read it—its symbols, you
know, the things behind things.

Toni Morrison

What I strive to do in my writing, and in general . . . is to
examine philosophical, historical, political, metaphysical
truths, or rather assumptions. I try to trace them through
various contexts to see if they work.

Toni Cade Bambara

After Toni Cade Bambara's death in 1995, the poet Amiri Baraka offered
a moving summation of her ethos, creativity, and commitment to feminism and Black community. Baraka described Bambara as:

. . . part of the rush of Black women writers that flowed out of the Black
Arts '60s, a smoking magma of the real . . . [w]ho converted the concrete
dialectic of our struggle into a complex reflection of people's lives and

minds. . . . She gave a living cast to our real life struggles. . . . She wrote of Black people, women, men, children, as workers, mothers, wives, husbands, sons and daughters, revolutionaries, militants, community organizers, nationalists, their families, the participants, the onlookers, bystanders . . . innocent or otherwise. She created a cast of the real people of our world. (2008, 109)

Baraka's words ring true because Bambara always sought to understand the whole of the matter, the "real life struggles." Although she counted among her friends and associates famous people like Toni Morrison, Ruby Dee, Ossie Davis, and Samuel L. Jackson, and her colleagues included such luminaries as Barbara Christian, Audre Lorde, Nikki Giovanni, and Addison Gayle, she also associated closely with regular folk on the block. She was humble, granting that she edited one of the most important Black feminist anthologies of the twentieth century (*The Black Woman*, 1970) and was revered by independent film circles. Her work leaned toward multiculturalism and multivalent voices and her life experiences and vision contributed mightily to her art, which has greatly influenced the direction of contemporary scholarship in the areas of feminism, Womanism, transnationalism, intersectionality, Afro-futurism, and post-Black aesthetic.

Bambara's life and work have influenced well-known black feminists like bell hooks, who wrote in her 1995 essay, "Challenging Sexism in Black Life" of the necessity to: "interrogate patriarchial masculinity to see ways it has been destructive to black males" and that we should "rethink our understanding of masculinity and manhood" (69). Hooks's epiphany is preceded by Bambara, who, in her essay "On the Issue of Roles" contended that: "black liberation struggle [is] strengthened when Black males and females participate as equals in daily life struggle . . . [and] we . . . need to rethink our notions of manhood and womanhood" (Bambara 1970, 68). A common motif in Bambara's fiction is her willingness to give voice to female characters and Black community in a manner that honestly critiques patriarchy with an eye on a larger liberation question. The ability to read what Morrison terms "the things behind things" (Holmes and Wall 2008, 97) was cultivated over time during her journey working as a community organizer, social worker, artist, comrade, and teacher engaging in practices of liberation that privileged individual consciousness, family, faith, and freedom.[1] Indeed, the distinct experiences, places, and people she encountered helped to shape the unique feminist and Afrocentric philosophy that resonates in her fiction that I call a spiritual wholeness aesthetic. The complexity of this aesthetic reevaluates Blackness, reconstructs popular notions of narrative and text, embraces innovation, and searches for truth—all without separating from African American culture or Black feminism. This delicate negotiation made her a "smoking magma of the real" that produced important revolutionary acts of language and artic-ulations of Black aesthetics and feminism in her art. She learned these skills at an early age walking "along 7th Avenue while [her mother] pointed out the Old Lafayette, places where the Dark Tower poets used to meet, and the bookstore-workshop of J. A. Rogers" (Lewis 2012, 62). She also learned important revolutionary acts of language as a child on "Speaker's Corner listening to trade unionists, Pan-Africanists, Ida B. Wells Club organizers . . . the Temple People" (62) and alongside her father at the Apollo, where she "learned that if you are going to call yourself some kind of communicator, you'd better be good because the standards of our community are high" (63). And she completed her training in the library which taught her "more about the oral tradition and our high standards governing the rap, than books" (63). Her fiction reflects this rich cultural education, which allowed her to be very adept at "read[ing] the world . . . its symbols . . . the things behind the things" (Holmes and Wall 2008, 97).

To effectively understand Bambara's fiction is to comprehend aspects of the life she lived; the evolution of her politics, her ideology, and the people-privileged ethos that shaped her intellectual and artistic vision. Her lived experiences inspired her unique liberation impulse that spoke to feminism, nationalism, transnationalism, self-determination and agency, Pan-Africanism, Black Nationalism, and the Black Arts Movement (BAM) aesthetics that influenced Black women's literature of the 1970s and early1980s. She extended ideas of second-wave feminism, which championed redrawing the map of how women could be perceived and emphasized women as individuals and not solely as caretakers. Bambara's art is equally influenced by the Black Arts Movement, which saw the artist and the political activist as one; equal shapers of the future reality. Her literary thrust parallels her thrust as a teacher, which was "to encourage and equip people to respect their rage and their power [. . .] To understand that your own experiences and knowledge of history make you an expert in regard to certain questions, namely the black agenda [. . .] I mean answering questions like: what are our prospects, what are the realities of our condition, and where are our arenas of power?" (Lewis 2012, 93). This empowerment and BAM notions of outer space, abstraction, and eccentricity that pivoted between collective mirrors and collages that gave Blackness depth (via the Black church, blues, spirituals, and folklore of the people) are prevalent in Bambara's fiction.[2] By examining the practices of her life as lived, Bambara's ethos that embraced the role of mother without abandoning the role of woman as warrior and protector of the community becomes even more legible.

Becoming Toni Cade Bambara

Toni Cade Bambara was born Miltona Mirkin Cade on March 25, 1939, to Helen Brent-Henderson Cade (Brehon) and Walter Cade II.[3] Both of her parents were from the South, and her mother came to New York from Atlanta. They lived in Harlem for the first ten years of her life, during a period of serious militancy in Harlem. Her mother, who played the organ in church, taught Toni to play the piano and took Toni and her brother, Walter, to bookstores, museums, and concert halls. Her father, an informal stand-up comedian with a passion for cinema, according to her brother, influenced Bambara's humor and interest in cinema. Her brother said that as children he and Toni would go to one of the many movie houses in their neighborhood to watch movies most of the day.[4] Her early formal education included attending private schools such as "the Mather Academy, a boarding school, and the Modern School, an independent black school" (Holmes 2014, 9).

Bambara attributes much of her early personal evolution to "living on 151st Street between Broadway and Amsterdam" and absorbing the jazz music of the forties and fifties, the culture of the Apollo Theatre, and the Speakers' Corner arguments of trade unionists, Rastas, and Pan-Africanists.[5] Her childhood in the 1940s and 1950s forced her to witness legal de facto segregation and a willful resistance to it. The Harlem of her youth taught her racial pride and consciousness as a staple. The examples of her parents and elders in her community taught her and other young folk how to organize to fight against the establishment and feelings of powerlessness. Bambara recalls how her mother would "walk [her] over to the Speaker's Corner to listen to the folks . . . talking union or talking race, we'd hang tough on the corner. . . . [T]he sermons I heard on Speaker's Corner as a kid hanging on my mama's arm or as a kid on my own and then as an adult had a tremendous impact on me."[6] These life and cultural lessons shaped her unique vision of wholeness. The sites, smells, politics, rhythm of language, and people of her Harlem youth are prominently featured in her first collection, *Gorilla, My Love* (1972). Jazz, blues, and gospel modes had an enormous influence on her choices of form: "The voice of my work has been, for a long time, 6/8 urbane be-bop in pitch and pace" (Lewis 2012, 9). She goes on to admit that her "repertoire" includes "the gospel and blues modes" (Lewis 2012, 10) and cites the presence of these modes in her first novel, *The Salt Eaters*.[7]

While Bambara credits her parents and childhood neighborhood (Harlem) as being instrumental in shaping her identity,[8] she lauds her mother, Helen, for providing her space to think and dream. According to Bambara, her mother granted her enormous space to *become*. It was so wide that the young Miltona felt free to change her name to "Toni" before she entered first grade. Moreover, she respected her mother and her generational perspective and wisdom so much that she asked her to contribute a historical reflective essay, "Looking Back," to her important anthology *The Black Woman* (1970). This particular essay details the love, hate, confusion, need, pride, and embarrassment of being a Black woman in different eras from 1915 to the 1960s in "white America, a capitalist democracy" (Bambara 1970, 290). Respect for elders surfaces as a theme in much of her fiction.

Bambara's evolution into a premiere Black woman writer during the 1970s and 80s who successfully negotiated Black Nationalism and a commitment to feminism really began to take shape during her teenage years and early twenties. When Bambara was a teenager, her family moved to Queens and she was forced to attend John Adams High School in Ozone Park. It was a crushing change because she missed Harlem very much. Although she managed to make new friends from different racial backgrounds and joined the staff of the high school literary magazine, *The Clipper*, she felt Ozone Park was an alien environment. To escape it she took a heavy course load so that she could graduate early. And soon after graduating she enrolled in Queens College to study pre-med. However, her interest in medicine was fleeting. Bambara alleges she left pre-med because she did not like "being up late at night in the stinky, smelly lab eating weird food out of a vending machine . . . [and she] felt much more comfortable with art majors and hanging around the art department" (Lewis 2012, 124). She also claimed that "writing courses and the theatre club in need of plays" lured her away from studying pre-med.[9] When she joined the theater club, she wrote film scripts, plays, and novels and even performed in the campus production of William Saroyan's play *The Time of Your Life*. Bambara graduated in 1959 with a B.A. in theater arts/English that she used throughout her life in the same manner that she would have used a degree in medicine: helping to heal people.

Only twenty at the time of her college graduation, Toni Cade was already publishing short stories, writing film scripts and plays, and "immersing herself in the local black jazz culture" (Holmes 2014, 11) of New York. This brought her into contact with the sights and sounds of Charlie Parker, John Lewis, and the Modern Jazz Quartet at local clubs (11), and the pitch, tone, and improvisation of this music resonated in her fiction. She also cultivated her transnational political appetite during this period, finding time to join local activist groups opposing US aggression in Asia, Africa, and Latin America. For example, "She also stood with black mothers protesting the Korean War" (11), and her transnational life practices come to life on the pages of several of her stories.

In 1959 she published the short story "Sweet Town" about a young girl's summer crush on a boy, her budding sexuality, her heartbreak, and her search for a healthy sense of self. Barely twenty-one years old and living in Greenwich Village in 1960, Bambara published "Mississippi Ham Rider." At the time she was writing and working as family/youth caseworker for the New York Department of Welfare to pay the bills. She held this position for two years and did not publish another story until "The Hammer Man" appeared in 1966. However, during the six-year stretch between publications the young Bambara kept writing and amassed several interesting life experiences that would later impact the content and form of her first collection of short stories that appeared under the title *Gorilla, My Love* (1972). Among those experiences was a fleeting marriage to Tony Batten after graduating from Queens College. She met Batten, an African American documentary filmmaker and actor, at Queens High School, and divorced him less than one year after getting married. One year after her brief marriage, she and a friend ventured to Europe, where she spent time writing and studying "mime and theater by enrolling in a course of study in Italy" (Holmes 2014, 12).

A closer look at her early journey reveals that in 1961 she took a job as director of recreation at Metro Hospital NYC, a psychiatric hospital. Her stint at Metro Hospital lasted only until 1962, but made her aware of the criminal discourse surrounding Black men and inspired the short story "The Hammer Man." Soon after her time at Metro Hospital, she became the director of the Colony Settlement House in Brooklyn. This position is quite interesting because it helped to shape the people-infused spirit motif in her fiction.[10] Usually settlement houses in poor urban areas recruited volunteer middle-class "settlement workers" to live among the poor, hoping that they would share knowledge and culture with and alleviate the poverty of their low-income neighbors. These organizations provided an array of services, from parenting classes, food assistance, and childcare to education for children and youth. Basically, their goal was to serve the needs of people in the communities where they existed.

Bambara riffs this history and her own experiences in the short story "The Lesson," where the children are confronted with the truth of capitalism and exploitation, in the hope that they will use this new consciousness to change their condition. Bambara's work as a director of the Colony Settlement House helped to shape the practices of liberation and the people-centric impulse that drive her fiction. The point is that Bambara spent many years working in the community as a cultural worker, working for change as either a caseworker or the director of a service program. This was an uncommon work history for a successful writer of her stature. She was on the ground as a cultural worker in different venues and capacities, helping working-class youth and families—the people—deal with and solve problems. Furthermore, while doing this service work she was studying for her master's degree, which she completed in 1965 at the tender age of twenty-six years old. After she graduated with her master's in American literature, she mostly focused on living a semi-Bohemian life in Greenwich Village, working with a theatre company, traveling, writing, and playing music on her guitar. During this phase of her life she was also hanging out with designers and theatre people, artist types and Bohemians with radical politics.

Armed with practical experiences and an enhanced understanding of literary theory, Bambara was prepared to make meaningful art. Also around 1965, Bambara ramped up her engagement in Black revolutionary politics, largely because the civil rights movement had erupted into Black Power demands. Bambara explained that "it wasn't until the sixties struck that I really finally felt at home in the world. I finally reconnected with a lot of things from childhood that I had lost. I had lost an edge somewhere while doing those college years, hanging out in Flushing. I always take Harlem as my standard of a viable community: Speakers' Corner, a place where politics are discussed and where there is critical response so that you do not become captive. . . . Harlem became my standard and very few neighborhoods fit this" (Lewis 2012, 125). So, with her degree in hand and her "edge" renewed, she shifted from being a cultural worker at Colony Settlement House to being a faculty member at City College, taking on the ideas that shape the world.

When Bambara's arrived at City College, it was a heated site of militant campus activity, and she joined the fight for radical change. The SEEK program became her base for organizing students and changing racist institutional policies and practices that blocked admission of students of color and offered curriculum that was irrelevant to them. Just as she had done at Colony Settlement House and as a social worker, as a SEEK faculty member she focused on raising her students' consciousness about race and gender realities. She explained her frustrations with institutionalized racism in education to Louis Massiah: "The SEEK program was 'Let's get these colored people in here, let them fail and flunk out so we don't have to be bothered with them again.' . . . The attrition rate at City College was something like fourteen percent, and in the SEEK program it was less than nine. We were very serious" (Lewis 2012, 128). She understood that the battle to be waged was against a "mainstream American culture . . . riddled with too much duplicity" (Lavan and Reed 2018, 15). Aware that the students were "weary of being lied to, tired of playing games," and tired of being "indoctrinated, programmed," and "ripped off," Bambara played a key role in organizing students and challenging the curriculum.[11] It is important to recognize that while Bambara was working with SEEK students during the 1960s, she was also witnessing on television children in Alabama being bitten by dogs and being washed down the street by the pressure of fire hoses as they sang "freedom."

Bambara, not yet thirty years old, was among the youngest professors at City College. According to Bambara, she was surrounded by: "a bunch of heavy folk up there at that time" (Lewis 2012, 128). She was privileged to have colleagues like poet Adrienne Rich, Audre Lorde, June Jordan, Barbara Christian, Addison Gayle, and Larry Neal. These associations seemed to significantly impact her ideological leanings, as her colleagues were some of the leading Black aesthetic and Black feminist thinkers of her era. It was during this period that Bambara became involved in different sociopolitical issues and community groups—something she would continue to do throughout her life wherever she resided.[12] Bambara's regular interaction with Black feminist thinkers like Lorde, Jordan, Gayle, and Neal (the editors of two seminal anthologies of the Black Arts era) allowed her to absorb diverse perspectives. In fact, these associations yielded her the courage and support to publish *The Black Woman* and *Gorilla, My Love*, which privileged Black aesthetics, feminism, and collaborative practices of liberation.

On the City College campus she helped lead the fight against intransigent resistance to integration that had the same sentiment as in the South—-absent the dogs, police clubs, and water hoses. As Bambara put it, the curriculum was "dripping out the old Anglo-Saxon bag, the snobbism and racism which has its roots in the Jamestown Settlement and was nourished from generation to generation by Anglophiles . . . who were committed to the belief that the Anglo-Saxon tradition was superior to all and that its purity and sanctity needed to be protected by the most sturdy of America's cultural-protectoral institutions—its universities" (Lavan and Reed 2018, 15). A regular critic of White northern racism, she suggested the name of one course "be changed to White Western History and that another course which . . . [would] offer an ideology other than the White Western one be offered" (Lavan and Reed 2018, 17). As a twentysomething Black professional woman,

Bambara found herself fighting ideological fire hoses and dogs on a university campus during a time of terrorism and violence. Bambara was unafraid to wage this battle because she was a child of the tumultuous 1940s and 1950s, which prepared her to be a cultural activist. For her there was only one choice and that was to "make revolution irresistible" and submerge "all breezy definitions of manhood/womanhood . . . until realistic definitions emerge through commitment to Blackhood" (Bambara 1970, 134). These ideas frame or serve as the core foundations of her practices of liberation in her life and art.

The 1960s and 1970s struggle for social and civil rights produced enormous upheaval that redefined the social and political landscape. It was an urban moment that was racially diverse, a politically charged environment that pushed the boundaries of civil disobedience. Indeed, it was an era of monumental culture wars in America. For example, nonviolent protest groups like Congress of Racial Equality (CORE) boarded students on buses and sent them to confront the Deep South about voting and civil rights. Activist groups were engaged in direct action to force the federal government to protect their rights, and Black and White students were participating in sit-ins across the South to desegregate lunch counters. Both high school and college students played a pivotal role in the struggle against Jim Crow. On college campuses, like the one where Bambara taught, there was a push to get Black Studies and women's studies classes approved and there was an ongoing struggle over free speech and civil rights. This was a moment of rising concerns among youth frustrated with blatant manifestations of racism and dissatisfied with America in general.

Young intellectuals like Bambara were redefining themselves in the midst of this moment. Not long after her first book was published, she became known as Toni Cade Bambara. She gave herself the surname Bambara because she claims she saw it on a trunk owned by her grandmother. Her brother Walter says he has no memory of such a trunk in their grandmother's home.[13] However, what is important is that she had an affinity for the Bambara people, claiming to have among her language skills "phonetic Bambara."[14] The Bambara people of ancient Mali reflected several values that align with Bambara's, including the spiritual wholeness aesthetic, which privileges the communal. For example, among the Bambara people, every household is responsible for providing for all of its members as well as helping with farming duties, and both men and women share the farming duties. The communal and unifying spirit of the Bambara people, who also privileged ancestors, appealed to her.

The Black Power movement and the Black Arts Movement, which honored prideful, purposeful, and communal values, offered broad possibilities for participants. Adherents of these movements were interested in collective emancipation and privileged the art of improvisation. They pushed the boundaries of tradition, using appropriation and recontextualization to challenge notions of White as normative, and invoked alternative cultural models as representative of their experiences. Black aesthetic adherents emphasized the efficacy of art developed from, directed to, and in the service of the full Black nation's desires for self-realization. Hence, the emergence of Black aesthetic principles shaped new artistic models and paradigms, evoking slogans like "Black is beautiful" and "Black Power" that helped provoke uprisings in society, education, and art. This appealed to Bambara and her peers as their generation rejected the values prescribed by the dominant culture and were not conflicted over DuBoisian "double-consciousness" about being Black and being American. Instead they took pride in being Black—period.

In short, Bambara's generation was unafraid to point out America's failure to live up to its promise—even if doing so cost them their lives. America's failure to fulfill the promise of democracy, equality, and freedom compelled them to fight for the hard-won rights. The White American public and American government's response to this generation was hostile, and repression was exhibited in the bombings, lynchings, mob attacks, rapes, police brutality, CIA surveillance and harassment of groups like the Student Nonviolent Coordinating Committee (SNCC), the Black Panthers, US Organization (sometimes referred to as Organization US), and others fighting for social and political rights.

As a child of the 1940s and 1950s, and only twenty-five years old when the March on Washington took place, Bambara was certainly influenced by protests against racial prejudice and economic oppression. At an early age she learned the importance of cooperating and organizing around a common cause. Bambara explained to Claudia Tate that this period taught her that: "a whole lot of organizations back then in the sixties floundered, fell apart, and wasted a lot of resources in the process, due in large measure to male ego, male whim and macho theatre" (Lewis 2012). Thus, her stories exemplify her determination as a writer, activist, and cultural worker to avoid these pitfalls. For example, "The Organizer's Wife" and *The Salt Eaters* are egoless iterations of communities organizing for action or needing to reorganize to reclaim some of the lost "resources" she laments to Tate about. For Bambara, revolutionary success required the revolutionary practice of cooperation; it obliged leaders to unite under one banner to make an event or movement successful. Practices such as self-determination, unity, and organizing for freedom were at the core of Bambara's lived and artistic liberation impulse.

Cultural Worker

What is amazing and unique about Bambara as a writer is that she paralleled her problem solving and gap-bridging impulse as an activist. Her fiction combines her practical experience as family and youth caseworker in the New York City Department of Welfare, as director of recreation at the Metro Hospital in New York City, and as director at Colony Settlement House.[15] Moreover, her life as an activist, cultural worker, and artist modeled her forays as cultural worker for the people in Black communities! As one of the few successful Black writers of this era with actual professional training and experience in performing cultural work, Bambara the cultural worker and Bambara the writer organized working-class people in urban communities and understood the bureaucracy and challenges these people faced.[16] She practiced what she wrote about.

Indeed, the confluence of these experiences dominate the focus and form of her early short stories like "The Lesson," "The Hammer Man," and "Raymond's Run" in *Gorilla, My Love*. She wrote what she termed "straight up fiction" (Bambara 1972, i). The stories are liberation lessons, tutelage in how to go about the business of practicing liberation, cultivating consciousness. Political awareness leads to enhanced self-knowledge and confidence that leads to self-liberation—the first step toward liberation on a broader scale. The elders in her stories represent the ancient wisdoms and the youth represent the future possibilities. There is no doubt that her art was influenced by her experiences working in urban centers servicing a diverse group of Black people between 1959 and 1965. The revolutionary 1960s, quipped Bambara, was "inspired, shaped and sustained by that incredible release of Black energy—poets, dancers, community organizers, health workers, seers, teachers, filmmakers, marchers, healers, historians, comics" (Holmes and Wall 2008, 12). This period, she says, created the space for her "to discover with greater and greater precision what [her] work in this world [was]" (12).

It was while teaching at City College's SEEK program in 1965 that Bambara says she began to narrow the focus of her "work in this world" to writing and published four short stories, including the tense story "Hammer Man," which later appeared in *Gorilla, My Love*. As Howard Rambsy points out in his important book *The Black Arts Enterprise and the Production of African American Poetry* (2011), intentionality was prevalent as many of the Black Arts writers and theorists were in dialogue about the state and direction of Black literature. For example, a leading Black Arts Movement theorist, Larry Neal, who also worked at City College during the time Bambara taught there (1968–69), was certainly engaged in dialectics with her. In addition to her City College colleagues, Bambara's circle included many important and influential artists and theorists, such as Amiri Baraka, Hoyt Fuller, Barbara Christian, Nikki Giovanni, and Alice Walker.

During this period Bambara also committed herself to being a teacher and cultural worker, and her students, like Linda Holmes and Nikky Finney, were transformed by her and went on to become important writers and cultural workers in their own right (Finney, a Distinguished Service Professor of English at the University of Kentucky, won a National Book Award for poetry and Holmes published the first biography of Bambara in 2014). Holmes and Finney are a sample of the "cadre of young folk at City College and the Livingston campus of Rutgers University" that Bambara impacted[17] because as a teacher, artist, and activist Bambara never placed distance between herself and Black people in the communities (Jackson 1982).

When Bambara accepted a position as assistant professor at Livingston College (at Rutgers), she continued doing what she had done at City College. First, she made an immediate connection with the students and the Black community in the area. Next, she became more than a teacher and was soon considered a mentor and friend to students and members of the community. According to George Levine, who organized the English Department at Livingston College, Bambara had "influence in a wide scope of activities and quickly became one of the architects of the educational experience for black students. . . . She had terrific ideas about education and she was amazingly strong as well as sensible" (Holmes 2014, 13). At Livingston, Bambara functioned as an organizer who advocated and cleared space for the underrepresented students to help them graduate from college as "whole" individuals.

Throughout her career, Bambara refused to separate the struggle for civil rights from a commitment to women's struggle for freedom, and she pragmatically infused her writing with the best of Black aesthetic theorizing and feminism. This was immediately clear in 1970 when she published the anthology *The Black Woman* and was confirmed when she published *Tales and Stories for Black Folk* (1971), as well as her first collection of short fiction, *Gorilla, My Love* (1972). Her anthology

The Black Woman focused on images of women and the connection of those images to women's oppression, in works ranging from position papers to poems, essays, and fiction. The anthology was unique and firmly rooted in the diverse experiences of Black women, both celebrating those experiences and critiquing popular stereotypes. While *The Black Woman* kicked the door open on contemporary Black feminism, demonstrating to the publishing world that there was a market for women's work, Bambara wanted it to broach even more than it did. Bambara explains that she originally had different aspirations for the project. Her original vision for the shape of *The Black Woman* was to gather women in leadership in the SNCC, CORE, and the Black Panther party to produce position papers: "[I] had read a piece by Rudy Doris about women and leadership and SNCC, so [she] talked to the women in the Panther party, women in CORE, Women in SNCC . . . to get some papers out of them and put them in a book. But the women said, 'No, this is in-house stuff. We are not interested in going public'" (Lewis 2012, 128). So, while waiting for papers from the Panther party women, she published *The Black Woman* in 1970 to get things started.

She began the process of compiling the book in 1968, and she credits three people for pushing her to put it together. One of them was SEEK student Francine Covington, who challenged her: "You've been saying this, that, and the other. Why don't you do a book, damnit?" She also credits Dan Watts, editor of the *Liberator*, who thought she "had an interesting take on things" and her City College colleague Addison Gayle, who told her: "I heard you deliver eight talks. Why the hell don't you write them down and get them printed?" (Lewis 2012, 128). The evolution of *The Black Woman* is classic Bambara. Her acts of teaching and organizing people led to a tangible, liberation-infused product. In this case, *The Black Woman*.

The anthology received enormous acclaim and positioned the thirty-one-year-old Bambara as a leading Black feminist voice. As Eleanor Traylor points out in her introduction to the reissued edition, "[Bambara] pluck[ed] the 'weasel' of thought and fire[d] the pistol of action," and the anthology emerged "as founding text of a 'womanist' evolutionary enunciation" (Traylor 2005, x). Indeed, the collection was necessary, masterful, and a founding text of womanist enunciation. Furthermore, as Traylor aptly contends, its prevailing power stems from the "voices [that] . . . were (and remain) active participants in an ever-evolving movement whose impact at mid-twentieth century was perhaps the most revolutionary cultural and intellectual re-imagining to have occurred in the United States since the birth of America in The Declaration of Independence" (Traylor 2005, xii).

On the heels of the success of *The Black Woman*, she published three stories in 1971 ("Raymond's Run," My "Man Bovanne," and "Gorilla, My Love") that were included in her first collection of short stories. *Gorilla, My Love* (1972) received favorable reviews that deemed it witty and refreshing. Bambara tells Claudia Tate that these stories, written between roughly1953 and 1970, were her "back-glance . . . on-the-block" stories focused on insuring "space for our children" (Tate 1983, 24). The stories staked feminist and nationalist ideals Bambara practiced as a social worker with the same focus, seriousness, wit, and balance that she had previously articulated in her essay "On the Issue of Roles" in *The Black Woman*. In that particular essay she famously shared aspects of her ideology that helped me frame the spiritual whole-ness aesthetic. Especially impactful was her declaration: "I am neither a man nor a woman who wishes to be a man—I tend to find no particu-larly rigid work assignment based on sex" (Bambara 1970, 124). This proclamation is a precursor to the spiritual wholeness aesthetic and the foundation for the vision and strong feminist voices articulated in her subsequent fiction. Indeed, *Gorilla, My Love* extended and practiced the work of *The Black Woman* and positioned Bambara as a leading Black Nationalist, feminist, and social activist of the era.

After the publication of *Gorilla, My Love*, she visited Cuba in 1973, where she met with women's organizations and women workers. This was an important trip because she credits it with inspiring her to think more seriously about the connection between writing and social activism, as well as about possibilities for women in the United States. Bambara tells Kalamu Ya Salaam, "I think it was in 1973 when I really began to realize this [writing] was a perfectly legitimate way to participate in struggle. . . . This counts too" (Lewis 2012, 129). As more international organizations became aware of her work and purpose, she also received an invitation to visit Vietnam as a guest of the Women's Union, and she arrived in Hanoi on July 21, 1975. The Women's Union was celebrating its forty-fifth anniversary. It is important to understand that at the time of this trip Bambara was a member of the North American Academic Marxist-Leninist Anti-Imperialist Feminist Women group.[18] Bambara and three other women were selected on the basis of their involvement in the anti-war movement. In her "Vietnam Notebook" that she kept during this trip, Bambara made an interesting observation:

> In the next ten days we learned a great deal about the efforts of the Women's Union to mobilize, organize, develop and defend women and their interests. We learned too about some of the earlier women's organizations, the precursors or prototypes of the Women's Union, and their efforts to recruit and train women, and to encourage women to be masters of their destinies—to take responsibility for the running of the country. . . . They are everywhere. There is not a single aspect of national life that is not the domain, the concern of the Women's Union. So we were able to get a thorough-going tour just through traveling from one Women's Union branch to another, from one district to another, from one province to another branch of the Women's Union. . . . The Vietnamese women in general are a hellifying group of women . . . quite stunning, very strong, warm, and gracious. . . . They gave me back my grandmother in the sense of being in the presence of these women renewed your whole love affair with your grandmother, and with those other women that we know who kept on keeping on.[19]

The impact of this visit resonates in her second collection of short fiction *The Sea Birds Are Still Alive* (1977), which is filled with strong feminist voices taking "responsibility for running" communities, organizations, and countries. Nearly every story in this collection depicts "hellifying" women engaged as community workers and organizers in local and international struggles for equality.

She wrote the bulk of the *Sea Birds* stories while living in Atlanta and attributed the expansiveness of her "vision" on display in this collection of stories to the city's "rich . . . metaphysical-training possibilities" (Jackson 1982, 42). Nearly every protagonist exhibits some duplication of practices that comprise a spiritual wholeness aesthetic. They take responsibility for leading or coleading the communities fighting for liberation. For example, "The Organizer's Wife" features Virginia leading a fight for justice after training to become a future leader. The story is an extension of Bambara's connection to the Earth Liberation Front (ELF) in the Sea Islands and North Carolina, which fought for land rights. In 1972 she visited Hilton Head, South Carolina (when it was a Black community), and in 1975 Bambara visited Penn Center in Frogmore, St. Helena's Island. She said, "The story would never have gotten past the notes stage had I not moved south and gotten involved, albeit [in] a modest, miniscule way, with independent farmers in the rural sector trying to hook up with tenants councils in the urban sector" (Lavan and Reed 2018, 42). Literary critic Eleanor Traylor offers an insightful assertion that in many of Bambara's stories she fashions "liberation zones" where her characters are "safe to grow and develop consciousness."[20]

The Seabirds Are Still Alive is Bambara's triumph of her commitment to using writing as a tool of social activism and her international liberation lens. She categorized these stories as being about "the international operation of colonialism and [the celebration of] the international nature of liberation struggles" (Lewis 2012, 19). *The Sea Birds* is a manifestation of Bambara's travels to various countries like Laos and Vietnam. The transnational focus of this second collection is clear, as it is filled with "liberation zones" where her characters are safe to grow and develop consciousness. Furthermore, this collection reflects Bambara's belief in eliminating the "[oppression] experienced by the colonized Third World and poor people in the United States."[21] Bambara makes this clear in interviews when she talks about the impetus of this collection of fiction aimed at critiquing "the international operation of colonialism and [celebrating] too the international nature of liberation struggles."[22] Thus *The Sea Birds Are Still Alive* is transnational in its focus on human transformation and reconstruction as essential practices that bring forth revolutionary change. Assisting people with their transformation and reconstruction was what she did as a social worker, artist in residence, and as a teacher, cultural worker, and activist.[23] As she explained to Beverly Guy-Sheftall: "The major question that corners me at the moment is what constitutes development for the systematically underdeveloped" (Lewis 2012, 18).

These experiences and her outrage at oppression are on display in *The Sea Birds Are Still Alive*. In fact, according to Bambara, the title story was based on stories the women told her in Vietnam. Bambara was horrified by Black people's "capacity for accommodation" and believed it defied "any kind of analysis and any kind of humor" (Lavan and Reed 2018, 36). The reason Bambara crafted women and children and the activists in the community trying to bring forth individual and group transformation and reconstruction in her first two collections of fiction was due to her anger that: "our children are being slaughtered, our men are being butchered, our women being massacred [and], any sense of community is being destroyed. With our consent" (36). In her life she practiced multiple strategies to halt this slaughter. The art of her story telling was bound up in political and social issues that she hoped would also save lives. In much of her work she is deeply concerned with exploring and placing attention on the role children and youth have played in the struggle for liberation. Thus, her fiction fulfilled her desire to use "learning theories, [and] educational models, to reveal how the training of children is being approached as a management problem rather than a *development* question" (Lewis 2012, 19).

As she had done at Livingston and at City College, Bambara completely immersed herself in the Atlanta community and, as she explains, "observed and absorbed the particular pitch, pace, and voice" (Lewis 2012, 63) of the region. During her tenure as writer in residence at Atlanta's Neighborhood Arts Center (NAC) she wrote and fostered networking opportunities for African American writers in the South. This was a different iteration of the teaching and social and cultural work she had done in New York and New Jersey. Although she had mixed success in Atlanta and at times found the work to be frustrating, she did help with the formation of the Southern Collective of African American Writers. In addition to her work at NAC, from 1977 to 1978 Atlanta University's School of Social Work hired her to teach two courses. Spelman also hired her as writer in residence for one year, and the following year she offered a workshop for writers interested in developing their craft and encouraged young writers to tap into existing outlets and expand new outlets for their work.[24] She remained in residence at NAC until 1979, and this was perhaps one of her most productive periods as a writer. Yet what made her writing productivity even more amazing is that she did all of this while juggling parenting a young child; organizing writers' collectives; working at NAC teaching creative writing and scriptwriting workshops; teaching at Spelman, Atlanta University, and Stephens College; and traveling around the country to speak at paid and unpaid events!

As was the case with her own life, her first novel, *The Salt Eaters* (1980a), avoided a linear trajectory. The structure she opted for was an inclusive circular narrative pattern that emphasized healing and wholeness. A unique quality of *The Salt Eaters* is that it features Bambara's creative use of a different kind of medium, as well as the expansiveness of her repertoire of rhetorical skills to produce "synthesis, transformation, and the future" (Lavan and Reed 2018, 49). The novel advances language and traditional notions of the role and status of the narrator to new heights and it represented a distinct shift as it sought a "new language that signal[ed] the birth of a new age . . . designed in the Afro-centric mode" (49). It was unlike anything else at the time. Bambara claims that the structure of the novel emerged as it did because she was: "in a state of altered consciousness in the sense that [she was] self-remembering . . . [or] acutely aware of dialogue . . . going on between me and the characters which are conjured . . . [and] I am acutely aware of myself as reader. I actually am aware of the relationship between what's going on in my head and what I can do with my hands" (Ya Salaam 1980, 49). The dialectic of the novel restructures, dissipated, and fractured energies of the 1960s and 1970s. Utilizing a deliberate pace and multiple characters, Bambara fuses the activists, warriors, and medicine people into a venerable force capable of forming a coalition because they recognize that they have a common agenda: liberation.

The Atlanta child murders consumed much of her time and emotional energy from 1979 to 1981 because Bambara was living in Atlanta at the time. This series of murders was committed in Atlanta from mid-May 1979 until May1981 and resulted in the death of at least twenty-eight children, adolescents, and adults. Wayne Williams, a twenty-three-year-old Black man, was arrested, tried, and convicted of the adult murders. Williams maintained his innocence. After his apprehension, however, the murders stopped. Several books appeared about the murders, and Bambara was a resource for some of the authors. In 1985 a film entitled *The Atlanta Child Murders* was produced. Bambara spent time gathering information and interviewing people for her own nonfiction book that evolved into a novel and was posthumously published as *Those Bones Are Not My Child* (1999).

Perhaps fatigued from her work on the ground and writing about the Atlanta child murders, and maybe a bit traumatized by dealing with this as an activist and writer and frustrated with what she deemed the limits of fiction, Bambara decided to shift to film. She believed the visual story conveyed with the camera and script was not readily accessible in fiction.[25] So after she met Louis Massiah, founder and director of the Scribe Video Center, she relocated to Philadelphia, where she started making documentary films.

The Scribe Video Center was a good fit for Bambara because it appealed to her interest in film and in being on the ground working with people from the community. At Scribe she also taught script writing, which fulfilled her passion for teaching and organizing. In this way she both appeased her individual passion and still remained rooted in community activism. She invited community members to work on and learn how to make films that told their stories. While working with Massiah at the Scribe Center, she improved her editing and her documentary filmmaking skills and became involved in and taught others about filmmaking. While Bambara humbly contends she learned much from working with Massiah, he is quick to point out that Bambara was quite knowledgeable about film before arriving in Philadelphia to work at Scribe.[26]

One of the first film projects she was involved with in Philadelphia was the extremely important documentary *The Bombing of Osage Avenue* (1986), which won the Best Documentary Academy Award. The film is about the May 13, 1985, bombing of the headquarters of the Black organization MOVE in Philadelphia's Cobb's Creek neighborhood. The structure of the film reflects a prime Bambara ethos, which is hearing from the ordinary people, the folk who were not what she calls "pimp flashy" (Lewis 2012). The documentary amplified the unheard voices of the community that had been drowned out by the mainstream media coverage. Bambara privileged the eyewitness accounts for this film. In a similar way to how she approached the writing of *Those Bones Are Not My Child* and short stories like "The Lesson," "The Apprentice," and other works, Bambara took to the streets of the Cobb Creek neighborhood to give *the people* an opportunity to tell their side of what happened. Bambara understood two things: first, the ordinary people, folk voices, must be heard if we want the truth, and, second, without the people there can be no revolution. She was as committed to the people as she was to her core audience. In response to White critics, she responded as follows: "It has been pointed out quite often that I do not cater to or even seem particularly cognizant of white readers . . . [but] I realize that the 'who' that can make or break this writer with a 'Amen, daughter,' or a 'Hold on, Mama,' or a 'Forget you, sister,' is the community that calls my name" (Lavan and Reed 2018, 43).

In a 1982 interview with Kay Bonetti, Bambara offered an equally apropos assessment of her artistry: "When I look back at my work with any little distance the two characteristics that jump out at me is one, the tremendous capacity for laughter, but also a tremendous capacity for rage" (Lewis 2012, 36). Indeed, this is a wonderful appraisal of her work. The former is wonderful and easy to spot. We laugh at the comical nature of the young protagonists at odds in a story like "Hammer Man" but are surprised by the protagonist's and our own rage when the police harass the young male at the end. The story "Gorilla, My Love" makes us laugh, and we are outraged that the protagonist is expected to conform to female behavior instead of assert her desire for running. The children in "The Lesson" are hilarious, but readers and the children become outraged when they see a different world in the toy store. Bambara's rage emanated from the injustices she saw in the treatment of children, the elderly, women, and the oppressed Black world. Also, Bambara was outraged when Black folk were afraid to act to change the conditions. She explains her frustration and philosophy: "We got grounded because we ate too much salt, but some folks say we got grounded because we opened ourselves up to horror—invited it onto the continent—that created tears. And it was that salt that drowned our wings and made us earth-bound" (Lewis 2012, 39). During this interview with Kay Bonetti, Bambara conveys to Bonetti a desire to function as "a new kind of narrator—narrator as medium . . . a kind of magnet through which other people tell their stories" (37). A careful inspection of her fiction reveals Black Arts Movement influences that sought to destroy double-consciousness and emphasized producing art by, for, and of the people, which led her to actively seek a narrator/medium role in her art. This unique narrator/medium approach allows the folk—past and present—to become visible in her fiction. Her writing was beautifully political, a seemingly effortless balance of ornate and simple language that was organic. She amplified several community voices simultaneously, capturing all of the divergent register of voices, issues, idioms, riddles, intonations, and vocabulary of the African American community, much like a jazz musician playing bebop. In her own words, she worked "to do justice to the cosmopolitan nature of the Afro-American experience—especially to counter the isolation and numbers game peddled by the downpressing mythmakers" (Lavan and Reed 2018, 45).

Bambara's fiction is remarkable, and it has impacted contemporary American literature, not just African American literature, because of her willingness to remain critical of patriarchy without excluding men or their issues from her narratives. A cursory glance at her essays and fiction reveal a spiritual wholeness aesthetic that is balanced and committed to depictions that nudge the gender politics dialogue in the most productive direction. Whenever Bambara discussed her fiction she was always mindful of social activism and the Black aesthetics of the 1970s and pushing back against "the grammar of the Western mind in general," which she saw as: "fragmentation/analysis/hierarchal as opposed to holistic, logical/rational/control as opposed to bicameral/understand harmony" (Lavan and Reed 2018, 47).

During an exchange with Gloria Hull about Bambara's novel *Those Bones Are Not My Child* she describes it to Hull as the product of a: "lot of notes [and the] process [being a] blending [of] this and that."[27] For Bambara, writing *Those Bones* was a long journey because her notes were originally for a nonfiction project about the Atlanta child murders. A major function or purpose that her novel performs is to act; to find the truth instead of accepting what Bambara called an "official version" of the truth:

All I'm asking, essentially, is do we understand what it means when you
buy into the official version of things? I mean, we know why we do it
because it's easier. To be responsible for your eyes or be responsible for
what you hear, what you know, it takes a lot of energy, a lot of courage.
In so many ways it seems easier to wait for that phony, bogus, official
version, even though you know damn well that it's not being composed
in our interest. At least it gives us something to gripe about. . . . I think
it's a funny addiction too; the addiction to official versions; to spend life
pushing up against 'em and reacting to them. I know many people who
are addicted. Can't wait for the official version to come out so they can say
[sucks her teeth and turns her head], something.[28]

There is no question that Bambara's novel represents a different version that contradicts, or at least challenges, the "official" one regarding
the Atlanta child murders. However, as the conversation intensifies
and draws to a close she makes clear that her interest had shifted to
film because she believed it provided her with a new language, and
because she found the writing profession to be too isolating. During
this exchange Bambara's liberation impulse of truth, activism, and self-
determination is visible and consistent with her life's work.

One constant about Bambara was her extraordinary commitment
to practicing a liberation impulse in her art and her life. She had an
uncompromising determination to convey the truth, because as she
pointed out "The concerns have not changed. Racism is still a problem,
sexism is still a problem. We are still at the bottom: 75 percent of us
are still in poverty [. . .] those conditions are fairly chronic" (Lewis
2012, 81). All of these realities catalyzed Bambara's interest in the parent
behind the child that became a successful adult, the husband or wife
who supported a famous spouse, the woman assuming a position of
leadership in her community, the man struggling with the meaning
of fatherhood, the women of the night, the folk listening to the speaker
on a soapbox, and the lament of parents who have lost a child but do
not receive answers from the authorities. Bambara was disgusted that

"This society has rewards for those who demonstrate skills in nimble avoidance of uncomfortable realities that threaten the bogus peace. But no mercy for those who dare penetrate the social garments and speak out on the emperor's clothes."[29] Indeed, her fiction examined the things behind the thing that made the people tick, and she fearlessly blew the whistle when the emperor was naked.

Perhaps the clearest way to understand the vision and charge of Bambara the artist, cultural worker, and person can be gleaned from her comments in a 1980 interview with Kalamu Ya Salaam. She tells him, "colored people, Negro people are fours. The thing about fours is that if they invest too much time looking at how they are boxed in on all four sides they never look up and know that they can build upward. To constantly be looking at those four sides is to stay in prison, is to collaborate with your captives, indeed is to lend them energy, which is the same thing as providing them with the power to keep you locked in" (Lewis 2012, 28). Indeed, to understand Bambara is to comprehend the spiritual wholeness aesthetic that does not limit her vision to "twoness" or "fours" because any form or fashion of constraint is simply not an option for her. The spiritual wholeness aesthetic in her fiction builds narratives that celebrate and examine the whole of Black community and conjure positives from the negative. The spiritual wholeness aesthetic that I examine in her fiction demands of its readers the practice of "try[ing] to break past" any and all constraints and limitations to develop what she calls "a whole new thing" (28). Bambara's life and art refused to be imprisoned, and therefore she exemplified a unique conflation of the Black feminist and cultural movements—both aesthetically and ideologically.

2

SLAYING GORILLAS TO EMPOWER SISTERS AND COMMUNITY

It is essential for continued feminist struggle that Black women recognize the special vantage point our marginality gives us and make use of this perspective to criticize the dominant racist, classist, sexist hegemony as well as envision and create a counter hegemony.

Toni Cade Bambara

I am about the empowerment and development of our sisters and our community. That sense of caring and celebration is certainly reflected in the body of my work and has been consistently picked up by other writers, reviewers, critics, teachers, students.

Toni Cade Bambara

In *Gorilla, My Love* (1972), Toni Cade Bambara practices the blueprint or framework of her liberation impulse. This impulse engages what I call a spiritual wholeness that coalesces an Afrocentric and feminist aesthetic dedicated to female and community empowerment that includes group, individual, and social transformation. Bambara's first collection of short fiction, *Gorilla, My Love*, which is jammed with the sites, smells, politics, and people of her Harlem youth, reveals her unique liberation impulse. The rhythms of bebop drive nearly every story. Her fond memories of living on 151st Street between Broadway and Amsterdam literally jump off the page, bringing to life the voices of Rastas, Pan-Africanists, and cultural lessons of the Apollo Theatre that she encountered as a child with her parents. These voices thrive in this collection of short stories and shapes the unique vision of wholeness in her fiction. What Bambara articulates in her fiction is nationalist Black activism and feminist-based practices of the Black liberation struggle that: (1) empowers and develops "sisters and . . . community" (Tate, *Black Women Writers at Work*, 15); and (2) highlights "the special vantage point [of black women's] marginality . . . and make[s] use of this perspective to criticize the dominant racist, classist, sexist hegemony as well as envision and create a counter hegemony" (Guy-Sheftall 1979, 242). This liberation impulse holds the community accountable and is central to her wholistic forms of progress and change that feature females in the Black nation imaginary.

The discussion of *Gorilla, My Love* that follows is within the trajectory of her groundbreaking anthology, *The Black Woman* (1970), which championed transformation, renewal, and conscious resistance. Like her anthology, *Gorilla* (1972) extends Black aesthetic theory, feminism, and activism to new heights. The anthology is important because it was firmly rooted in the diverse experience of Black women. It celebrates that experience, critiques popular stereotypes, and claims new space about gender and the meanings of Black womanhood. *The Black Woman* received enormous acclaim, positioning the thirty-one-year-old Bambara as a leading Black feminist voice. The evolution of *The Black Woman* is classic Bambara.

The same practice of activism she brought to her classroom and the community contributes in major ways to the content found in *Gorilla, My Love*, *The Sea Birds*, *The Salt Eaters*, and *Those Bones Are Not My Child*. One of the most notable essays that appeared in *The Black Woman*, "On the Issue of Roles," models her approach to negotiating male/female relationships in much of her fiction. As Eleanor Traylor points out in her introduction to the reissued edition of *The Black Woman*, Bambara emerged as a leading voice of womanism who produced "[a] founding text of a 'womanist' evolutionary enunciation" (Traylor 2005, x). Certainly, as Traylor aptly contends, the book's impact at mid–twentieth century was an important "revolutionary cultural and intellectual re-imagining" (Traylor 2005, xii).

Gorilla My Love is comprised of fifteen short stories written between 1959 and 1971 that capture the essence of Bambara's diverse experiences servicing people and learning about the world and herself. Bambara's early endeavors in jazz clubs and hanging out on the Greenwich Village scene were ubiquitous in focus, shaping stories in *Gorilla, My Love* like "The Lesson," "The Hammer Man," and "Raymond's Run." Additionally, "Playin with Punjab" and the title story, "Gorilla, My Love," are influenced by her experiences as a social worker. Many of the stories are liberation lessons in how to practice the business of liberation and cultivate consciousness, self-knowledge and confidence. For example, "The Lesson" is from the perspective of youth and "a culture worker who belongs to an oppressed people [who believes her] job is to make revolution irresistible" (Lewis 2012, 3). In her art self-liberation is the first step toward a broader notion of change and resistance. This is the energy that is manifested in *Gorilla, My Love*, because Bambara made crafting art that raises consciousness "[her] work in this world" (12).

It is important to recall how she came to this "work in the world." When she completed her master's degree in 1965, Bambara spent time as a cultural worker in different venues and capacities help-ing working-class youth and families deal with and solve problems. These experiences impacted her and gave her the perspective that guided the tone and themes found in *Gorilla*, but also helped her shape what she has termed the whole of the matter, the things behind the things. Indeed, there are many parallels between her stories in *Gorilla* and this period of her life, which models and theorizes prac-tices of liberation. Her stories articulate different forms of conflict, and the practices of resistance, transformation, and renewal required to uphold covenants with self, family, community, and nation. Her approach is attuned to poet Sonia Sanchez's focus on family and wholeness. I use the phrase "practices of liberation" because Bam-bara is concerned with the process of liberating the self and commu-nity. Her characters and communities are rebellious nonconformists engaging in the practice of finding pathways to freedom in order to become whole. Through this process not only are Black girls and women transformed but dispossessed and displaced Black boys, men, and elders coalesce to build a nation. Bambara explains the unique nature of her work that guides my analysis of the practices of liberation in her fiction:

> What informs my work as I read it—and this is an answer to the fre-quently raised question about how come my "children" stories manage to escape being insufferably coy, charming, and sentimental—are the basic givens from which I proceed. One, we are at war. Two, the natural response to oppression, ignorance, evil, and mystification is wide-awake resistance. Three, the natural response to stress and crisis is not break-down and capitulation, but transformation and renewal. The question I raise from "Gorilla" to "Sea Birds" to *Salt* to "Faith of the Bather" is, is it natural (sane, healthy, whole-some, in our interest) to violate the contracts/covenants we have with our ancestors, each other, our children, our selves, and God? (Bambara 1970, 47)

Judging from these comments, it is evident that Bambara is a "revolutionary" writer who has decided that neither White racism nor male sexism will exercise control over her or her work. Her impulse is emancipatory. Therefore the people of her fiction are transformed and renewed through the language of resistance to oppression. Bambara's fiction is a continual act of discovery that succeeds in reclaiming the spirit or "contracts/covenants we have with our ancestors" (Bambara 1970, 47) via myriad Black cultural expression and perspectives. The goal of this approach is making liberation or emancipation irresistible.

Another constant subject in the *Gorilla* stories is a positive frame of understanding the social experiences of the group, specifically the caring "networks that exist between men and women, men and men, women and women, children and elders" (Guy-Sheftall 1979, 244–45). Such healthy networks are key to her liberation impulse. This impulse stems from a commitment to faith in self, wholesome male/female relationships, and family/community traditions as components of freedom, which coheres with Bambara's own proclamation that her writing is focused on issues of war, transformation, renewal, and wide-awake resistance. Several of the stories' themes revolve around adherence to contracts and covenants with self, children, and ancestors. This cross-generational and cross-gender chorus of voices becomes a mainstay in her fiction, running through the seams of her art until her death. The artful manner in which she presents these voices as a practice of liberation further situates Bambara as a pioneering voice among fiction writers of the 1970s. She is a feminist, "revolutionary" Black writer who engages in a continual act of discovery. To be sure, she strives to reclaim what in *Black Feminist Criticism* is described as Black women illuminating their situation to reflect their identity, growth, and relationship to men, society, children, history, etc., as they experienced it (Christian 1985, 156).

In her important essay "On the Issue of Roles" in *The Black Woman* (1970) Bambara also asserts that the individual, the family, and the home are necessary sites of revolution. She says: "If your house ain't in order, you ain't in order" (135). For Bambara the most significant stage of revolution, the most important revolutionary unit is the self (133). Her goal was to produce literature that helped transform or replace the current social order with a new vision of community that extended cultural nationalism as sets of practices of liberation. Bambara outlines this ethos in "The Education of a Storyteller," where she says her fiction is steeped

> in the tradition of Afrocentric aesthetic regulations who trained [her] to understand that a story should be informed by the emancipatory impulse that characterizes our storytelling trade in these territories as exemplified by those freedom narratives which we've been trained to call slave narratives for reasons too obscene to mention. . . . She [Grandma Dorothy] taught that a story should contain mimetic devices so that the tale is memorable, shareable [*sic*] that a story should be grounded in cultural specificity and shaped by the modes of Black art practice—call-and-response . . . that bespeaks a communal ethos. . . . [she goes on to explain how] the bebop musicians [she] eavesdropped on while hanging around fire escapes and in hallways were teaching [her] about pitch, structure, and beat, and the performers and audiences at the Apollo and the Harlem Opera House were teaching [her] about the community's high standards regarding expressive gifts. (Bambara 1996, 249–50)

For artists and critics of the Black Arts Movement (BAM), revolution and liberation were core impulses of the art. As her words above reveal, Bambara's narratives are modern freedom narratives that privilege practices of revolution that involve small liberation acts of organizing, inscribing, and self-discovery. To "make revolution irresistible," her stories "[bespeak] a communal ethos" that articulates a collective of community voices. This collective finds form in Bambara's depictions of regular people. Indeed, the regular folk in her fiction represent the grass roots, the 90 percent majorities that fuel the movement; it is the antithesis of a "leader" model that can be compromised. Bambara's liberation impulse abandons the Black upper/middle class reformism approach and privileges *the people*. Her focus is the Black people that represent the 90 percent majority. Bambara avoids paragons or caricatures in an effort to capture ordinary people facing real traumas—a capacious "Blackness." Thus, it is to be expected that, in her own words, she writes "straight-up fiction" (Bambara 1972, x) that contains "mimetic devices so that the tale is memorable, shareable [*sic*] . . . [and] grounded in cultural specificity" (Bambara 1996, 250) of the women men, children, and elders who represent the Black aesthetic commitment past and renewal.

In addition to grassroots representation and cultural specificity, the women in *Gorilla, My Love's* liberation impulse evoke an alternative feminist reading—a new womanhood—that encapsulates Black aesthetic values, and counterhegemonic feminist consciousness. This gives rise to an ethos that conveys the African American tradition of resiliency via a chorus of voices. As one of the pioneering figures of a new womanhood, in her fiction Bambara is committed to communal solidarity—men and women as equal agents of resistance, renewal, and transformation. The feminist and Black aesthetic principles of transformation, renewal, and resistance, along with African spirituality, drive the practices of liberation in her fiction. These principles privilege freedom, family, and faith (in self and community).

At the core of Bambara's ethos of African American resiliency is a new womanhood committed to communal solidarity that positions women and men as equal agents, partners in acts of resistance, renewal, and transformation. The emphasis on polyvocality leads to a correspondingly more expansive construction of the Black aesthetic and liberation that is accessible to women, Black men, youth, and elders. The "people" in her fiction participate in a capacious discursive framework. Perhaps poet Amiri Baraka best explained Bambara and her literary impulse best when he said: "Toni . . . created a cast of the real people of our world" (Baraka 2008, 109). As Baraka points out, the cast of "real people" in Bambara's impulse incorporate feminist and Black aesthetic principles of transformation, renewal, and resistance and African spirituality. Thus, she produces fiction where people learn to love themselves and build a nation. The iteration of Black aesthetics Bambara puts forth is expansive and fluid and inclusive of the history and diverse experiences of women in the struggle for liberation and resistance to masculine biases.

My lens for viewing her work respects the speculative, inventive, reconstructive, and transcendent thrust of her work. The liberation impulse powering her fiction also entails a spiritual and psychological act or practice that must occur with the elders and the youth who represent the future. She manages not to alienate other voices. Another striking feature of her work, specifically the story "Gorilla, My Love," is the language and themes of social protest and ghetto stylizations. The aesthetic driving most of these stories privileges jazz's unique pitch, collaborative structure, and beat. Often the characters are a separate voice, instrument, or medley that, taken collectively, approach a "whole" cultural representation of community. The community of voices in her stories is a medley representing the unique individual and communal ethos of Black literature and culture. While the situations of each character are distinct, similar obstacles of internal and external oppression must be navigated to unify them. For example, "My Man Bovanne" interrogates Black Nationalist politics and generational issues, balancing the important contributions of youth and elders. Meanwhile, "Raymond's Run" balances the seemingly disparate self-definition of young Hazel and male/female familyhood via the achievement of her brother Raymond.

In the spirit of the Black aesthetic search for a lost spirit and its emphasis on building heroes and legends that restore self-esteem, Bambara conjures positive myths, heroes, and legends for both genders simultaneously. This evenhandedness enables her fiction to expand the Black aesthetic emphasis on politics and cultural investigation of a lost spirit. Actually, her stories cull the African spirit of proverbs and folklore as a teaching tool regarding femininity and contemporary Black experiences, making full use of "those most distinctive features of twentieth-century black culture—dozens, toasts, prayers, sermons, slang, and signifying" (Berry and Blassingame 1979, 252). In her stories there are times when females are antagonists, partners, and leaders of Black men. Yet unlike those of some of her 1970s contemporaries, Bambara's female protagonists are critical of sexism while also maintaining the focus on males as partners or comrades in the project of nation building.

Bambara's Afrocentric/feminist aesthetic thrives in many of these stories via generational, gender, or cultural conflicts whose resolution demands a resistance and renewal that moves women, youth, and elders from the margins of discourse to a position that encourages a new centeredness of female, male, cultural, and community reclamation and transformation. That said, one can make a strong claim that Bambara's 1970s fiction was a paragon of what Black male feminist Michael Awkward decades later proposed as the function of contemporary "black womanism":

> Black womanism demands neither the erasure of the black gendered other's subjectivity, as have male movements to regain a putatively lost Afro-American manhood, nor the relegation of males to prone, domestic, or other limiting positions. What it does require, if it is indeed to become an ideology with widespread cultural impact, is a recognition on the part of both black females and males of the nature of the gendered inequities that have marked our past and present, and a resolute commitment to work for change. In that sense, informed Afro-American male participation heartily welcomes—in fact, insists upon—the joint participation of black males and females as comrades. (Awkward 1995, 52)

Bambara's paragon Black womanist status is theorized in *The Black Woman* and practiced in the stories collected in *Gorilla, My Love*. She preceded her contemporaries in formulating a womanist outlook that challenged notions of roles and welcomed the joint participation of Black males and females as comrades in struggle for liberation. Put simply, Bambara settles on "wholeness," an existence that premises African spirituality and progressive feminism and is critical of men without excluding them from discussions or representations of African American culture. The *Gorilla* stories achieve what Addison Gayle instructed should be the focus of Black art, which was to draw from the "unique cultures that the enslaved developed out of the conditions and imperatives of their lives in the U.S." (Shockley 2011, 4). Indeed, what she achieves is a portrayal of Black people that accurately represents their political situation while offering usable lessons for struggling effectively for collective power (Shockley 2011, 4). This is an impulse that provokes a quest for freedom and movement toward a progressive state of being for individuals, community, or nation. As I argue in this chapter, *Gorilla* reveals Bambara's praxis of liberation that corrects gender and generational inequities as well as counterproductive emancipation and liberation practices.

Honoring Contracts and Covenants

"Sweet Town"

In 1959 Bambara published "Sweet Town" in *Vendome*. While the story's focus is most likely semi-autobiographical, "Sweet Town" veers closely to her self-proclaimed "straight-up fiction" (Bambara 1972, x) that portrays the real-life struggles of the people. Here Bambara presents an ordinary young girl struggling with something as seemingly mundane as budding sexuality and morality, but Bambara insists it is an important topic for the community to consider. Kit, the protagonist, is ravaged by a period of "sweet and drugged madness" (122) that threatens her dignity. In other words, she has gone "boy crazy," causing her to violate covenants with her family and herself by having sex at a young age and running around with a boy named B.J. When the story opens we know that things are askew because the protagonist reveals to us she has written the following note on the bathroom mirror to her mother: "Dear Mother, please forgive my absence and my decay and overlook the freckled dignity and pockmarked integrity plaguing me this season" (121). She admits that her wild behavior, which includes writing "mad cryptic notes on the kitchen sink with charred matches" (121), is the antithesis of the dignified conduct and covenants she has been taught. But her mother, in the Black vernacular tradition of signifying and humor, lets her know she understands the conflict—within limits—when she quips back "on the kitchen table in cake frosting . . . 'My dear, mad, perverse young girl, kindly take care and paint the fire escape in your leisure,'" dotting the I's "with marmalade" and crossing the t's "with orange rind" (121–22). Kit's mother's cryptic response to her behavior is figuratively and literally bittersweet.

Bambara's interest in traumas as simple as a young girl losing her moral and emotional bearings because of a hormonal metamorphosis initially seems not to fit the liberation impulse model. However, Kit's internal conflict is worthy of inspection because it runs parallel to her subsequent retransformation, renewal, and resistance. A recurring theme in several of Bambara's stories involves characters enduring a multilayered process of liberation that always begins with them seeking inward for emancipation. The spring and summer heat jeopardizes Kit's bearings, her moral compass. She explains that she is struggling internally with "the cosmic interrelationship between the cellular attunement of certain designated organs and the fermental correlation with the axis shifts of the globe" (122). These internal physical shifts have unsettled her, compelling her to violate her covenant with herself, and that with her family. Kit laments this loss, explaining the cause of her demise that she cannot control as a situation whereby: "the glands always win and the muses and brain core must step aside to ride in the trunk with the spare tire" (122). Indeed, her inability to break free of this spell compels her mother to threaten her "with disinheritance. And [her] old roommate from camp actually turned a hose on" her (123). Actually, she is so scattered that when B.J. dumps Kit to run away from home with his buddy Eddie, she considers abandoning her plans to go to college, thinking she might instead: "bum around the country. And in every town . . . ask for them as the hotel keeper feeds the dusty, weary traveler that [she assumes she will] be" (125). Although she struggles with being "sticky with the rotten apricots oozing slowly in the sweet time of her betrayed youth," she resists the urge to betray herself and her family. Kit comes to her senses, realizing that in the future, once her "sweet time" has passed, she will recognize him as "an enchanted frog" (125) and not the sexy guy she thinks betrayed her. Her instincts tell her it is not natural, sane, or wholesome to follow him and violate covenants with herself or her family. Bambara's point is that an important initial step in the practice of liberation is always to first and foremost be oriented in the self. Kit realizes that she is not the problem but rather B.J.'s poor judgment and her raging hormones are the cause of her near violation of covenants with herself and her family. This seemingly mundane story thus captures Bambara's commitment to a psychic, spiritual, and intellectual wholeness that demands principled behavior.

The Johnson Girls

In "The Johnson Girls," Inez, Gail, Great Ma Drew, Thumb, and Sugar characterize a multivoiced community debating the best path to healthy relationships. Among the practices of liberation on display here is what Bambara terms a "caring network that exists between men and women, men and men, women and women, children and elders" (Lewis 2012, 16). "The Johnson Girls" revolves around a note Inez receives from Roy announcing the end of their relationship and that he has moved to Memphis (perhaps to cure his blues) because she does not want to marry him. The narrative explores how to have healthy male/female relationships and the best strategy for getting Roy back. Although Roy is critiqued, he is never labeled an adversary and pushed to the margins. In Inez Bambara portrays another strong Black female character that is strong, complex, and human. The reader comes to understand the deep, dialectical nature of her relationship with Roy, and that men are not perfect, nor are women. Inez has a great career and is independent and respected by her family and community. In fact, her independence keeps her from wanting to marry Roy. Through Inez Bambara champions a feminist revolution that helps wounded relationships between Black women and men that are the foundation for strong families and liberated communities. Inez loves Roy but also loves herself and her career and is distraught over the loss of him. For 1970s women, negotiating relationships, family, and career was a new challenge that created enormous strains that Bambara herself faced. After graduating from college Bambara was briefly married for one year and seems to have dealt with similar tensions.

Several community and family members—both male and female—offer Inez advice for getting Roy back because the pulse of her liberation philosophy embraces the notion that "there is no *the* woman or experience or *the* profile" (Lewis 2012, 7). Because of this stance the advice Inez receives is both modern and ancient. Bambara's status as a self-declared feminist and nationalist elucidates her simultaneous embrace of female independence, family building, and nation building without sacrificing any one of them. Actually, we are told that Inez's guy "is something special" (Bambara 1972, 171). Bambara would likely reject the notion that a man completes Inez because she believes that strong, healthy, sane family units are essential to the emancipatory aims of community and nation. Sugar intimates as much to Inez about her union with Roy: "the two of you kept my faith in the blue-plate-special [the perfect man she desires who has it all]" (171) and Gail confirms but complicates her praise of them, admitting "I'll give Roy his due, he's groovier and more solid than most men, but he's still a man, his mama . . . left the job of polishin him off to manhood to other women" (175). Although critical, Gail also admits that Roy is "worth all the trouble that his sulky exit is causin [Inez] and [her] best friends" (176). Two things are evident from this exchange. First, Bambara believes in healthy female/male unions and is concerned about the "caring that lies beneath the antagonisms between black men and women" (Lewis 2012, 15). Second, as these conflicting perspectives about men and, in particular, Roy, confirm, Bambara recognizes that negotiating relationships is complex. Indeed, she disbelieves in a single solution or approach, and thus she has Inez consider both modern and ancient advice, a fact that is evident when Thumb advises Inez, "Stead of burning roots, you could send Roy a telegram sayin you comin" (Bambara 1972, 164), advice that Great Ma Drew quickly refutes, advocating she instead "set up some counter juju and get that man turned around again" (164). Ultimately the assertion of multiple, even antithetical perspectives serves the greater purpose of transformation and renewal.

It is not uncommon for Bambara to construct fictive communities amenable to myriad perspectives. Bambara practices a liberation impulse that eschews the essential Black subject and identity boundaries. Indeed, her communities are open to a diverse range of perspectives, which is why the unknown young college-aged female at the conclusion of "The Johnson Girls" orients the group of women when it is time to get down to the business of dealing with Roy's note. This explains why Inez, who has been established as the self-assured, serious ringleader, defers to the leadership of the younger, college-aged female narrator. Inez does this because her objective is finding the best strategy to help her get her man back. Bambara's emancipatory impulse creates space for different individuals to have equally prominent voices—it does not discriminate between the young, the old, female, or male.

The multiple perspectives on display in "The Johnson Girls" are akin to a bebop session about love and relationships as different characters take turns giving solo advice. The mood of the story is grounded in a call and response and communal ethos. This collection of stories represents Bambara's distinctive liberation and emancipatory impulse narrative that privileges a jazz pitch and pace sprinkled with call and response. She transforms gender and generational tensions and neglect between youth and elders in stories like "The Johnson Girls," "My Man Bovanne," and "The Hammer Man" into positive shouts of joy. For example, in "My Man Bovanne" Hazel overcomes her children's shortsightedness while the younger Hazel in "Hammer Man" overcomes her conflict with Crazy Manny to protect him against police abuse. Through these Hazel characters Bambara riffs on police brutality and community solidarity. These stories are variations around Bambara's theme of negotiating gender tensions and female self-definition as a route to wholeness. Many of the characters and stories play a similar tune of gender and community unity on their own instrument, so to speak, in a manner befitting their individual style. Bambara intimates in an interview that one conflict she is interested in trying to resolve or at least interrogate is

> the caring that lies beneath the antagonisms between black men and black women . . . the usable lessons . . . the caring networks that exist between men and women, men and men, women and women, children and elders. (Guy-Sheftall 1979, 244–45)

For Bambara there is no singular truth but many impressions of it. The jazz/bebop ethos offers usable truths, variations on the themes of family and gender participation, which are imperative practices of liberation that promise sane, healthy and wholesome existence. The diverse internal truths and solutions via a jazz emerge from myriad voices. Thus Inez receives different riffs of advice from her peers, an elder, a male, and a younger woman regarding the best path toward transformation and renewal with Roy. Bambara is sensitive to the reality of wounded relationships between Black men and women. "The Johnson Girls" is her pronouncement that there is no recipe but we must be willing to sample a veritable "blue plate special" of advice to heal wounded relationships and fortify existing ones.

"Happy Birthday"

When there is no male/female unity to negotiate, Bambara presents a story like "Happy Birthday" to force us to focus inward at neglected aspects of the liberation struggle. This story is a reminder that covenants with children cannot be violated in the quest for liberation. The avant-garde nature of Black aesthetics emphasized aesthetic freedom, which Bambara's fiction answers. "Happy Birthday" falls into this category. It fits the Black aesthetic criteria of being "accessible" to those members of the Black working classes who have little patience for difficult literature. It achieves the Black Arts aspiration to establish a new set of cultural reference points and standards that centered on "the needs and aspirations" of African Americans—correcting family and community neglect of young women. While on the surface it appears to be a seemingly meaningless story, it is part of Bambara's covenant with all of the people in the community to birth a new day of behavior that upholds our contracts with our children, especially the celebration of their birthday. Bambara was especially sensitive to how children and elders were treated. She deemed their function in the family and community essential to the future of a healthy nation and to the emancipatory project of the 1970s.

The protagonist, Ollie, is sad because the day is nearly over and nobody—not even her parents and grandparents—has remembered to wish her happy birthday. She roams the neighborhood looking for someone to play with or talk to so she can let them know it is her special day. But on this day not a single person can be located: "Everyone was either at camp, or at work or sleeping" (Bambara 1972, 64). Even Chalky the superintendent and the older guys who usually sent her on errands, or made comments like "Here comes Miss Freshmouth" (63) ignore her. Making matters worse, Ferman, "the nut from across town" (63), asks her: "Ollie when are you going to learn to play with dolls?" (63), before telling her "Go away, little girl" (64). Ollie feels neglected, rejected, and misunderstood. Through Ollie, Bambara instructs us that wholesome liberation requires healthy treatment of children and that men, women, and elders are complicit in forgetting this, in the same harmless manner that they forget a child's birthday and ignore her disappointment.

As a former social worker, Bambara was sensitive to children's feelings and their role in building a healthy nation. The conjuration of Ollie's birthday blues trauma or birthday slight resonates a larger caution against breaking the covenant as a community not to neglect youth, who represent future and hope. Ollie's status as a female makes this cautionary tale even more poignant. It is a reminder not to expect "particular" behavior of little girls and to recognize that the new womanhood Ollie represents is "too big for dolls" (63). Bambara is criticizing the lack of space for the liberated spirit of young girls. She reminds us that to effectively enact a liberation impulse a community must be sensitive to the nurturing needs of young girls.

Although Ollie is a tough little girl who hangs around the older boys and is not interested in dolls, Bambara reminds readers that such girls are vulnerable human beings equally in need of nurturing. Not even Reverend Hall recognizes that Ollie's spirits are low because he tells her, "You go play somewhere else" (65). However, when Ollie explains there is "nobody to play with," he continues to lack empathy for her, rebuking her further, "Little girl you can't act up here in front of the church" (65). Ironically, not even the leading religious community member is attuned to or willing to nurture the spirit of this young girl. Aware of his reticence, Ollie challenges him by asking "How come you always calling me little girl, but you sure know my name when I am walking with my grandfather?" (65). Just for a moment Bambara reminds us of the feisty side of Ollie, to stifle vulnerable tragic empathy. This is confirmed when Ollie whispers to the pigeons, "Wish me happy birthday" and when they do not she yells, "Better wish me happy birthday or somebody around here is gonna get wasted" (65). Not even the elder female, Miss Hazel, who leans out her window to discern the commotion, recognize Ollie's frustration or is willing nurture her. Bambara's point is that even elder women who should know better can fail to uphold the covenant to nurture youth. Unlike some of her feminist peers, Bambara was not interested in narratives that limited themselves to male neglect or mistreatment of women. Anybody breaking covenants that were essential to liberation was a target in her fictions. Ollie says, "You should never have a birthday in the summertime," to which Miss Hazel says, "Well, don't cry sugar. When you get as old as me, you'll be glad to forget all about it" (65). Miss Hazel's dismissive behavior is as problematic as Reverend Hall's behavior. Symbolically Bambara has Miss Hazel's misunderstanding and flawed wisdom break Ollie, evoking a dramatic show of tears from her and capturing the attention of others. Bambara also complicates the feminist moment with a confused Miss Hazel having no idea why Ollie is upset, telling her own great-grandmother, "Beats me... [I do not] understand kids sometimes" (65). Bambara's point seems to be two-pronged: (1) if we desire wholesome, healthy future communities, this requires upholding the covenant of taking the time to "understand" our children; and (2) central to the emancipatory impulse is a willingness to embrace and critique men, women, youth, and elders.

Miss Hazel's failure to take the time to understand the place from which Ollie's pain stems breaks the covenant and is unacceptable. As far as Ollie is concerned, family and community are not supposed to neglect children. Bambara is suggesting that the most minor of breaches can upset the emotional balance of community members, creating unhealthy behavior like Ollie's declaration of war on the pigeons and her burst of uncontrollable tears. The dismissive treatment of the new womanhood Ollie represents threatens to disrupt community liberation efforts. This story is a reminder that a strong community begins by upholding the covenant to nurture its youth. Failure to take the time to pay attention to youth or something as simple as a birthday can cause irreparable damage, rendering the Ollies of the world less useful in the project of feminist and community revolution.

Rejecting Gender Restrictions

"Raymond's Run"

Bambara's often anthologized story "Raymond's Run" continues the trajectory of vocal and confident young protagonists exhibiting wide-awake resistance. The Hazel of this story is complex, bold, courageous, and nurturing. She implodes gender norms and hierarchies while redesigning a domestic nation that includes women and men functioning in sisterhood and brotherhood. At work here is Bambara, the "Black Nationalist" and "feminist," creating art that models a nuanced and balanced perspective dismissive of gendered norms.

Hazel immediately informs readers that she is not to be messed with; that she takes on all rivals, including the new girl, Gretchen, and her crew. When tension between the young girls is revealed early in the story, there is little question whether Hazel, who: "walk[s] straight on through them or even over them if necessary" (Bambara 1972, 26), is a tough little girl. Symbolic of the new female resistance we are about to be introduced to, she proclaims herself "ready to fight cause like I said, I don't feature a whole lot of chit chat" (26). Clearly, Hazel rejects the role of the passive or accommodating girl in favor of one willing and able "to just knock you down right from the jump and save everybody a lotta precious time" (25). This stance transforms passive notions of feminine, while also effectively signaling that a different type of girl and woman will be the focus of the story. Further, the attention Bambara pays to female/female conflict in this story extends her visionary feminist ideas and her quest for wholesomeness and liberation. Her feminist emancipatory impulse is critical of any behavior that conflicts with strong families, communities, or nation—-even if the source is female:

> Gretchen smiles, but its [*sic*] not a smile, and I am thinking that girls never really smile at each other because they don't know how and don't want to know how and there's probably no one to teach us how cause grown-up girls don't know how either. (26–27)

Here again Bambara uses her feminist voice to criticize and correct. She seizes the moment to correct the inner conflicts that exist between women. Thus she stresses the importance for women of figuring out how to first get right with self so they can resist fractured female relationships and bond with each other for the sake of a united sovereign community.

Throughout this story, as in other stories in *Gorilla, My Love*, varied internal truths and representations emerge whereby female protagonists discover or proclaim self then challenge and redefine sexual borders. They slay gendered and social gorillas, if you will, that would normally hold their development and free expression captive. This "slaying," Bambara suggests, is the first step toward a spiritual "wholesomeness" that revolves around transformation and renewal. A salient theme in these stories usually involves female protagonists rejecting gendered norms or expectations that burden the freedom of their spirits, or scaling walls of communication that impugn healthy male/female relationships. The young girls and women freely speak their minds, bucking "traditions" and asserting femaleness on their own terms while challenging institutions and ideas rather than succumb to victim status. This story is among those that also conjure a sort of initiation rite of passage for her young female protagonists who challenge social norms and redefine themselves.

In the spirit of the Black aesthetic advocacy for oppositional or alternative texts that deconstruct ideological assumptions underpinning Western constructions of reality, this story challenges the patriarchal assumptions of society that minimized the role of women. However, it does so without separating politics from modes of multidimensional Black cultural discourse, or feminist revolution from the goal of nation building. The first evidence of this is Hazel's role as Raymond's protector. The second sign occurs when Hazel allows "ole Raymond [to get] on line on the other side of the fence" (30). Hazel says: "I was going to yell at him but then I didn't. It burns up your energy to holler" (30). Bambara implies that to subvert Raymond's desire to run is counterrevolutionary; fighting in this way only "burns up your energy" (30), which is harmful to her personal goal to win the race and achieve the common good. Also, Hazel's decision to retire and refashion herself as Raymond's coach aligns with Bambara's emancipatory feminist/ liberation impulse because Hazel establishes herself as a winner and the community respects her individual achievement. This frees her to be whatever she desires: a champion runner, coach, spelling bee champion, or piano star—the options are limitless.

Indeed, this revolutionary feminist impulse frees Hazel to determine how she will venture her female self. When she will be cocky. When she will be gracious. How she will nurture or protect her brother Raymond. She fashions her own reality on her own terms, something young Hazel deems imperative because she is aware of her existence in a society that is "too busy [making girls] flowers or fairies of strawberries instead of something honest and worthy of respect . . . you know . . . like being people" (32).

As a matter of fact, Hazel signals to the reader early on that she is unlike other girls, making it clear that she openly rejects domesticity and that "[her] mother does that [cleaning]" (23). This information is her declaration that she represents a new generation, a new type of womanhood. Yet as a new woman, young Hazel's self-pronounced goals are negotiating running and watching her brother Raymond, who is "not quite right" (23). This matches Bambara's own complicated feminist/nationalist identity outlined in her essay "On the Issue of Roles" that privileges self and nation. Indeed, young Hazel's toughness, boastfulness, and athleticism, as well as her willingness to care for her brother, redefine and challenge traditional female stereotypes of women. She models the type of feminist-based Black liberation struggle that Bambara advocated. The parameters of Hazel's confident new womanhood are also made clear in her proclamation that she is not a flower, passive, or averse to being physical, and her elucidation that she is such a master of the fifty-yard dash that they call her "Mercury" because "No one can beat [her] and that's all there is to it" (24). She also cautions men against judging her by her seemingly weak appearance or gender, "even if [she is] a little girl with skinny arms and a squeaky voice" (23). The point is that strength comes in different packages and we must see all community members as potential champions. Hazel's resistance to limited definitions such as "fairy" or "flower" and to being called "squeaky" by her male coach corroborates this point (27). The feminist-based Black liberation womanhood Hazel models permits her to be a prideful runner and a protector of her older, "not quite right" brother, Raymond. Although she acquiesces and looks out for him, it is on her terms, which force him to keep up with her while she trains. Hazel's revolution begins in the self and with the self; she does not sacrifice herself for Raymond but negotiates a way to take care of herself first and help to take care of him. Further, Bambara turns the model of leader upside down by making the younger sister protect the older brother. This scenario forecasts a larger message to the 1960s and 1970s Black feminists and nationalists. Positioning Hazel in this manner emphasizes the sane, healthy, wholesome behavior Bambara believed was necessary for revolution or emancipation. By means of creating Hazel in this manner, Bambara is suggesting that the possibilities for young women like her are limitless—for them womanhood and liberation struggle are not in an either-or position but can be negotiated without sacrificing self-development. Doing so derails a feminism that is required to rebuke reproductive or "female" attributes. Portraying Hazel like this is subversive without rejecting behavior that nurtures others and community. Bambara recognizes that this is a dilemma but contends that family and nurturing are key covenants with our ancestors, each other, our children, God, and self; this dilemma is part of the process of resistance, transformation, and renewal that must be negotiated effectively.

Individual liberation, Bambara suggests, is the first step toward transformation and renewal of the community or nation. Hazel recognizes the conflict of prescribed notions of "girl" and rejects it:

> The biggest thing on the program is the May Pole dancing, which I can do without, thank you, even if my mother thinks it's a shame I don't take part and act like a girl for a change. . . . You'd think she'd be glad her daughter ain't out there prancing around a May Pole getting the new clothes all dirty and sweaty and trying to act like a fairy or flower or whatever you are supposed to be when you should be trying to be yourself, whatever that is, which is, as far as I am concerned, a poor Black girl who really

can't afford to buy shoes and a new dress you only wear once a lifetime
cause it won't fit next year. (27)

Hazel's rejection of contrived roles for girls in her candid critique of the
merits of the maypole event bucks "traditions" and asserts femaleness
on her own terms—as a runner. Making Hazel a runner—an activity
that requires constant motion—is significant to Bambara's feminist and
emancipatory impulse. It symbolizes the constant forward motion that
will produce progress or the act of "trying to be yourself, whatever that
is" (27). The discovery of the yet unknown self suggests that the possibilities are endless, especially when institutions and ideas like the maypole are challenged. Rather than succumbing to victim status within
her gendered or cultural environment, Hazel deconstructs the maypole
as an obstacle to her honest discovery of self. Moreover, Hazel's rejection of the archetypal idea of the feminine in our culture in favor of
defining her humanity or femaleness void of imposed prescriptions
of who or what she should be—even if the prescriptions come from her
parents—is refreshing:

> I was once a strawberry in a Hansel and Gretel pageant . . . being a perfect
> fool just so my mother and father could come dressed up. You'd think
> they'd know better than to encourage that kind of nonsense. I am not
> a strawberry. I do not dance on my toes. I run. That is what I am all
> about. (28)

The first stage of young Hazel's liberation is to know what she is not. Yet
again, Bambara is critical of cultural codes that encourage "the kind of
nonsense" of women Bambara makes them betray getting to know self
or make society know what women are "all about." This is a prerequisite
for women to develop healthy self, female or male relationships, and
communities in many of Bambara's stories because she knew black folk
had to deal with racism and sexism in our communities and create feminist revolutions.

At the end of "Raymond's Run" Hazel considers uniting with Gretchen in the cause of teaching her brother, Raymond, to run effectively. She says: "Maybe she'd like to help me coach Raymond; she obviously is serious about running . . . and she nods to congratulate me and then she smiles. And I smile. We stand there with this big smile of respect between us" (32). This final exchange between Hazel and Gretchen is symbolic of Bambara's visionary feminist/nation liberation impulse that sought to cultivate the possibilities for female/female and male/female bonding. The point seems to be that harmony and unity allow victory for Hazel, Gretchen, and Raymond. Hazel wins the race and she and Gretchen become allies working together to give Raymond effective instruction that will develop his running skills. Bambara uses her feminist/nationalist impulse to critique and correct. She seizes the moment to stress the importance of women figuring out how to get right with self so they can unite with each other and then lead a sovereign community toward freedom.

Also, because Bambara was in the people business—Black people, to be more specific—cultivating narratives that advocate mutual respect among young women was a promising sign for the community's growth and feminist goals: "We stand there with this big smile of respect between us. It is about as real a smile as girls can do for each other considering we don't practice real smiling everyday" (32). The shift in their spirits creates space for real female bonding to ensue, which is an important component of "wholesome, sane, and healthy behavior" for people interested in salvation. In essence her decision to add Raymond as "a great runner to the family tradition" (32) and to unite with Gretchen to train him is in keeping with the family, self, and ancestral covenants that were essential practices of liberation for Bambara.

Bambara's protagonists represent everyday "forms of transgression in which existing borders forged in domination can be challenged and redefined" (Awkward 1995, 9) in the interests of individual and community resistance, transformation, and renewal. Indeed, Bambara's fiction links theory and practice; it exemplifies her personal connection to diverse Black communities. Through Hazel Bambara models and negotiates the simultaneous making of self and community in a revolutionary manner. Her characters make self and then proceed to make others in the community better. Once that self is established, the person becomes a vital member of the community, contributing to efforts to achieve liberation. This is a process that, as Hazel demonstrates, may not always be neat or uncomplicated, but can improve the lives of many. For example, while Hazel tells an antagonist of her brother, "You got anything to say to my brother, you say it to me" (Bambara 1972, 27), she is not willing to sacrifice her running, which represents her identity. So when Mr. "Beanstalk" Pearson suggests she lose the race to Gretchen, she rejects this proposal and gives "him such a look he couldn't finish putting the idea into words" (29). While she is willing to fold watching Raymond into her training schedule, she will not sacrifice her running reputation—it is her identity. The myriad Hazel characters and other females in *Gorilla* all find a similar balance between individualism and communalism. Bambara's female protagonists model an iteration of self-expression that enhances group harmony and makes brothers (like Raymond) better.

Furthermore, while the "self" is important there is no question that communalism, the common good of the people, was the "business" that appealed to Bambara. However, the first line, mode, or impulse of liberation in her art usually involves building a stable self that can fashion a liberated community through strong family bonds and feelings of connection to a communal spirit that is poised for freedom. In "Raymond's Run" Hazel follows the practice of self, family, and community when she includes Raymond in her exercise routine. Raymond, while placed in the background of this story, is never quite out of sight. How he functions reflects Bambara's feminist-based liberation model that privileges women but does not ignore men. Thus Raymond tags along with Hazel, is forced to keep up with her pace, and in the process he also gets in shape! The outcome of this approach is that she inadvertently forces Raymond to become a skilled runner too. As a member of her community, he is important to her, but she does not sacrifice her dedication to the art of running, her selfhood, for him, and instead grows her family of runners. Her primary focus is her training schedule; Raymond is secondary. Hazel's assertion of feminism in this story cultivates personal, familial, and communal resistance efforts.

Cultural Work(er)

"The Lesson"

Bambara's other heavily anthologized story, "The Lesson," is also one of the best of her stories that display the art of her praxis of a liberation impulse. She created art that was activist-driven from her real concrete work experiences. Perhaps influenced by her experiences as family and youth caseworker in the New York City Department of Welfare, and as director at Colony Settlement House in the 1960s, "The Lesson" exemplifies her liberation impulse of activism and cultural work *for the people*. Like Bambara, the protagonist of this story practices liberation that directly aids the Black masses as they negotiate the daily struggles of life. Everywhere she ventured, Bambara was about the business of teaching real-life applications. Even as an instructor at Livingston and City College Bambara used the institutions to forge social justice and change, conjuring assignments for her students that were always geared toward real-life applications (Holmes 2014, 58). Among the Black writers of her era she had actual professional experience performing cultural work. She was actively engaged in practices of organizing working-class people in urban communities and academic institutions and therefore personally understood the bureaucracy that impugned help for the poor. Indeed, Bambara practiced what she wrote; she wrote what she practiced; she practiced liberation in art and life.

The way the character Miss Moore in "The Lesson" interacts with the children mirrors the duties of a settlement house director or counselor. The "settlement houses" concept emerged near the end of the nineteenth century but peaked around the 1920s in England and the United States (see Jeffery Scheuer's *Legacy of Light: University Settlement's First Century* [1985]). They were established in poor urban areas with the goal of bringing the working classes into contact with other classes, specifically the university educated, in an interdependent community. Hoping to share knowledge and culture with the poor to help alleviate the poverty of their low-income neighbors, these organizations provided an array of services, from parenting classes, food assistance, and childcare to education for children and youth. Bambara's stint as the director of the Colony Settlement House in Brooklyn aligned with the practices of liberation that privileged individual then family and community that we see in a story like "The Lesson." Thus, the character's name, Miss Moore, is symbolic of her role in helping the children recognize *more* options in life. Bambara, being Bambara, has the fictional Miss Moore offer the children *more*—she offers them "knowledge and education" *about poverty* in order to spark revolution rather than cultural assimilation.

In "The Lesson," Miss Moore is a grown-up iteration of the Hazel protagonist from "Raymond's Run." Like Bambara, Miss Moore has gone to college and returned to help a group of neighborhood youth understand the world, and recognize conflicts, while she arms them with knowledge that will assist their practice of self-liberation. Her engagement with the children is intended to produce resistance and recognition of their conflict or oppression, which is found in their economic inequality. Miss Moore is steeped in the Black aesthetic idea of collective art and community responsibility. In the tradition of Bambara's advocacy of "wide-awake" resistance and transformation, Miss Moore returns to the people more "beautiful" or educated than when she departed for college. Also, she is committed to the community, as is evidenced by her self-imposed "responsibility for the young one's education" (Bambara 1972, 88). Miss Moore models an emancipatory female character, willing to perform the real cultural work on the ground, among the people, assuming the "responsibility" of leadership—an organic intellectual. Miss Moore wants the children to know *more* of the world beyond their immediate community. She is illustrative of the range of female possibilities when "gorillas," or gender conventions, are lifted and replaced with guerilla consciousness training tactics like the trip to a wealthy Manhattan toy store. Miss Moore labors through the process of making revolution irresistible for these children. She also is in the tradition of civil rights struggle, which had a plethora of female leaders who skillfully cultivated the process of political consciousness and resistance without imposing their will. Thus Miss Moore is a radical example of a sane, wholesome practitioner of wide-awake resistance, self-defined and committed to a Black collective.

This story is a cue that revolution and transformation is never a simple or easy proposition and that the theory of revolution is a process that must be put into practice at the most basic level—a toy store. Indeed, liberation, community, transformation, and renewal are complex and complicated, which is why the young antagonist Sylvia is angry at the world and perceives Miss Moore as: "this nappy-headed bitch and her goddamn college degree" (89) instead of as a college-educated asset willing to share what she knows. Sylvia utters her disgust with Miss Moore as the group of neighborhood children is herded on a "field trip" to the FAO Schwartz toy store. In the true spirit of liberation and developing consciousness, Miss Moore situates the educational activity in the lived experience of the participants. During the field trip Miss Moore remains patient as she imparts serious lessons about money, economics, socialism, and capitalism. Initially Sylvia is cynical of Miss Moore's explanation for the purpose of the trip: "She boring us silly about what things cost and what our parents make and how much goes for rent and how money ain't divided up right in this country" (89). However, she slowly comes to realize that there is some merit in Moore's "boring" lecture when the children get into the toy store. Their inspection of expensive microscopes, paperweights, clowns, and a handcrafted fiberglass sailboat completely alters their world, rendering them at once both intimidated and angry. This reduction coupled with Miss Moore's teachings seems to anger Sylvia the most, and she shares her outrage at the social inequities while perusing the store:

> I could see me askin my mother for a $35 clown. "You wanna who that cost what?" she'd say cocking her head to the side to get a better view of the hole in my head. Thirty-five dollars could buy new bunk beds for Junior and Gretchen's boy . . . the whole household could go visit Grand-daddy Nelson . . . [it] would pay for the rent and piano bill too. Who are these people that spend that much for performing clowns and $1,000 for toy sailboats? (94)

Clearly Sylvia's analysis indicates Miss Moore may have succeeded in turning the toy-store outing into a lesson in wealth disparities. Miss Moore's dialogical pedagogy on democracy, capitalism, and socialism is far from heavy-handed socialist rhetoric. It is in the tradition of the critical pedagogy of Paulo Freire's and Antonio Gramsci's dialectical education of liberation. Miss Moore leads the children through dialogue and suggests but never pushes or acts on the children, instead working with them for answers. Inside the store, the poor are empowered to name the world. This approach empowers the children to transform their reality using a plethora of evidence to construct their own conclusions—which Sylvia and her "crew" begin to do. We see additional evidence of this when Sugar remarks, "You know, Miss Moore, I don't think all of us here put together eat in a year what that sailboat costs . . . this is not much of a democracy if you ask me" (95). While Sugar's comment agitates Sylvia, the true source of her anger is Miss Moore's indictment of them as "all poor and live in the slums" (89). This, says Sylvia, "[she] don't feature" (89). The truth about her class status in the world angers her more than anything else.

Actually, this story is a continuum of Bambara's notion of wholeness that dictated recognizing a conflict and the praxis of resistance for freedom, transformation, and renewal. The guiding question Bambara repeatedly has her characters in *Gorilla, My Love* ask or meditate on is whether it is natural, sane, and healthy to violate the contracts or covenants with ourselves, our families, or our community to know and love self and to be free. In "The Lesson" Bambara's objective is getting the children to understand where they stand as individuals and outside of their immediate community. Most important, she wants them to recognize that they are at war with the dominant class for a place at the table. Sylvia's recognition of this conflict and her status leaves her feeling displeased:

> We all start reciting the price tag like we in assembly. Handcrafted sailboat of fiberglass at one thousand one hundred ninety-five dollars. "Unbelievable," I hear myself say and am really stunned. I read it again for myself just in case the group recitation put me in a trance. Same thing. For some reason this pisses me off. (92)

In other words, how Sylvia's community and her toughness compare to her status in the larger world is an equally important part of achieving a whole existence or sense of self. Of course, the issue of Sylvia's and the other children's consciousness is as important as Bambara's suggestion that a community must practice agency and self-determination. This is why Miss Moore reminds the children, "Where we are is who we are. . . . But it don't necessarily have to be that way . . . poor people have to wake up and demand their share of the pie" (94–95).

Part of the beauty of "The Lesson" is Miss Moore's effortless instruction of what Bambara terms "wide-awake resistance." Miss Moore nurtures the process of being and becoming; she teaches in the spirit of an educator for liberation, instructing but avoiding being dogmatic or sounding monolithic. Furthermore, she also deemphasizes her role as the unilateral educator, cognizant that true liberatory practice requires problem posing and transcending the divide between teacher and learner. The practice of liberation the children engage in forces each individual to come to states of consciousness on their own. So when the children recite the price of the sailboat and they "look at Miss Moore and she lookin at us, waiting for I dunno what" (92), Bambara perfectly models in her art the element of conscientization—developing consciousness. At the moment that she stares back at them for answers she commits class suicide as unilateral educator, hoping they will become agents of their own liberation. In fact, Bambara invites readers to recognize the conflict, go through a transformation with the children, and figure out a path of resistance. Miss Moore's patience with the process of this dialectical exploration of class and economics comes to fruition when Q. T. proclaims: "Must be rich people shop here" (92).

A true *lesson* in this story is its tutelage in the practices of the liberation. The process requires creating space for an emancipatory consciousness to emerge organically. Miss Moore's liberation pedagogy captures Sylvia's attention, compelling her to ask Miss Moore, whom she dislikes, "how much a real boat costs" (93). This is a defining moment. Earlier Sylvia remarked that she would never talk to Moore and "give the bitch that satisfaction" (93), but when Miss Moore responds to Sylvia's boat question with a suggestion that Sylvia "check that out and report back to the group" (93), it angers Sylvia, who wants "some answers" (93). However, Miss Moore's dialectical liberation impulse privileges a sustained consciousness. It is the best way to transcend the divide between teacher and learner. Miss Moore actually demands *more* of Sylvia. True liberation practices require Sylvia to not only pose problems but have the power to transform her reality and close the divide between teacher and learner. The hope is that this practice will produce another Miss Moore, able and willing to embrace the dialectical process of liberation, thereby extending the pedagogy of hope that can be carried forward. Bambara simultaneously channeled the Black aesthetic directives of politically committed, purposeful art and a feminist-based Black revolution impulse. "The Lesson" reflects these intentions, as well as the potential of dialectics.

The story also instructs us about leadership and agency in the practice of liberation. For example, the children are nudged to enter the store but not pushed or led. They must enter the doorway to consciousness on their own. While their entry into the toy store is a comical scene, it confirms the awkwardness of taking the first step toward liberation:

> she don't lead the way. So me and Sugar turn the corner to where the entrance is, but when we get there I kinda hang back. Not that I'm scared, what's there to be afraid of, just a toy store. But I feel funny, shame. But what I got to be shame about? Got as much right to go in as anybody. But somehow I can't seem to get hold of the door. (93)

While Sylvia, Sugar, and the rest of the kids try to decide if they have the agency, Mercedes acts. She is described as "squeezing past" them, "smoothing out her jumper and walking right down the aisle." In stark contrast, "the rest of [them] tumble in like a glued-together jigsaw done all wrong" (93). Leadership rises naturally. In this instance it is Mercedes. For Bambara an essential art of liberation was the practice of eliminating hierarchies. Thus, Mercedes does not wait for Sylvia or Sugar to lead. She claims her agency, stepping forward to "walk down the aisle" toward freedom when the *leaders* of the group are afraid to take the lead.

Bambara intentionally leaves the ending open. When Sugar tells Miss Moore "this is not much of a democracy if you ask me. Equal chance to pursue happiness means equal crack at the dough," we are hopeful that Sugar is closer to consciousness. Next Miss Moore asks the children to "Imagine for a minute what kind of society it is in which some people can spend on a toy what it would cost to feed a family of six or seven" (95). Sensing Sylvia's budding consciousness, Miss Moore looks in her direction and bluntly asks, "Anybody else learn anything?" (95). To this Sylvia walks away. However, her retreat is not rejection but a reaction during the early stages of resistance before transformation and renewal. Sylvia's retreat is to process her recognition of the conflict, which is a prelude to resistance, transformation, and renewal on her own terms. Although Sylvia has a renewed vision of her inner self and herself outside of her Harlem community, it is unclear how she will ultimately process the information. Sylvia's consciousness has been triggered but is not yet "wide-awake" as she shrugs Sugar's arm off her shoulder on the way to the candy store, but there is hope that she may yet achieve "wide-awake resistance" when she says, "I'm goin over to the West End and then over to the Drive to think this day through" (96). While it is possible that she may take an unequal share of "the dough" and fail the test, it remains unclear how she will process the day. If she spends the cab fare she will have flunked the lesson about equity, greed, and democracy, and will prove herself no better than the toy store's patrons. Yet Sylvia's vow to take some time to "think this day through" (96) extends hope that she may have ascertained the lesson Miss Moore was trying to teach. The conclusion is open-ended for the reader's benefit and to afford Sylvia space to partake of the process of becoming.

The Hammer Man

"The Hammer Man" is yet another variation around Bambara's theme of feminist-based Black liberation that adroitly negotiates gender tensions and self-definition as a route to a wholesome sense of self and commu- nity. The story interrogates problems with conventional "girl" behavior that conflicts with efforts to cultivate sane, wholesome communities and community members—namely women. Bambara crafts another protagonist that rails against gender limitations. We are told that our narrator's mother wants her to join the local center in an effort to get her "out of [her] pants and stay in skirts on account of that's the way things were at the center" (Bambara 1972, 38). While she obeys the covenant of respecting her mother, who wants her to "fix [her] hair right and wear skirts all the time just so [her] mother would stop talking about her gray hairs, and Miss Rose would stop calling [her] by her brother's name by mistake" (38), the covenant with self is stronger. We learn that she "got thrown out of the center for playing pool when [she] should have been sewing" (39). This story challenges gender conventions and tries to heal antagonistic male/female relations without sacrificing critical realizations of self and community sovereignty. "The Hammer Man" explores covenants with self, family, and community.

A specific focus is the insanity of expecting girls to behave a particular way and the insane way that little boys like Manny believe they must act. In fact, Manny's insanity stokes a conflict between him and the protagonist that leads to unhealthy community relations. Bambara's focus on children aims to show us the roots of contentious male/female relationships, and that a solution to many of these conflicts requires changing the gender covenants with our children. Manny's insanity is similar to the insanity of the men in another story in the collection, "Talkin 'Bout Sonny," where Sonny's madness results in him stabbing his wife. The narrator is bothered that Delauney, the guy she is dating, casually dismisses his friend Sonny's violent act as "periodic" rage. In "The Hammer Man" Bambara examines similar antagonisms, but from the perspective of children. The unnamed female narrator has a conflict with Manny, who is also mentally unstable. The narrator, another one of Bambara's atypical females, is chastised for "hang[ing] around with boys" and "fight[ing] with them too" (35). Bambara's use of children as conduits to transform or reconstruct social expectations, contrived gender roles, and male rage is an exceptional idea because the youth represent hope for future change.

However, before any social customs are altered or any bonding takes place between the two children, a contentious relationship ensues. The conflict and its repercussions erupt "after [our narrator] called [Manny] what [she] called him and said a few choice things about his mother" (35). Bambara, a self-proclaimed feminist and nationalist, acknowledges Manny's insanity but it does not deter her from casting a female character as the instigator of disharmony that proves to be detrimental to the common good of the community. Manny threatens her life and spends days sitting outside of her home with a hammer, hoping to "kill" her "first chance he got" (35). Manny's lack of "sense of humor" and his determination to harm her triggers a case of "yellow fever" (she is afraid) that keeps the feisty narrator homebound (36). This seemingly harmless conflict between a little boy and a little girl is a metaphor or warning to Black communities that internal rage and violence is insane behavior that threatens a liberation impulse. It diminishes community harmony, making the larger community vulnerable to other fractures. The children's conflict has repercussions that splinter other relationships and upset spiritual balance in the neighborhood. For example, Miss Rose, who defends the narrator, gets into a fight in the streets with Crazy Manny's mother, whereby "they commenced to get with it, snatching bottles out of the garbage cans and breaking them on the Johnny pumps and stuff like that" (36). The conflict also spreads to our narrator's father and Manny's brothers and uncle when her father "happened to ask Manny one night why he was sitting on the stoop like that every night" (37). When Manny explains that he plans to kill our narrator, her father has "a few words with Manny first, and then he got hold of [Manny's] older brother, Bernard, who was more his size" (37), jamming "Bernard's head in the mailbox" (37). This leads to her father receiving "messages from Bernard's uncle about where to meet him for a showdown" (37), which causes her father to spend days mumbling to himself and arming himself with her "stickball bat" (37). These internal frictions are contrary to Bambara's desire for Black folk to understand that they are "at war" and must practice "wide-awake resistance" in order for transformation and renewal to ensue.

Fortunately, Manny's insanity, which contributed to the conflict in the first place, calms the situation when he ventures onto and literally falls off of an unstable roof. Manny's fall is symbolic of how far the community has fallen from its purpose. The openly adversarial behavior is a violation of the covenant to unite against a common enemy. Bambara was sensitive to any behavior that threatened liberation. This included antagonistic male/female relations at all levels. Her fiction seeks to detonate gender conflict without sacrificing critical realizations, while stressing principles such as healthy gender relations, united family, and community. Her point seems to be that internal conflict—even among children—leads to chaos within a community that violates the covenant of transformation and renewal. While our protagonist's resistance against contrived gender behavior is positive for the community's growth, her conflict with Manny stifles the larger goal or impulse of community salvation.

"The Hammer Man" emphasizes that gender conflicts also stifle liberation for the group. In this scenario unhealthy mocking behavior provokes a mentally unstable boy to react outrageously, which disrupts the delicate balance of harmony in the neighborhood. When Manny approaches the narrator and a group of children playing in the school-yard, she launches into a verbal attack, yelling, "You had enough, Hammer Head. Just bring your crummy self in this yard and I'll pick up where I left off" (38). Despite Manny's insane behavior (a symbol for the larger issue of male sexism) leaving him with his head bandaged and his leg in a cast, our narrator, ignoring the previous unrest her signifying has caused, further instigates conflict with the injured Manny. Her taunts threaten the covenant of peace that was established after his fall. The attack on wounded Manny is antithetical to the feminist-based liberation impulse Bambara champions in much of her fiction. Temporarily positioning her female protagonist in a less than positive light is a cautionary message from Bambara that it is important to be critical of all insane behavior that threatens or violates the larger covenant of healthy, wholesome community. Bambara was committed to truth. The conclusion of the story bears out Bambara's unique and complex feminist/Black aesthetic philosophy that privileges pluralism, consciousness, transformation, and renewal.

These things come to fruition in the park when Manny is practicing layups and minding his own business after park hours. Suddenly the police arrive on the scene and begin to question Manny, but he continues shooting imaginary layups without responding or acknowledging the police. The narrator, who had been standing watching Manny practice long before the police arrived, intervenes to speak for Manny. She sarcastically explains to them the obvious: "He's doing lay-up. I'm watching" (40). But when the cop slaps Manny and calls him "black boy" because he ignores them, she exhibits a commitment to the covenant of unity and consciousness: "when somebody says that word like that, I gets warm . . . crazy or no crazy, Manny was my brother at that moment and the cop was the enemy" (40). She goes on to tell the cop, in Manny's defense: "You better give him back his ball. Manny don't take no mess from no cops. He ain't bothering nobody. . . . Just trying to get a little practice in before the softball seasons starts" (40). Bambara, whose goal was constantly to unify the nation, models salient concerns for Manny and the narrator despite their combative history; she chooses a path or practice of liberation that unifies her with Manny against a common adversary. What is equally masterful is how Bambara subverts cultural and gender conventions, making her female narrator the protector of a male. Indeed, like young Hazel in "Raymond's Run," who protects her brother, Raymond, the narrator in this story protects her "brother" Manny from police harassment. Bambara's fiction consistently reveals the dialectical and complicated nature of liberation. While the narrator might not have resolved her conflict with Manny, she understands that the larger war or battle is against a salient enemy that oppresses them both indiscriminately. Her harsh treatment of Manny when he is down is a critique but she also models when and how to unify against common enemies when she bonds with Manny in an emancipatory manner, telling the cops: "I damn sure can't be your sister seeing how I am a black girl" (41). However, in the same salvo, she calls Manny her "brother." Here again Bambara emphasizes her recurrent theme that male/female bonding and communal solidarity are important emancipatory elements for nation-building.

There are several important final things to note about this story. First, the narrator's decision to unite with Manny, whom she regards as her "brother at that moment," when faced with the cop's harassment of Manny models a unique feminist-based liberation politics. Second, the narrator never denies that she and Manny have a conflict. In other words, her nation-first stance does not mitigate her critique of Manny's crazy (subtext for sexist) behavior that threatens to "kill" her (perhaps symbolic of how sexism threatens the spirit of women). However, "the cop was the enemy" at the moment. Third, Bambara is critical of any negative behavior that obstructs unity or provokes internal conflicts (such as that between our narrative's father, Manny's mother, brothers, and uncles, and Miss Rose) or tensions in a community rather than harmony. Fourth, Bambara impresses upon the reader the importance of being able to suspend personal disagreement to unite against common enemies. Thus our narrator allies herself with Manny and risks also being arrested in the schoolyard. Finally, once again Bambara's complex, feminist-based liberation impulse masterfully positions females as leaders and equalitarian protectors of their "brothers." As is common with Bambara's protagonists, our narrator's sense of self remains unscathed. Until the end of the story the narrator strategically remains unnamed or undefined; she maintains her dungarees and brash, strong demeanor. Although at the end she does participate "in this very boss fashion show at the center" (43), this concession, we are assured, is on her own terms. Of equal note is Bambara's refusal to define her narrator as merely a feminist protagonist who acts like a boy. She is whole and heroic in her negotiation of her femininity. Not only does she wear pants and ditch sewing class to play pool with the boys but she also agrees to participate in the fashion show. She is complicated, evolving, in a state of becoming. And while we are unsure if she will ever attend a sewing class, her willingness to model clothes that others sew demonstrates a nuanced and evolving sense of what it means to be female that seems a worthy practice to model.

Generational Conflicts

"My Man Bovanne"

The story "My Man Bovanne" continues Bambara's liberation focus but shifts the subject to overlooked elders, who are equally essential to liberation. In this instance Bambara compels a critical examination of internal threats to nationalist politics and community salvation when the intentions are honorable. Instead of being the culprit of misunder-standing and miscommunication, in this story the elder Miss Hazel undergoes a traumatic experience similar to what young Ollie faces in the story "Happy Birthday." Here Miss Hazel protects herself and the blind Mr. Bovanne from her young daughters and sons, who are organizing the community for social justice. Ironically, her daughters and sons, in their revolutionary zeal and organizing efforts, are blinded from appre-ciating the agency of the people they are working to organize—people like Bovanne and Hazel. The message of respect for elders in the wake of Black Power is in line with the covenant of ancestral embrace. Bam-bara's story is a reminder that a core contract or covenant is valuing the wisdom and guidance of ancestors and elders. The youth err by taking elders for granted or giving them diminished priority. However for Bambara these wisdoms were an important part of the process of the practice of becoming liberated. Miss Hazel assesses the youth, saying, "Black Power got hold to their minds and mess em around till they can't be civil to ole folks" (3). The story is a cautionary tale about an issue that was a concern among many writers of the Black aesthetic that privileged the ancient and the future. Bambara, an activist by nature, was critical of any dogma, hierarchy, or exclusionary behavior that might threaten the agency and freedom of the Miss Peoples of the world. Bambara was interested in the process of becoming of the "Black" mind and the next steps that would guide the process of a healthy nation in the future.

"My Man Bovanne" forces a critical examination and revision of blind spots regarding politics and community organizations that threat-ened covenants with elders, youth, women, or a healthy nation. The contribution of every community member is invaluable in the process of liberation—particularly the wisdom of elders. In her essay "African American Women Writers, Black Nationalism, and the Matrilineal Heritage," Joan S. Korenman correctly points out that: "Bambara seems apprehensive that black nationalism may be endangering vital aspects of African American life, in particular the bond between genera-tions and the wisdom black elders have traditionally offered to family and community" (1994, 149). Thus, there is nothing arbitrary about the symbolism of Mr. Bovanne's blindness. In Bambara's expressions of Black aesthetic adherence to the process of Blackness and the practices of liberation, the elders are a valuable aspect of the search for a viable legacy. Moreover, "My Man Bovanne" is another model of wholesome, healthy representations that contribute to immediate and future goals of nation building. It depicts Black Nationalism and feminism in a balanced, critical, and honest manner. Indeed, her liberation impulse cautions youth against being "blinded" during the process of becoming liberated from appreciating the value and wisdom of elders.

"My Man Bovanne" teaches two great lessons: (1) it shows how to balance Afrocentric and feminist sensibilities; and (2) it cautions against and models how to mitigate generational conflict that threatens the larger liberatory project. While Miss Hazel cedes leadership to her children, she refuses to languish into the background or have her sense of *being* limited in the name of "revolution." This is why Miss Hazel rebuffs the "community" and her children from stifling her self-definition regarding her sexuality and politics in relation to Bovanne. In terms of feminism, her daughter's leadership role is as prominent as that of her sons. Once again Bambara's fiction characterizes females as leaders as a common and necessary occurrence. Not only does she confirm the presence of female leadership but she also shows that the men are not in opposition to it. Hazel proves that the individual can belong simultaneously to both him- or herself and the community. We first see this when she disputes her children about her attire, telling them, "I can still wear me some sleeveless dresses without the meat hanging off my arm" (6). Bambara challenges the limits of consciousness and self-expression that were at odds during the 1960s and 1970s, teaching a great lesson about negotiating gender, generational, and cultural tensions.

No lesson is larger than Miss Hazel's decision to dance with the blind man Bovanne despite the disapproval of her children, who consider him a "tom." In many ways "My Man Bovanne" imparts a great illustration of effective practices of liberation. It negotiates gender and cultural tensions about the true nature or the legacy of communal and familial resistance. The reader learns that the best practice is one that elides essentialism in Black aesthetic or feminist sensibilities—both must embrace balance. There is no *either-or*, only *and-but*. Miss Hazel refuses to languish into the background, and her daughter's role as a leader is not an issue for the community; once again her brothers work in partnership with her as organizers. While the brothers and sisters work together, Miss Hazel refuses to allow stagnant notions of liberation to stifle her self-definition in terms of her sexuality or politics. Bambara alters slightly the African spiritual belief that the individual belongs to the community as a whole. Through Miss Hazel she asserts that the individual must first belong to self in order to best serve the community—in this way both interests can be served simultaneously.

In story after story Bambara engages an emancipatory impulse that privileges a humanistic, gender-balanced, cross-generational focus within a liberation impulse that features patience and respect for the process of becoming and being. Bambara is committed to feminism, community, and liberation that are dialectical, which allows her characters and their respective communities to expand boundaries. Miss Hazel's children need her to organize the elders but they also disapprove of her behavior (dancing with Bovanne and wearing sexy clothing), which they deem antithetical to their vision of liberation. Not only is their notion of liberation and nation building divergent, their words are injurious. Moreover, the rift between mother and daughter has Miss Hazel in the most pain:

> it was the girlchild [her daughter Elo] I covered in the night and wept over for no reason at all. . . . And how did things get to this, that she can't put a sure hand on me and say Mamma we love you and care about you and you entitled to enjoy yourself cause you a good woman? (8)

Here, Bambara is critical of revolutionary youth, who in their fervor for freedom lose faith in family and feelings of respect and trust of the elders who represent a more tangible "African" past. For Bambara, a successful practice of liberation is one that invites a chorus of voices—gendered and cross-generation—to be heard; it is one where the daughter puts "a sure hand" on her mother. Bambara uses her art to present such a chorus representing the scope, breadth, depth, and nuisance of liberation, Blackness, and community. In essence, the young people's rigid understanding of consciousness or revolution "blinds" them to the inherent "good woman" spirit of their mother and Mr. Bovanne as well. Miss Hazel and Mr. Bovanne symbolize the importance of recognizing internal cultural values, the intrinsic goodness of individuals despite peripheral impressions because the pathway to liberation can be capacious.

This story exemplifies Bambara's consistent practice of liberation that privileges African reverence for elders and adoration of children. Thus, when Hazel's children confront her obtuse notions of emancipatory behavior without including her in the process, she rejoinders their last-minute request that she talk "with [Reverend Trent] . . . about giving us his basement for a campaign headquarters" (8), as follows: "if grassroots mean you kept in the dark I can't use it. I really can't" (8). Bambara is not shy about critiquing emergent revolutionary youth who, in their fervor for freedom, lose sight of the covenant of faith in family and feelings of trust and respect for elders like Bovanne that connect them to a rich past. This also punctuates Bambara's compulsion for practices of liberation that are wholesome and capacious, have breadth and scope, and do not dichotomize Blackness. It is a continuum in her work. A core practice in Bambara's liberation impulse is a belief in cross-generational community and culture so that true spiritual growth is achieved.

The dialectics surrounding what it means to be conscious in this story support the BAM mantra of being and becoming that Bambara regularly explores in all the stories in this collection. The characters, even those with intellect and wisdom make mistakes and are in a perpetual stage of growth—the girls are not taught to cater to the egos of boys and men but raised to be competitors, without shame or silence. Bambara models in her fiction women, men, and communities emancipated or liberated from social conventions and gender prescriptions. In essence, her revolutionary children miss the inherent "good woman" spirit that their mother possesses; they are equally blind to Bovanne. Such "generational gaps" or fissures betray internal cultural worth, communal wholeness, and the intrinsic goodness of individuals. The capacious liberation impulse in Bambara's fiction does not dichotomize along the lines of gender or age. In fact, her negotiation of youth and elders is her iteration of a Black aesthetic negotiating ancient past and future.

"The Lesson" represents an early example of Bambara's notion of wholeness that stresses fundamental and pragmatic inclusion for all members of the community, specifically "grassroots" elements like Hazel and Bovanne, who are excluded because of age, gender, or other handicaps, or, as Hazel points out regarding Bovanne, "cause he blind and old and don't nobody there need him since they grown up and don't need they skates fixed no more" (9). Bambara insists that he remains an important member of the liberation chorus, which is in sync with Black aesthetic reverence for ancestral spirits and wisdom.

Like Bambara, Miss Hazel comprehends the symbolic ancestral importance of Bovanne and tends to his spirit herself, which compels her to decide to purchase him "some dark sunglasses," invite him to dinner, and give him "a nice warm bath," because, unlike her children, she recognizes the importance of taking "care of the older folks" (10). Miss Hazel's union with Bovanne consummates a reverence for male/female unity and cross-generational practices. Her embrace of Bovanne when all others find him detrimental or useless symbolizes effective negotiation of the nationalist covenant with ancestors, self, and community. Through Miss Hazel Bambara nudges Black Power politics (the youth in this story) toward a more capacious freedom, transformation, and resistance. Despite their misgivings, her faith in the youth is unwavering because she values their ability to "help us get the breakfast program goin, and the school for the little kids and the campaign and all" (9–10). The process of liberation, like Blackness, is complex, nuanced, and discursive, which is why Miss Hazel is correct and she sees value in what the youth espouse.

The discursive reality of Hazel's commitment and contributions are vital to the project of emancipation. What we glean from Miss Hazel's discursive exchange with her children is that effective practices of liberation require fidelity to covenants like respect for parents and people like Bovanne—the elders of the world. In Bambara's fiction, turning a "blind" eye to these covenants is not a sane, wholesome, or healthy practice, but rather antithetical to an effective liberation impulse. Bovanne symbolizes the possibilities and meanings of a wholesome notion of liberation, whereby our consciousness and emancipatory zeal do not blind us to the role of the people. Such a notion is open to becoming, without settling on being defined as a particular thing or behavior. Thus, Miss Hazel submits that for revolution to be "whole" it is important to nurture the entire community. This is a vision of life that is at once spiritually driven and whole. The children's mistreatment of Bovanne is not a good practice of liberation. Through Miss Hazel Bambara offers a reminder against neglecting or being blinded to recognizing the value of faceless members of the community. Bambara revisions notions of Black liberation without abandoning core principles that drove the Black aesthetic. This story, like others, practices these ideals. What she demonstrates is that liberation is a complex state of becoming and evolving—it is never stagnant. She culls the Black aesthetic legacy, etching its full potential to make this point. It is for these reasons that Bovanne's emotional status, his individual human spirit, and the *whole* of him as a person is tended to in the story. The messiness and complexity of liberation as it refers to community and individual spirit is a recurring theme in Bambara's fiction.

Miss Hazel's last name, "Peoples," speaks volumes about the community/individual conflict and effective practices of liberation. The name embodies Bambara's explanation to her own daughter that "Black people are her business" (Deck 1999). The people are her work in the world, and her name is symbolic of the people (elders, women, children, regular folk) that are the focus but not seen prominently enough in the struggle for liberation. "The People" become real persons in Bambara's art. Indeed, the plight of Black people was her business. Not only was her art her praxis of liberation, but also praxis of liberation was a central theme in her art. Bambara's emancipatory impulse was capacious, incorporating the blind, the old, and the young as essential to the struggle for liberation.

Black people were indeed Bambara's business. Furthermore, she wanted young activists not to be blinded to *seeing* that even the old and seemingly useless are essential, or at least viable contributors to the struggle for salvation and liberation. Thus Hazel rejoinders: "old folks is the nation. That what Nisi sayin and I mean to do my part" (10). She reminds her children, the 1960s Black radicals, that to neglect elders is to neglect the spirit or faith in African American heritage, which robs the younger generation of the spiritual wholeness necessary for survival and freedom. Elders are part of the ancestral past that the Black aesthetic championed; respecting them is a sacred covenant for which betrayal is inconceivable. Bambara, a self-declared "feminist-nationalist-activist," was critical of any narrow perceptions threatening wholesome evolution of Black consciousness because *all* of the people and their freedom were valuable to her liberation impulse.

"Gorilla, My Love"

The title story of the collection, "Gorilla, My Love," maps Bambara's assertion that there is war going on and that transformation and renewal can be achieved with the proper dosage of self-definition, recognition of conflicts, resistance, and upholding contracts and covenants. Bambara's feminist/nationalist liberation impulse of being and becoming is on full display here in the title story. What appears to be a harmless story of a little girl with a crush on her uncle, whom she calls Hunca Bubba, is packed with immense symbolism and a complex message about personal, community, and family covenants of respect and resistance. It also continues Bambara's theme of empowering young women to manage narrative. Ironically the first thing the narrator tells readers is that she is "sittin in the navigator seat with a wet thumb on the map," which indicates she is in charge of the story; she will map its coordinates. She guides while Granddaddy, who calls her "Scout," drives and Uncle Hunca Bubba (Jefferson Winston Vale) and Baby Jason sit in the backseat, a place she "don't feature" (13). Her role, the role of future young women, is one of leadership, which is why she "study the map" and is "the navigator" (14). Bambara's impulse or model of collaboration across genders and generations is manifest in this story.

The story situates a young female protagonist sitting in "the navigator seat," and while the story's central conflict stems from Hunca Bubba's decision to change his name "back" to Winston Vale and his announcement that he is getting married, the true focus is a young female and the covenant adults must have with youth. Winston Vale's proclamation frustrates our narrator because he breaks his promise to marry her when she grows up. Despite her toughness, Bambara reminds us that Scout is still a complex and vulnerable human being who, while a confident leader, is afraid to ride in the back because she fears "maybe a rat [is] in the buckets" of pecans (13). Later she reveals that although tough and high-spirited, she "sleep with lights on and blame it on Baby Jason" (13).

She is also vulnerable to Hunca Bubba's (Winston Vale's) photo of the "skinny woman in a countrified dress with her hand shot up her face" (14) that he plans to marry. Unwilling to acknowledge Hunca Bubba's fiancé or his imminent marriage, Scout spies a movie theater in the background of the photo, which shifts the story's focus to the time she and Big Brood and Baby Jason revolted at the RKO Hamilton movie theater. This reflection is another example of betrayal and demonstrates that she will not tolerate broken covenants without resistance and demanding justice. The conflict she recounts centers around the film *Gorilla, My Love* (a film about Christ's crucifixion, most likely *King of Kings*) that they expected to be a film about a gorilla but it was not. Scout was angered that they were getting "messed around with Sunday School stuff" (15), and her reflection on this incident confirms that Scout's leadership extends beyond Granddaddy's navigator seat. First we learn how when the matron "with her chunky self, [flashed] that flashlight dead in your eye so you can give her some lip" (14), she was the one "turning out the show if the matron get too salty" (15). Further, she reveals how when the "bad boys in the park take away Big Brood's Spaudeen from him" she is the one that "jump on they back and fight awhile" (15). The point is that in the face of betrayal or conflicts she leads a "wide-awake" resistance for justice in the wider family and community legacy of rebellion—-sometimes nonviolent and sometimes not.

Hazel (Scout) elucidates that she is not angry about the movie because she does not have "anything against Jesus" (14). However, she is angry because she feels violated, and is frustrated with adults who consistently break covenants with kids:

> Grownups figure they can treat you just anyhow. Which burns me up. There I am, my feet up and my Havmore potato chips . . . in my lap and the money safe in my shoe from the big boys and here comes this Jesus stuff. (15)

To protect their humanity, Hazel leads the children in a revolt against this injustice. She leads the children in antics of "Yellin, booin, stompin and carryin on . . . to wake the booth up" (15). And, when "the matron ropes off the children section and flashes her light all over the place," a full revolt ensues (15). Hazel and her crew protest the injustice of being confined by running all over the place to create chaos, informing the reader that "it take more than some dusty ole velvet rope to tie us down" (15). While flinging popcorn and "Baby Jason kickin seats" (15) may on the surface appear to be merely a scene of badly behaved children, it illuminates the importance of engaging in resistance, even for an injustice as miniscule as a film. Instead of sit-ins or throwing rocks, they stand up, run around the theater, kick seats, refuse to stay in the roped-off section, and throw popcorn in protest of the deceptive advertising tactics of the movie theater.

The revolt she leads adheres to her family's covenant of justice, integrity, and resistance. This liberation impulse, taught by her parents, is that it is not sane to undertake cultural ideas that challenge her family's teachings, which includes paying for a film that was advertised as something entirely different. Her outrage when describing the film reveals the teachings of her emancipatory impulse:

> [The film] is not so simple as it is stupid. Cause I realize that just about anybody in my family is better than this god they always talkin about. My daddy wouldn't stand for nobody treatin any of us that way. My mama specially. (15)

While she is not against Jesus, what she has been taught compels her to reject and resist being oppressed. The dialectics of transformation, renewal, and liberation she has been taught conflicts with the practices of taking place in this film. She informs the reader of her conviction that her parents would take direct action to get the family member off the cross. Hazel imagines her "Daddy yelling to Granddaddy to get him a ladder" or her "mama and her sister Daisy jumpin on them Romans beatin them with they pocketbooks" (16). Hazel's (Scout) parents' advice and their teachings of resistance, nourishes and empowers her natural emancipatory impulse. It is central to her identity. Moreover, the covenant of resistance that has been instilled in her is to always speak the truth and stand up for justice finds expression in the movie theater revolt. She informs the reader that her mother has taught her to "speak up and let the chips fall where they may . . . And daddy look up from the paper and say, You hear your mama good, Hazel" (18). Not only is this powerful because it orients readers to Hazel's core value system, but once again Bambara places a female voice in the forefront of consciousness raising. Also, Bambara smoothly neutralizes patriarchy when Hazel's dad echoes his wife then insist that her detractors "com see [him] first" (18). In short, she places faith in her family's love for her and their collaborative teachings of resistance. For her, the premise of the film is "stupid" because it conflicts with the covenants of family, community and the legacy of active resistance she has been taught.

This legacy of resistance is what compels her to yell "We want our money back," which "gets everybody in chorus" (16) during the movie. Hazel, tired of grown-ups' persistent violations of children's trust "cause they little and can't take em to court" (17), resolves to "kick the door open wider and . . . sit down and tell the man about himself and that I want my money back and that goes for Baby Jason and Big Brood too" (17). Notice that once again Bambara channels the dominant voice of resistance through a female voice because her emancipatory impulse privileges looking out for people. Hazel also demands a refund for the male members of the group she leads. Yet when these tactics fail she is more than willing to resort to more "active" forms of resistance that threaten the economic sensibilities of her enemy. Bambara chastises family members and the adult community for failing to adhere to a better code when dealing with children when she has Hazel remark, "even gangsters in the movies say My word is my bond" (18). Thus she sets a fire under the candy stand, "which closed the raggedy ole Washington down for a week" (17). While they do not get their money back, their oppressor loses his ill-gained profits in the cost of rebuilding and in losing a week of profit. The transformation and renewal she achieves is temporary, but it is a start. What drives Hazel is an unwavering adherence to the covenant of resistance that her parents have taught her.

The code her parents have taught her honors self-determination, self-respect, and justice. The depth of this code is tested when her father discovers it was she who set the fire. Hazel rationalizes her behavior using her parents' teachings of consistency: "if you say Gorilla, My Love, you supposed to mean it" (17). Her defense, steeped in core family covenants, gets her "Daddy [to] put his belt back on" (18). She explains her father's impartiality to the reader: "Cause that's the way I was raised. Like my Mama say in one of them situations when I won't back down, Okay Badbird, you right. Your point is well-taken" (18). They have taught her about integrity, truth, justice, and wide-awake resistance. However, the movie theatre and her uncle Hunca Bubba violate the covenants she has been taught. In fact, we are told that even Granddaddy Vale, who "got no memory to speak of," if told he has promised something always responds, "Well if that's what I said, then that's it" (18). These teaching guide her moral compass and compel agitation with her uncle, whom, she says, promised "to wait" to "marry [her] when [she] grew up" (19). His response that he was "just teasin" is rejected and compels her to call him a "lyin dawg" (19–20) for behaving in this manner.

In the end, Hazel, the leader and navigator, the tough little girl also known as Scout who can turn a movie theater out is still a vulnerable kid in the process of becoming whose feelings need protecting. However, despite her uncle's betrayal and her vulnerability, she nevertheless holds the map. She has temporarily lost her "bearins and don't know where to look" (20), but her possession of the map is an indication that she will find her way. It is refreshing that Jefferson Winston Vale's betrayal does not diminish Hazel's belief in female/male bonding, nor her commitment to family values. Her Granddaddy and Baby Jason are the remaining males in her family who can still be counted on for support. In fact, Baby Jason cries along with her in emotional solidarity, "Cause he is [her] blood brother and understands" (20). Furthermore, Hazel's emancipatory impulse allows her to understand that: "we must stick together or be forever lost" (20). Bambara seems to want her male and female readers to understand that for every Winston Vale there is a Baby Jason and a Granddaddy who represent the future and ancient wisdom.

Stories like "Gorilla, My Love" exhibit Bambara's interest in resistance, renewal, transformation, and faith in family. Whether battling sexism or any other forms of social oppression, her characters and the communities they inhabit explore capacious avenues to expressions of self, Blackness, and liberation. Moreover, her fiction traces and revises cultural nationalist ideology of the period. She forges strong feminist positions that critique patriarchy but embrace male/female bonding over dichotomies. In this way Bambara manages to remain connected to Black Nationalist politics and the Black aesthetic without sacrificing her nation- and female-centered politics of resistance, transformation, and renewal. This is a difficult task, yet Bambara finds a successful balance that fuses race, gender, community, cultural, and political concerns in her narratives. As Bambara explains, she does not

> find any basic contradiction or any tension between being a feminist, being a pan-Africanist, being a nationalist . . . and being a woman in North America. (Guy-Sheftall 1979, 239)

Rather than allow a single discourse to assume privilege, she successfully balances male and female discourses to achieve what her life and fiction is all about: wholesome, healthy, sane communities, capable of recognizing conflict then engaging in wide-awake resistance against obstacles to the covenants with self, family, children, and each other that impugn transformation and renewal. Therefore her Black aesthetic ethos is capacious, emphasizing pluralism in African American political and cultural representation.

The stories are variations on the themes of female self-definition, individual and community cultural renewal, and emancipation or freedom of some sort. Each story is a separate voice, instrument, or medley. Taken collectively these separate voices represent a revolutionary cultural and intellectual reimagining that is a "whole" cultural representation of self-definition and community, feminism, Black Nationalist politics and generational balance. Bambara, a self-declared "pan-Africanist-socialist-feminist" used her art to compel people to pay attention. Indeed, the art of her cultural work was intended to nourish souls and make "revolution irresistible." The stories in *Gorilla, My Love* are a wonderful example of this impulse channeled through Black feminist and Black aesthetic influences. There is no question that the special vantage point of women's marginality in these stories effectively criticizes the dominant racist, classist, sexist hegemony and creates a counterhegemony of daily life resistances that are vital practices of liberation.

3

IRRESISTIBLE LOVE AND STRUGGLE IN *THE SEA BIRDS ARE STILL ALIVE*

The job of the writer is to make revolution irresistible.

Toni Cade Bambara

Revolution begins with the self, in the self.

Toni Cade Bambara

We are at war, and that war is not simply a hot debate between the capitalist camp and the socialist camp . . . it's not just over . . . who has the right to utilize resources for whomsoever's benefit. The war is also being fought over the truth . . . the truth about human nature, about the human potential. . . . My responsibility, to myself, to my neighbors, my family, and the human family is to try to tell the truth . . . so I work to tell the truth . . . I work to celebrate struggle, to applaud the tradition of struggle in our community.

Toni Cade Bambara

A key impulse or practice in the fiction of Toni Cade Bambara encompasses a revolutionary love that privileges feminism and an approach to revolution that is initiated inward or with the self and spirals outward to partners, family, community, nation, and internationally. Her 1977 collection of short fiction, *The Sea Birds Are Still Alive*, written after major trips to Vietnam and Cuba, splendidly represents the power of the liberation impulse of spiritual wholeness aesthetic. In most of these stories Bambara offers a fluid and balanced negotiation of what it means to be "both a feminist and a warrior in race struggle."

Given Bambara's views of womanhood/manhood and revolution, when one views Bambara against her contemporaries, she was less concerned with the hurt of it all and chose to handle Black male-female relationships differently in her fiction. As Beverly Guy-Sheftall adroitly points out, Bambara's fiction omits the "bitter residue of bad feelings between women and men," opting for a more positive "net social effect" (Guy-Sheftall 1995, 15). This approach stemmed from Bambara's love for her community, which included men, women, elders, and youth, and her dedication to the "net social effect" that would ultimately lead to liberation. Thus her love for the community was revolutionary and it was a revolutionary love. As Linda Janet Holmes details in her wonderful biography of Bambara, *A Joyous Revolt*: "Bambara's writing is much more than a marker of time. As an essayist, editor, and fiction writer, Bambara envisioned multicultural movements that crossed geographic boundaries including forging alliances among women of color" (Holmes 2014, xviii). Therefore, she populates this collection of stories with characters that are cultural workers out among the folk, doing the business of helping the people discover and create possibilities and Afrocentric models. Thus, these stories model a society that is egalitarian, with new masculine realities that feature a more responsible Black manhood that is less sexist and believes less in patriarchy.

The revolutionary love on display in *The Sea Birds* tackles racism, sexism, and classism, manhood and womanhood, to grow personal relationships in a healthy and holistic manner and establish or renew faith, family, and community. The stories in *The Sea Birds Are Still Alive* represent new realities of Black women as protagonists united with each other and with Black men against racist, sexist, and classist oppression to displace unhealthy and stereotypic images. The people assembled in these stories practice an audacious commitment to the survival and wholeness of all the people—the females, males, children, and elders. The impact this collection makes is how artfully the stories "celebrate struggle" and applaud "the tradition of struggle" without sacrificing narrative complexity and craft. Bambara offers additional insight into what she is doing in *The Sea Birds*, and her general approach to revolutionary love in her fiction that separates her from her peers:

> I'm much more concerned with the caring that lies beneath the antagonisms between black men and black women. There is a great deal of static that informs our relationships, above and beyond the political wedge that has been jammed between us by myth-makers of the oppressor class . . . the hurt doesn't teach me anything and I'm concerned primarily with usable lessons. (Lewis 2012, 15)

Bambara offered a vision of future liberation activity for all Black folk that privileged united effort. She did not believe "that black women . . . or any sector of the community . . . [were] any more in command of [how to deliver liberation] or in touch with it more than any other" (9). In fact, her vision of liberation was transnational and multicultural.[1]

Bambara's goal was to make revolution irresistible, and she often succeeded in getting characters to fall in love with liberation or at least explore the possibility of embarking on a love affair with it. This collection emerged at a time when Bambara had come to terms with the relevance of her own writing as an effective way to be involved in political struggle. Several of the stories collected here were inspired by stories of "fierce interrogation and torture heaped upon women" (Holmes 2014, 82) that she heard while visiting the Women's Union in Hanoi in

Vietnam. In her notebooks Bambara articulated the unbearable pain she felt from the stories the women shared with her.[2] As one reads these stories it is clear that her early 1970s international travel inspired her to think more seriously about the connection between writing and social activism, as well as about possibilities for women in the United States. Nearly every story in *The Sea Birds* involves some act or practice of making revolution irresistible. From "The Organizer's Wife" and "The Apprentice" to "The Sea Birds Are Still Alive" and "Christmas Eve at Johnson's Drugs N Goods," Bambara offers a capacious rendering of nation building that unifies and mobilizes the power of the people. The stories reveal a connection between spiritual wholeness and commitment to family, faith, feeling, and freedom or liberation. The assembly of cultural workers in these stories helps people recenter themselves and work for liberation.[3]

The term practice of liberation, as used here, is concerned with the process or way to liberate self and community, either simultaneously or in that order. Women are central to every aspect of life in these stories, and her protagonists are strong, stunning, warm, and gracious. These women take responsibility for running the community or fighting for its survival or liberation. Many of these stories mirror what critic Eleanor Traylor calls Bambara's "liberation zone."[4] The characters and communities are rebellious nonconformists engaged in practices or acts of liberation inside of a liberation zone (community center or neighborhood) where they can safely cultivate consciousness. In liberation zones Bambara's characters fulfill and exceed all of the expectations of Black Nationalists or feminists because they find pathways to freedom that are safe, patient, and make community whole. The irresistible love in *The Sea Birds* requires characters to forge new pathways to freedom that are tethered to holistic love of the people. In story after story Bambara offers models of self-reliance, self-development, and an independent, self-sustained Black economic base mixed with the resistive spirit of Black culture.

The political organizers and cultural workers in *The Sea Birds* align with the Black Arts aspiration to establish a new set of cultural reference points and standards that centered on the needs and aspirations of Black people. Indeed, the reader is often presented with a new nationalism that combines an unmistakable feminist impulse. The women characters represent the strivings of people for clarity of vision and health. The protagonists strive for spiritual wholeness that emphasizes the positive development of current and future generations in stories like "The Apprentice," "The Organizer's Wife," "The Sea Birds Are Still Alive," and "Broken Field Running." In Amiri Baraka's *Kawaida Studies: The New Nationalism* (1972), he outlines Kawaida's emphasis on future generations. A quick glance at aspects of Kawaida reveals some principles that parallel Bambara's spiritual wholeness aesthetic. However, there is clear divergence when it comes to Baraka's ideas regarding male/female relations. For example, Bambara's feminist/Black Nationalist ethos in *The Sea Birds* tweaks Baraka's notion of "symbiotic understanding" of "nature revealed" and "the cosmos" of men and women (40). Upon closer examination, Bambara's stories can be deemed to embrace and extend Baraka's assertion in *Kawaida Studies: The New Nationalism* that

> We mean only good faith and good works and beauty to the world. . . . We live in a world now, where the real work cannot be spoken of clearly. We believe our children will get to the real work. We will make the real work possible. Before the real work can be done, the disease, the power of evil, must be cleared away. (Baraka 1972, 41)

Stories such as "Broken Field Running" and "The Apprentice" clearly depict protagonists doing the "real work" and "good works," seeking to bring "beauty to the world." They help clean up restaurants, patrol streets, visit old folk, monitor the police, and walk children from the community home from school through dangerous housing projects and teach them positivity. Baraka theorizes about "schools and temples and factories and laboratories and studies in which to function . . . [and] cities in which to move freely among the most sympathetic of environments so that they can study, and meditate, and create, and formalize the new learning and concretize the new vision" (41–42). The entire collection *The Sea Birds Are Still Alive* delivers a multitude of environments filled with liberation zones where a new Black reality can incubate and "concretize." Bambara's art practices aspects of Kawaida with modifications that emphasize spiritual wholeness and feminism.

Indeed, *The Sea Birds Are Still Alive* embodies revised aspects of Baraka's paradigm and hews close to what Baraka calls "the reins of a nation, a whole people" (42). This is not a wild assertion, as Bambara and Baraka communicated with one another and *The Sea Birds Are Still Alive*, published five years after Baraka's *Kawaida Studies: The New Nationalism*, tropes the ideas. Bambara's iteration of a liberation impulse meant to free spirits of "the alien value system" takes Kawaida to its highest level because the entire collection features strong females who drive the action of Black Power themes such as self-determination, self-respect, educating children who are the future, and self-defense. Her infusion of a healthy dose of anti-patriarchy and a spiritual wholeness aesthetic makes Kawaida more holistic and powerful.

The Sea Birds seems to heed and expand upon Baraka's 1972 call in *The New Nationalism* for women to "learn the priorities of nation-building and be an example of why we want a nation" (Baraka 1972, 29). She also uses her fiction as an artful corrective to trope Baraka's misguided assertion that women "must complement [men], complete [men]" (29). Thus in stories like "The Organizer's Wife," "The Apprentice," and "Broken Field Running" Baraka's flawed reliance on patriarchy forces her to erect a "new vision" of "whole people" who recognize women in equal and complementary relationships that are reciprocal. Her single and sometimes married women are all fiercely independent women supported by men as these women assume leadership positions. This type of re-visioning makes possible Baraka's call for "A nation" that "is a whole people" (29). A spiritual wholeness aesthetic is in tune with Baraka's assertion that: "The black woman must be the one half and the black man must be the other half of our life sign," however, Bambara's reiteration eliminates an *either-or* choosing to privilege "one half" or the "other half." In Bambara's iteration leaders rise according to what they bring to the table. Spiritual wholeness in *The Sea Birds* demands practices such as Black women and men moving and being together, "absolutely in tune, each doing what they supposed to" (29). The primary concern is sustained reemergence of the nation, which requires strong female and male leaders and male and female nurturers of youth. Bambara's feminist/Black Nationalist iteration of Baraka's new nationalism is a sustainable and holistic liberation impulse. I would also argue that in these stories Bambara asserts this unique revolutionary love while continuing her project of recuperating African American foremothers, ever mindful of bridging acrimonious gender divisions. Bambara clears obstacles to whole representation of liberation because she offers mechanisms for healing and facilitating conversions that recognize men and women's basic oneness and their connections.

Liberation Zone and Transnational Liberation

As previously mentioned, several of *The Sea Birds Are Still Alive* stories model liberation zones. In these narratives safe space is carved out for the youth to cultivate practices of self-love, love of the people, and love of the notion of liberation using principles of spiritual wholeness: faith, family, feeling, and freedom. These principles are on full display in such stories as "The Long Night" and "The Sea Birds Are Still Alive," where liberation is broad, complex, and too global to be confined by any parameters. The liberation zones conjured in these stories provide spaces where irresistible love is nurtured and gender norms and hierarchies are imploded. The domestic and global nation is redesigned to include women, youth, and elders functioning polyvocally to achieve liberation and revolution. Bambara's women slip the dichotomy of choosing between race and gender as the source of their oppression in favor of a nuanced and balanced perspective that privileges any male or female who is serious about revolution. For instance, the story "The Long Night" features an unnamed protagonist hiding from the police in a bathtub. Like the female protagonists in stories like "The Apprentice" and "The Organizer's Wife," she is an activist/organizer. Not only is she unnamed but Bambara also purposefully makes her racial and ethnic background unclear. What we do know about her, what is salient, is her commitment to struggle against oppression and for freedom, as evidenced in her thoughts such as "Harriet Tubman's work must continue" (Bambara 1977, 96) and her concern about the box filled with "posters, photos, statistics . . . and all that work" (96). The unnamed protagonist could be any of the female characters featured in the other stories. We also know that she has hidden away addresses of other activists, a gun, and negatives of campus agents somewhere. The concept of a box is of great significance to Bambara and her global feminist vision because Bambara once described Black people as "fours" who can only see obstacles and are limited by the four sides of a box rather than seeing a way out of the box.[5] In "The Long Night" Bambara does not limit the sides of the box or its contents—literally. Bambara plays with the idea of a box in unique ways. The female protagonist, whom we assume is a member of the FLQ in Canada, is concerned that the police will find in the box political slogans that say: "Africa Supports Us. Asia Supports Us. Latin Ameri . . . The PRG [people's revolutionary government—Grenada] Supports Us. The FLQ [Socialist group in Quebec] Supports Us. FLN [National Liberation Front in Algeria] Supports Us" (97). The ideas in the box are actually radical and outside the norms or mainstream messages people follow. Bambara perhaps chooses to focus on organizations such as FLQ because of her interests in transnational liberation; Holmes's biography (2014) makes the case that Bambara was influenced by and admired liberation struggles in Algeria and Cuba.

It is well known that the art of the African Liberation Movements was neither romantic, tribal, nor protest in form but rather instilled with national political consciousness directed at the masses to give them inspiration and courage to carry on their struggle against oppression. Bambara's second collection of fiction reflects her awareness of the struggles of the African Liberation Movements and the commitments the people made, or knew they must make, to win their freedom—practices of liberation. Bambara's stories here perform a similar objective and commitment. She transcends protest, which is but a prestage of revolutionary literature, and produces literature of combat or literature of action that engages in the process and practices of liberation. One might contend that *The Sea Birds* is a great example of counterpropaganda meant to condemn capitalism, patriarchy, and other forms of oppression to give the oppressed across the globe viable pathways to liberation. As Linda Janet Holmes skillfully points out in *A Joyous Revolt*, "Bambara's writing is much more than a marker of time. As an essayist, editor, and fiction writer, Bambara envisioned multicultural movements that crossed geographic boundaries including forging alliances among women of color" (2014, xviii).

The stories assembled make references to African countries immersed in liberation struggles, which reflect Bambara's transnational reach. "The Long Night" reminds readers of the Pan-African struggle for liberation in Mozambique (the Mozambique Liberation Front [FRELIMO], as well as in Angola [the MPLA], and Guinea-Bissau). The leaders of these countries all plotted revolutionary strategies to recapture the African minds and force liberation from European powers. Bambara's art had as its objective to help the people better understand their struggle by making them aware of the Pan-African or global struggle against colonialism, and she uses her protagonist and her lover Carl to stoke this consciousness. In fact, one could very well argue that all of her fiction is characterized by its functionality that is tied directly to the people's struggle. Her art becomes the living voice of their pains, defeats, and joys, except she allows them to speak for themselves.

Spiritual wholeness is complicated and inspirational because it inspires people to continue to fight against oppression and is a catalyst to help build morality, consciousness, and voice. It is educational; it teaches people what struggle is about and why it must persist if liberation is to be won. It is political because it fosters greater national consciousness and solidarity among the people. It is instructional because it prescribes without demanding positive direction that will help the people in their struggles for freedom. In short, Bambara's art arms the people's hearts and energizes them to strike back at forces that appear to be insurmountable. She arms them in the fight against Western imperialism with intellectual weapons they can wield safely.

The Organizer's Wife

The Seabirds Are Still Alive is Bambara's triumph of her belief that writing can be a tool of social activism, conjuring "irresistible" love. The first story in the collection, "The Organizer's Wife," presents a "bristling girl-woman" protagonist, Virginia, who expands the complexity of the Afrocentric and feminist concerns broached in *Gorilla*. Virginia represents the process that makes revolution become irresistible. Indeed, her transformation transcends resistance or faith in an individual in favor of the sustainable spirit of liberation. To have evolved to this state of consciousness is a holistic revolutionary love; such liberation cannot be stifled if one leader is gone. Virginia's world is initially turned upside down after her husband Graham has been arrested for being an "Outside agitator . . . [d]isturber of the peace . . . trying to incite a riot" (Bambara 1977, 18) when in truth it is because he organized the community against capitalist forces trying to take their valuable land. "The Organizer's Wife" lovingly sows the seeds of Bambara's spiritual wholeness motif, in that it calls for a renewal of cultural and spiritual values and themes found in the spirituals: family, faith, freedom, and feeling. Virginia leads the community of southern Black farmers against the granite company. In an interview Bambara explains that her goal in this story is to present the balanced "empowerment and development of our sisters and our community" (Bambara 1996, 245). "The Organizer's Wife" illustrates not only that it is possible to achieve this balance but also that success in both can occur simultaneously.

Virginia and her husband Graham are conduits through which a spiritual wholeness aesthetic can negotiate female equity and community liberation. Their story mimics the call and response of the spirituals. Bambara also culls the spirit of distinctive aspects of Black vernacular culture (such as spirituals, work songs, blues, and jazz) in all its complexity to tell her story. Thus, her critique in this story parodies the spirituals' call and response between audience and singer and also demands direct action. It mimics the harmonic and structural devices and vocal techniques of spirituals, work songs, and blues and pragmatically advances her urgings for spiritual renewal on multiple levels.

The story opens in the aftermath of Graham's arrest. The "men from the co-op school . . . [are] squatting in [Virginia's] garden" (Bambara 1977, 3), which is in disarray. This statement is significant because not only does it suggest that individuals are separated from the land and the community is disorientated but also, like a blues lyric, it immediately signals that there are troubles to speak of and troubles to come. In addition to giving the story a tone of lost hope, Virginia's dying garden signifies a new womanhood that will be harvested. The first description of Virginia is a physical one. We immediately are made aware of her size and that "none [of the men are] taller than she," (5) which forces the reader to acknowledge her stature in the community and look up to her as a leader. The physical description of Virginia as a tall woman who has neglected her garden, in which men squat in deference to her "dislodging slugs, raising dust. . . . scraping rust from the rake [Virginia] hadn't touched in weeks" (3), and the men's unusual silence, both combine to announce a new, complex womanhood that has yet to be harvested. We also learn that Virginia is a woman in motion, evolving rapidly, "Growing so fast from babe to child to girl to someone, folks were always introducing and reintroducing themselves to her. It seems at times that the walls wouldn't contain her, the roof wouldn't stop her. Busting out of childhood, busting out of her clothes, but never busting out of this place" (9). This story echoes the theme of transformation found in much of Bambara's work, only here it involves maturation from girlhood to womanhood and balancing feelings of community responsibility against those of family and individual.

In the opening scene Virginia mistakenly reads the men's silence negatively, calling them "Good-for-nuthin" (3) as she departs her yard. In spirituals and jazz, the space this silence takes up is necessary for response, for listening to and understanding other singers and musicians. Virginia misses the signs, reads the men's silence, or space, incorrectly because she has lost hope. Her spirit is not with the people; she has lost faith in "the courage of the youth, the hope of the future" that Graham constantly preaches about (5). To her the men's silence means they have no answers or words for her, have abandoned her in her time of need. What Virginia fails to understand is that they have come to help, but they do not know how to approach her. As Graham's star pupil, "the orator, whose poems and tales and speeches delivered from the sound truck had done more to pull the districts together, the women all said, than all the leaflets the kids cluttered the fields with" tells the men that even he can do "no better than yawl do" (5–6). They want to speak to her, but as the orator explains, "no one knew any more how to talk to the bristling girl-woman, if ever any had" (6). Bambara used this story and scene to address the male/female issue of her era as more underdeveloped communication than volatile antagonism. Truth was very important to Bambara. The men's coming to terms with their limitations clears obstacles in the way of clarity and spiritual renewal. Individually they failed to save Graham or console Virginia; however, they band together as a whole community to survive and save what is left.

The opening discord shows that Virginia has lost faith not only in the land but also in the spirit of the people. This is important because faith is essential to a spiritual wholeness aesthetic. Virginia's open neglect of her garden is symbolic of the people that she refuses to tend to and of the fact that she had surrendered the struggle they had been waging. Void of faith, she makes up her mind that she will:

> ask for nothing . . . [and] when she saw Graham that afternoon she
> wanted the thing stitched up . . . wanted to be able to say she asked

for nuthin from nobody and didn't nobody offer up nuthin. . . . They'd
set bail and she'd pay . . . the bail and unhook them both from this place.
Let some other damn fool break his health on this place, the troubles. (7)

Out of love with the people and the idea of continuing to work with them as a family, Virginia feels imprisoned and readily admits that "She'd been leaving since the first day coming" (7) and planned to have Graham, "whether he knew it or not . . . take her away from this place" (12). She also admits that she never entrenched her spirit or hopes in the place or the people.

This is the antithesis of Graham, who has faith in freedom and the people. He is "convinced that folks would battle for his release, would battle for themselves, the children, the future, would keep on no matter how hard the thief, no matter how little the rain, how exhausted the soil, cause this was home" (16). This also raises the complex issue of individual versus communal concerns—a consistent struggle during the Black Power movement and an obstacle to feminist concerns. How does female self-definition and freedom coexist with the needs of the community? At this juncture, Virginia moves from observing a source of knowledge, Graham, to developing her own awareness and intuitive perceptions. She is challenged to move from her personal, quite narrow goals of familial needs and adopt Graham's visions of empowerment for the people. In "The Dance of Character and Community," Martha Vertreace suggests that "Self-awareness within the community setting allows the individual to move beyond a concentration on exterior knowing of disconnected particulars to an interior awareness, knowledge as indwelling" (1989, 164).

This scene relies on the tradition of spirituals, with their renewal of cultural and individual purpose and their use of work songs, which are filled with mock prayers, sermons, and other parodies of the celebrated forms of the church. In doing so, Bambara sets Virginia at odds with the community and on course to spiritual redemption. However, before undergoing a spiritual conversion, Virginia repeatedly tries to ignore her "callin," much like someone would resist a religious conversion. The first time Virginia ignores the call is when the choir woman gives her money. She resents the woman for "trying to attach her all over again, root her, ground her in this place. Just when there was a chance to be free. Virginia clamped her jaws tight and tried to go blank. Tried to blot out all feelings and things" (Bambara 1977, 9). In choosing "the choir woman" to be the first to assist Virginia, Bambara plays around, like a jazz musician, with the idea of a choir answering Graham's (who is a preacher of sorts) call to unity, faith, and deliverance (freedom). The choir member is also symbolic of its parody of the term "preaching to the choir." Perhaps Virginia knows all too well that the choir must respond to the preacher's call, and thus the choir woman's claim that "He share our hardships, we bear his troubles, our troubles" has only a slight impact on Virginia, who, though moved, is not converted (8). That she is "moved" indicates a feeling, which is equally important to a spiritual wholeness aesthetic. This is another example of Bambara's variation on the spirituals' themes of feeling and freedom. Virginia has lost her feeling of commitment or connectedness to the community—her freedom lies outside of them and their problems.

Noteworthy here is Bambara's play with spirituals and the idea of spirituality in a biblical sense. One could make a connection between Graham's teachings, his imprisonment, and Jesus's betrayal. Like Jesus, Graham teaches principles of daily living rather than rules of daily living. Read this way, one might make a strong argument that Bambara has a problem with rules, such as edicts about "Blackness" or the exclusivity of some feminism, and other binaries that limit creativity and hinder true representations of pluralism in African American discourse. Indeed, she seems to suggest that the freedom to play around with the basic principles of African American culture is necessary for spiritually whole explorations to occur. The point here is that both Jesus and Graham paid dearly for teaching to their people. Jesus taught a spirituality that revolved around daily living, and he was betrayed by one of his disciples and was jailed, was crucified, and rose from the dead on the third day. Similarly, Graham organizes the community (performs "miracles"), he is betrayed (by the preacher), his leading disciple (Virginia) denies his teachings, he is imprisoned, and a resurrection of Virginia's love and commitment to liberation occurs. My purpose in constructing this parallel is to point out the variations of Bambara's Afrocentric and feminist spiritual wholeness motif. The principles Graham uses to develop the spirit of the community revolve around ideas of the sacredness of the land, which is home. In one scene he tells the people that the earth is:

> Not . . . for digging in or weeping over or crawling into, but home . . . where ancestral bones spoke their speak on certain nights if folks stamped hard enough, sang long enough, shouted. . . . Where "America" was sung but meant something altogether else than it had at the old school. Home in the future. The future here now developing. Home in the future. Home liberated soon. And the earth would recover. . . . The ancient wisdoms would be revived. The energy released. Home a human place once more. The bones spoke it. The spirit spoke it. The spirit spoke, too, through flesh when the women gathered at the altar, the ancient orishas still vibrant beneath the ghostly patinas some though right to pray to, but connected in spite of themselves to the spirits under the plaster. (Bambara 1977, 16)

Graham teaches people how to love and capture the principal uses of the earth, to see "the spirits under the plaster," to revere its true historical and cultural values. These teachings reflect practices—love of self, family, the people (the land), which are a key component of Bambara's spiritual wholeness message. The earth, the soil, holds the ancestral bones, the spirit of the ancestral people; it is called "America" but has different meanings than those given in a schoolroom. In this instance Bambara is clearly negotiating Black aesthetic nostalgic longings for Africa. Graham tropes this idea of Africa as the motherland with his preaching that spiritual energy and history, spiritual, and cultural past on American soil are equally rich with "ancient wisdoms." Graham urges people to look beneath the soil's surface to know its true richness and value. This helps explain why Bambara inverts the traditional African American idea of the flying African or the need for African American men to "fly" from their roots, as described by Ralph Ellison, Richard Wright, and Toni Morrison. She grounds Graham and does not allow him "fly" away.

Overall, the earth is the spiritual principle around which Bambara develops the story (it is central to her first novel as well). It is the basis from which the people's spirituality can grow, but they must hold on to it, maintain these important roots. The unique thing about this particular soil is that its very composition suggests pluralism, stoutness, and wholeness. The soil that the farmers in this community own lies down in the valley or "the pit" near dirty gullies that hold "the current that flushed the garbage down from the hill where the townies lived, to the bottom where the folks lived" (10). Notice the pun on the term "folks," which suggests that the community is the down-to-earth sector; the matrix of society lives at the bottom of the earth. Immediately the reader is saddened to read that they live among the filth. However, that feeling is brief, for Bambara also informs us in the next breath that "the co-op brigade" takes this garbage and "[makes] compost heaps" for independence, laughing as they do it. Two key components of the spirituals jump out in this exchange: first, the compost heap mimics the spirituals' trait of taking tears of sorrow and working them into tears of joy; second, the scene mimics or places emphasis on the idea of communal creativity, solidarity, and interaction necessary for survival. The people take garbage and transform it into fertilizer, just as Black folk have taken the garbage of hate and racism and transformed it into fertile love and spirituals and folklore and blues. This is a creative act and a necessary one. For Bambara the people represent the land; it is fertile ground for sowing her Afrocentric and feminist aesthetic of spiritual wholeness.

What is most ingenious is Bambara's use of the metaphor of the compost heap to represent an aspect of spiritual wholeness as a process that occurs over space and time. Compost is a mixture that consists largely of decayed organic matter and is used for fertilizing and conditioning land. If land is a principle element for spiritual renewal, then it needs fertilizer to be healthy. More specifically, compost represents the plural contributions—the mixture of Black feminism, Afrocentric aesthetics, spirituals, jazz, and blues—all elements that contribute to make a rich, whole product that can nourish the spirit of the people. This organic matter—equally important components of Black culture and interpretation—is integral to holistic cultural representations.

Land possession is at the center of this story. The land is the spirit of the people. And the fact that the type of rock Bambara happens to choose is granite is significant because granite is an intrusive igneous rock that happens to be the major component of the continental crust and composed of a multitude of elements like quartz, feldspar minerals, and micas. The people and their history is like the rock—coarse grained and composed of a multitude of elements from which its strength is derived. Like the once-molten rock, the people have cooled and need to be ignited to form a fluid, organized movement in order to keep the granite company from taking away the land from the farmers. The idea that the true value of the land lies in the granite beneath the earth also plays on the idea of inner spiritual strength, which is integral to liberation in Bambara's fiction. In this story, the inner spirit or strength of the land lies deep within and, like granite, is difficult to penetrate. The granite company, with its evil religion of avarice, is the enemy trying to unearth the granite and threatens to harm the people's inner spirit.

This idea of the land's value is relayed in Virginia's epiphany, while walking to confront the Revun, that the Granite company wants "to maim . . . rape . . . plunder it all with that bone-deep hatred for all things natural . . . leaving for the children their legacy, an open grave, gouged out by a gene-deep hatred for all things natural, for all things natural that couldn't turn a penny quick enough to a dollar" (Bambara 1977, 17). This conversion occurs via her encounter with three signs painted by the co-op that Virginia encounters on her way to meet the Revun. First, she sees the mural "Face Up to What's Killing You." Next, she spots the triangle below the statement depicting a fat fanged beast living well, in smart clothes, "lounging on the backs of, feeding off the backs of, the folks at the base, crushed almost flat trying to get up" (16). Finally, she looks at the sign outside the wall of the church that says, "WE CAN-NOT LOSE" (16–17). The conflation of these three signs moves her to act.

At this point Virginia understands the principal importance and value of the land in relation to spiritual renewal or wholeness and she come to terms with her feelings. She tries "to speak on what was happening to her coming through her shell. But [she] had trouble stringing her feelings about so many things together" (20). However, Virginia's newfound faith helps her convey her feelings to Revun Micheals in an unconventional testimony of blows to his head with a ruler. She chastises him for trying to sell the people's land, telling him: "You didn't have to. Enough granite under this schoolhouse alone . . . if we developed it ourselves. . . . Outside agitator, you said. And [Graham's] roots put down here long before you ever came" (18). Here again, Bambara plays with the metaphor of Judas's betrayal of Christ, likening Revun Michaels to Judas, with Virginia asking him: "Thirty pieces of silver, maybe? That what you preach, tradition" (18–19). For Bambara, any people or traditions that strip people of what is important to their spirit, development, and future are the enemy.

Virginia's literal attack of Michaels attacks the flawed values or spirituality that place more importance on making a profit than on people's everyday needs. I would like to point out here that the co-op brigade, a one-room shack where Graham organizes and teaches the people, is situated on church land. The symbolic importance of the co-op's geography is that its political instruction of "truth" does not separate it from the community's religious traditions, it connects the youth to the elders. Thus, Graham's "creed" is not a separation from religion. During the civil rights movement the church was the foundation upon which the movement was built. In fact, Virginia's attack of Michaels is an attack of an individual void of true spirituality; he has lost faith. It is also significant that Virginia "testifies" to Michaels in the classroom instead of the church regarding his sins, and uses a ruler to beat him. The metaphor is one of a teacher punishing a disobedient child—harshly but not detrimentally. Of course, the use of the ruler is also significant, in that it suggests an inversion of order: the Revun Michael's is no longer the ruler of the people's spirits. When the ruler breaks, it suggests that spirituality without traditional rules is what is required for the future for the community; thus, Virginia breaks old rules when she secures a new place of leadership among the men in the community.

It is also important to note a few points about Virginia's feminism. Although she is literally a towering example of Bambara's self-defined feminism, she never equates this feminism with spurning motherhood. At every point of the story, Virginia acts with "the baby's carry straps around her waist" (5). She has the baby when she walks past the men in her garden on her way to confront the Revun for selling the land, and while she is beating the Revun for selling the land, "[t]he baby cried" (5). In fact, at the height of her acceptance by the men she pulls out her breast to nurse her hungry child in a car full of men. What Bambara is saying is that mother and activist/leader can coexist.

"The Organizer's Wife" is a wonderful example of how Bambara's fiction, like the spirituals, is an unceasing variation on family, faith, freedom, and feeling. Thus she challenges notions of tradition, gender, race, even Black Nationalist political discourses—all in the name of a "spiritual" reorientation or wholeness infused with her own vision of feminist and Afrocentric doctrine. Bambara uses this story to suggest that something different is necessary and possible regarding gender, Black culture, and politics. The story mirrors her theory in the essay "On the Issue of Roles" that:

Perhaps we need to face the terrifying and overwhelming possibility
that there are no models, that we shall have to create from scratch.

Doctrinaire Marxism is basically incompatible with Black nationalism;
New Left politics is incompatible with nationalism; doctrinaire socialism
is incompatible with Black revolution; capitalism, Lord knows, is out.[6]

Critical of the inherent cultural and gender limitations in these models or philosophies, Bambara consistently uses her fiction to present a feminist and Afrocentric agenda that is honest and recognizes that all is not praiseworthy, or honorable, and that culminates in a new spirit via older African and African American spirituality. This agenda clears space for a new model of leadership to emerge that Virginia and the community cultivate in the soil. Bambara scrutinizes gender conventions and aims an equally critical eye at spirituality, politics, and culture, and specifically the spirituality and politics of Revun Michaels, who worships capitalism or avarice instead of community. At the end of "The Organizer's Wife," as in many of her stories, what is clear is that Bambara understands the need for diverse renewal that challenges gender, politics, and spirit—the whole; and she incorporates myriad aspects of Black vernacular and culture to make these interrogations and explorations. A constant conduit of hope and striving for spiritual wholeness is "the courage of the youth, the hope of the future" (Bambara 1977, 5). It is fitting that she concludes "The Organizer's Wife" with such hope, as Jake, the first to lose his land to the granite company, has the spirit to laugh at his sorrows: "they sat right down to table and stole the chickens. . . . Now that's the truth, Jake said, laughing. His laughter pulled Virginia forward, she touched his arm, moved. That he could laugh. His farm stolen and he could laugh. But that was one of the three most moving things about Jake" (22). Besides biblical reference to things occurring in threes, this is an important lesson for Virginia in faith and hope for impending freedom. Jake has not given up on the community. Despite his personal misfortunes he maintains his responsibilities as a teacher.

Whether the community saves the church land remains uncertain, but what is important is that Graham returns and Virginia, who has "her strength . . . back," understands her feelings and knows "exactly what to tell him" (23). Of course, "The Organizer's Wife," with its variations on the themes of individual, community, faith, feeling, freedom, female self-definition, and unity, is not the definitive last word, but it is an excellent start toward "slaying gorillas" and clearing obstacles that stifle the growth of Virginia's garden, which at story's end she vows "she sure as hell was going to keep up" (23). Bambara's suggestion in "The Organizer's Wife" that we "start from scratch" might appear subversive on the surface, but what she actually advocates is an Afrocentric and feminist model infused with and guided by a spirituality that seeks individual freedom, family and community cohesiveness, and wholeness.

The irresistible love Bambara conjures in this story is multileveled and creates space for the men to look to Virginia to lead the people to save the next Black property owner from being duped. That Virginia runs this meeting while nursing her baby indicates acceptance of a new vision of leadership and feminism. Furthermore, the story ends with Virginia's love for Graham still strong and her faith in their struggle renewed, which is reflected in her strength for tending her once-ignored garden. "How else," she says, "to feed the people?" (23). "The Organizer's Wife" pushes the boundaries of Afrocentric cultural politics and Black feminism—showing that one does not have to be sacrificed for the other, they can, must, exist simultaneously, as does compost, to produce something rich that can fertilize future hopes for liberation. This is a fine example of the spirituals' mantra: working tears of sorrow until they become tears of joy, hope, and faith.

The Apprentice

The second story in *The Sea Birds Are Still Alive* is "The Apprentice" and it picks up where "The Organizer's Wife" ends. It is a continuum of Bambara's efforts to clear paths to spiritual wholeness and freedom via nourishing all the members of the community: elders, women, men, and the common man and woman who are often overlooked.

Here, among other things, she tropes the Black Panther Party's street policing, food co-op, and community center programs. Elliot Butler-Evans believes the "major thrust of the collection is the awakening of the cultural nationalist and feminist consciousness" (1989, 121). In "The Apprentice," love of the people, belief in the people, working tirelessly for the people, the actual work and mechanisms required for revolution, and communitarian spirit are explored. Key elements of the ethos Bambara espoused in her "Preface" to the anthology *The Black Woman* emerge front and center in this story. The cultural workers make the notion of art and activism meaningful, as they are on the ground, among the people, making changes from the bottom up, so to speak. In several essays and interviews Bambara is clear that struggling for liberation from racism, sexism, and corporate control of society demands the practice of being in touch with the people and unifying them. For her a primary liberation act is to look inward and get truthful and correct with the self. "The Apprentice" ventures into a day in the life of an unnamed narrator receiving training from Naomi, a community worker and activist. Naomi is teaching the narrator positive and productive liberation practices for being an effective change maker in her community and how to positively perform love of struggle. The story is a lesson for the people, for the nation, and for budding revolutionaries about the spiritual wholeness of work, commitment, and love required to be an effective cultural worker. While the apprentice is the narrator of this story, she is clearly not in control—Naomi drives the narrative with her actions. We learn from the narrator that she is under the tutelage of Naomi because her "work attitude ain't too progressive" (Bambara 1977, 32) and she has been told in "group criticism sessions" that she is negative. To correct this ineffective practice, she has "been teamed with Naomi" who "views everything and everybody as potentially good, as a possible hastener of the moment, an ushering in of the new day. Examines everybody in terms of their input of making revolution an irresistible certainty" (33). The story models several key practices for making revolution irresistible to the people. The young apprentice has been told she must learn the requisite patience and wisdom as a leader, activist, and revolutionary to "develop the progressive forces, win over the indifferent, and isolate the diehards. . . . A diehard is one energetically working to disrupt unity, fighting against health, sanity, delaying willfully the liberation of the people" (32). This story paints a pluralistic picture of community struggle that, in the mode of spiritual wholeness, values the role of all "workers" and places women in leadership positions. Mindful of the value of elders and their wisdom, Bambara has Naomi, an older female, teaching the young narrator what it means to be a leader in the community.

The story opens with Naomi and her unnamed female mentee policing the community and protecting people against police. They approach a police officer who is brutalizing a Black male motorist on a routine traffic stop. This was a common tactic of the Black Panther Party. Yet to deemphasize the myth that the Panthers were only men and were violent, the two women do not approach the officer with guns (a common practice of the Panther Party was to carry unloaded weapons). Naomi's and her apprentice's weapons are note pads, their brains, and pencils. Naomi demonstrates to the apprentice how to use her mind to disarm the officer, asking, "Excuse me, Officer . . . I have no intention of interfering, but I wondered could I ask this gentleman here if there's anyone he would like us to call on his behalf. If that's all right . . . sir." (25). Immediately Bambara makes the point that her politics, while the same as those of other Black Nationalist groups, have a different approach that also conjures results. The threat of Naomi's knowledge of the law and charisma stop the harassment, and the officer informs her, "No need for that. . . . Just a routine check" (25–26). Reminiscent of young Hazel in "The Hammer Man," Naomi is unafraid to challenge police authority. And like young Hazel, Naomi also comes to the aid of a male who is being harassed by the police. However, Naomi is a mature, more evolved version of young Hazel.

Still, both of these confrontations with police solidify Bambara's belief that freedom and liberation require men protecting women and women protecting men. For Bambara, a successful struggle for liberation is not limited by patriarchy or confining gender roles. In addition to continuing her inversions of patriarchy, and conjuring effective female protectors, she reminds us that racism is the real enemy of Black men and women. Bambara also evokes notions of spirituality in her description of Naomi during her confrontation with the cop: "Naomi looked so sure, standing there, legs apart like a tree standing in the water—Naomi was not about to be moved" (28). Here, Bambara parodies a popular spiritual about freedom and stubbornness, suggesting that spirituality, feeling, and faith are important components of freedom. Hazel was less effective in "The Hammer Man" because her budding feminism and activism lacked the power of the spirituals. Naomi, like Virginia in "The Organizer's Wife," succeeds because she evokes this dimension in her liberation repertoire.

Taken at face value, it is easy to misread aspects of this story as a simple exercise in "narrow" Black Power or feminist rhetoric. Yet, a closer examination reveals much more. First, Naomi's stance simultaneously engages nationalist and feminist ideology that establishes links with the larger community, and, these links are integral to Bambara's notion of wholeness. Naomi is a protector who has the entire community under her care, but she is far from a traditional or stereotypical depiction of Black women as caretakers. Actually, this story is a wonderful example of the "struggle and resistance" that is possible but "without suppressing the real heterogeneity" of interests and identities, as Stuart Hall broaches in his essay "New Ethnicities." According to Hall, effective political boundary lines can be drawn "without fixing those boundaries for eternity."[7] This story reflects Hall's emphasis on recognizing the central issue of race through various approaches such as through the categories of class, gender, and ethnicity (Hall 1995, 166). It is heterogeneity that enhances African American cultural representation, and the spiritual wholeness aesthetic embraces this idea. Bambara's fiction represents all of these approaches and clears obstacles to movement toward a whole and heterogeneous representation of community and liberation. As the old man in "The Apprentice" says, "You got to let the people in. . . . They got to be a part of the whole musical thing or whatever's the program" (Bambara 1977, 30).

Bambara clearly understands the importance of recognizing the extraordinary diversity of perspectives, social experiences, and cultural identities that comprise Black life. While the story clearly privileges a feminine perspective, this does not eliminate conflict and tension. This is evident in the interaction between Naomi and our narrator, who share a diversity of interests. While they are unified as female activists, they have different ideas about what an effective approach to the struggle for racial and social justice is. The narrator acknowledges this divergence early in the story when she tells us that, unlike her, "Naomi assumes everybody wakes up each morning plotting out exactly what to do to hasten the revolution" (27). Bambara is not naïve enough to believe "Blackness" or feminism is a Utopia for the Black community. Our narrator and Naomi are engaged in a generational and ideological conflict, but Naomi's embrace—literal hug—of our narrator after chastising her for being tired is symbolic of the types of practices that are necessary if a new, more "whole" political ideology of freedom is to emerge and spread.

On two other occasions in the story the young apprentice is introduced to practices of liberation that are not "pimp flashy" or newsworthy but essential for liberation and spiritual wholeness. The first practice she learns is when they visit the old folks' home and the second is while helping to clean Larry's restaurant. What is of importance here is Naomi's (like Bambara's) comfort among the people who are her focus. At the old folks' home, Naomi, seeking a way to connect with the people, "goes upstairs to the old folks' lounge to mess around on the piano and fill up the bulletin board with clippings and flyers. Music always draws a crowd and provides an occasion for rappin" (28). Although our narrator does not join her mentor, Naomi demonstrates for her mentee the importance of finding a way to capture the Black masses' attention and gain their trust. Taking a different route, our narrator is a self-described "listener" who prefers "the downstairs laundry room," where she listens to the women talk. She later admits to us that she is slowly learning the patience and varied practices that leadership and liberation require and demand:

> I cleared my throat and was fixin to ask them if they supported the Right to Eat Food Co-op's demands and were they coming to the rally. But that ain't no way to come at people, head-on, blunt. I been studying the way Naomi do it and am amazed at all this patience she got stored up. (29)

The point here is that the there is no panacea; pathways to liberation and revolutionary consciousness are limitless, so to speak, and a similar outcome can be achieved using varied tactics. Bambara's wholeness aesthetic imbibes from a multitude of strategies, tactics, and cultural traditions to achieve spiritual wholeness and change. One of those strategies or practices is to recognize that progress and revolutionary love are about "always teaching," which is something Naomi takes every opportunity to do. For example, at a public housing hearing earlier in the day the young apprentice informs us she was amazed when Naomi

> just got up with no warning—less you want to count a mumble and some heavy teeth sucking—and strolled up to the table to in front where the legislators and the housing authority biggies sitting, pours herself a glass of water. Then she pours some more, taking the mayor's glass even, and puts them on her clipboard and proceeds to serve the folks. And in that one gesture she makes us all aware that them folks at the table are sitting two feet higher than we are, got all the ashtrays, got two pitchers of ice water and we ain't got shit. Meeting completely changed up after that. Naomi something. (36)

What is striking about these two examples is Bambara's penchant for using her art to adjudicate conflicts in the process of striving for liberated people—in other words, she is about the business of the people, which leads her to seek sustainable practices of liberation.

The senior citizen apartment house functions as a continuum on the theme of ancestral spirits, elders, community, and the importance of the Black church in nourishing spirits. Bambara, mindful of the power of spirituals, uses the seniors to shift the focus of the story to the idea of roots and the importance of ancestral knowledge in an urban setting. The visit to the seniors represents another version of soil from which African and African American spirituality can grow. Of course, Bambara references the church because she valued its spiritual strengths, its belief in uplift, renewal, collaborative effort, and hope. Thus, she coveys this when an elderly gentleman from the apartment house gives a mock sermon to Naomi and our narrator, evoking call and response. Here African spirituality further expands the spiritual wholeness framework to include men in the act of spreading the gospel. The gospel he preaches reminds them that struggle is "just like church, . . . Sermon's only as good as the congregation make it. Preacher can't do much lessen you give him some encouragement, lend him your energy, your fire" (30). To this they both answer as a congregation answers its minister, "That's right" (30). He calls, they respond.

This is what is so unique about the spiritual wholeness aesthetic in Bambara's fiction. Stories like this one, which on the surface is decidedly "revolutionary" in tone, are subtly filled with visions, signs, and a mock-sermon that teaches things like "The man got to know his words are speaking to your life, Like when I was young and . . . I sang in the choir, . . . I'd fill in the empty music spaces asking, Am I spoilin ya?" (30). Actually, in using an elder to mimic a sermon, Bambara culls the African idea of spirituality, which claims to be involved in every aspect of one's life, whether work or play. The man in the apartment house reminds us that because each life is different, the words must change to meet different needs. As in spirituals, variation is paramount; it is how life must be approached—with flexibility. Further, it is also significant that Bambara chooses an elder male to speak to Naomi and our narrator about wholeness and spirituality. On one level, it connects men to the process of wholeness. On another level, it reminds us that as members of the community, elders (and men) also have a stake in female self-definition and development. The old gentleman makes a very important point that is central to Bambara's notion of spiritual wholeness. When he concludes his mock-sermon he reminds them:

> You got to let the people in, ya see. They got to be a part of the whole musical thing or whatever's the program. . . . Take this community, for example, . . . Many people here still movin on, fightin for rights, scuffling to keep goin. But they got to tarry a while and ask us old folks, 'Am I spoilin ya?' And we got to answer, say amen, take part in the thing. You understand what I'm saying? (30–31)

Besides the effectiveness of this speech in presenting language that emphasizes a method of call and response, it is also a reminder that unity, determination, and ancestral knowledge are important practices if the community hopes to achieve spiritual wholeness. That "spirit" is one that values the importance of one's ancestors and spiritual past. The apprentice and Naomi seem to understand his words, which is most evident at the conclusion of the story because both Naomi and the nameless narrator help clean the kitchen at Larry's. Bambara reminds us that leadership and liberation require being "part of the whole musical thing," from the most glamorous to the dirtiest jobs. A spiritual wholeness aesthetic also values each individual spirit, from the eagerness and inflexibility of youth to the patience and wisdom of elders.

The visit with Edward Decker, head of the Brothers of Canaan Lodge, is a great example of how a spiritual wholeness aesthetic negotiates gender tensions, artistically encodes fiction with positive images of African Americans, and promotes unity, feminism, truth, and healthy resistance. Decker exemplifies a flawed heroic or romantic notion of the Black aesthetic and liberation. The apprentice sees this and wants to avoid Decker and "go straight on to the tenant's council and meet

[Naomi] later at the public housing hearing," but "Naomi gave [her] a look" (31). The look itself is a reminder of Bambara's commitment to the complex project of honest criticism, without sacrificing male/female unity. It is equally important to note that Bambara analyzed, even laughed at, any Black male ego that she deemed an obstacle to political change and real progress. Decker represents what Bambara would consider counterproductive male ego that requires critique and patience. Our narrator is impatient with Decker as he gives them "a tour of the house, made long speeches about the framed citations on the living room walls and was the general drag [she had] always found him to be" (31) because he believed "Black folks had spoiled his triumph" and "would not acknowledge [him] as leader" (31). Bambara introduces Decker to suggest that he and all the Deckers of the world miss the true "spirit" of struggle because they cannot see past "I" and "me." Decker uses "I" and "me" repeatedly during his discussion with them. Still, when the narrator mumbles a disparaging remark about him Naomi gives her a look that shames her behavior. Spiritual wholeness aesthetics in Bambara's fiction privilege deft negotiation of gender tensions and dialectics because the ultimate goal is liberation for the nation. Naomi's harsh look reminds our narrator that

> Cynicism, sarcasm, smugness was defeatist, benefited nobody but the enemy. . . . The job is to develop the progressive forces, win over the indifferent, and isolate the diehards. . . . And the diehard was not just any ole body I didn't like, as the group instructed me at last criticism session, folks I hastily bumped off out of a reluctance to work. A diehard is one energetically working to disrupt unity, fighting against health and sanity, delaying willfully the liberation of the people. My work attitude ain't too progressive, I been told more than once at the group criticism sessions. I am negative. I guess that's why I've been teamed with Naomi. She views everything and everybody as potentially good, as a possible hastener of the moment, an usherer in of the new day. Examines everybody in terms of their input to making revolution an irresistible certainty. (32–33)

This statement clears more obstacles and effectively explains the foundational tenants of spiritual wholeness. It demands an embrace of family (unity), faith in liberation and freedom, and feeling at ease with a wholeness perspective. Thus in the same breath that Bambara interrogates male ego, she is equally critical of any self-righteousness, including female, that poses equally detrimental threats to "the liberation of the people." These practices of liberation guide spiritual wholeness in her fiction and allow her to express feminism without cynicism, sarcasm, or smugness. It is a great example of Bambara's mantra that revolution begins with the self in the self.

The exchange between Naomi, the narrator, and the workers at Larry's restaurant represents another political obstacle clearing of sorts. It functions as the practice of religion or faith after reading and accepting signs. Communal cooperation and food nourish the spirits of the characters in this story. Food is a recurring symbol of spiritual nourishment throughout the story. First they try to enlist the elders in the Right to Eat Food rally, then Decker offers them food when they visit him but takes it away before they get a chance to eat, and finally they nourish themselves at Larry's then proceed to help clean up. Nourishment of body and spirit is also essential to spiritual wholeness.

Of equal importance is Bambara's emphasis on collective work and responsibility. Naomi knows this and is trying to teach the narrator that there is no single role in the struggle for freedom; one must be diverse and flexible. This is why Naomi engages in "scrubbing and mopping and sweeping and carrying on like she getting time and a half for overtime," while our narrator is again more comfortable performing the role of listener. She explains that she is: "there for the stories. . . . It seems to refresh them and that's cool. I figure I am doing my part keeping the folks going" (42). This scene reveals Bambara as an early advocate for diversity and heterogeneity, as well as a process of call and response. She constantly emphasizes the importance of listening as a route to understanding and moving toward wholeness. There is little question that Naomi strongly resembles Bambara, who, like Naomi, spent time in Cuba and has a transnational perspective of revolution and realizes there is nothing sexy about the work required to attain it. The apprentice/narrator imagines as Naomi is shouting "just like in church . , . Oh, Lawd, let it come in our lifetime [revolution]" that she is thinking about time she spent "in Cuba" and with "them folks in the Sea Islands who organized against the golf-course developers and even got the Arabs to put up some money in front to beat out the Jew landbarons. Organized their farms collectively, built a school and trained some organizers, sent some folk to law school and still moving, plus like to party ole Naomi in the ground to boot" (38).

Perhaps the true beauty of this story is its culmination in Larry's Diner. Naomi and the narrator (her apprentice) eat their dinner then proceed to enter the kitchen after a heavy dinner rush, and Naomi without any hesitation punctuates the lesson of tireless work as a primary practice of liberation. The narrator explains that Naomi: "goes through the swinging doors and squeezes out a rag in the sink and commences to clean" (40). As they begin a conversation with Mama Mildred and Pop Feather, who also works in the kitchen, Bambara again emphasizes the importance of cross-generational dialectics and cooperation as practices of holistic liberation. These two elders share wisdom with Naomi, the apprentice, and other young workers. But when Pop Feather tells them "colored folks always on some soup line or other. And always will be, I guess" (41), Naomi's polite disagreement reinforces the faith and freedom that are central to Bambara's liberation impulse. She tells the old gent "Naww . . . Not always, Pop Feather. You know good and well that ain't the truth. We got a brighter future than that" (42). Pop Feather's quick agreement is a great example of the present in the past, future focus of the BAM because Feather's next statement is a disclosure of his dream to have his own gumbo joint with a "folk-price menu," and Mama Mildred volunteers to join him in this venture to feed the souls of the majority of the people—the "folk."

The final scene details the communitarian spirit of the era, and displays Bambara's nuanced practice of the BAM notion of emphasizing

Black culture from the ancient to the future. Mama Mildred and Pop Feather impart wisdom while the young and old work collectively, performing different tasks to clean up the greasy kitchen. Furthermore, although the apprentice does no physical labor herself, Bambara the artist seems to rationalize the value of every role (no matter how large, small, or indirect) as essential to the whole practice of liberation. Equally important here is that Bambara gives voice to the people in multiple ways and has a holistic understanding of liberation that values all contributors.

The full scope of their day of cultural work, which entails monitoring a cop, visiting the old folks, Decker, a tenants meeting, a public housing meeting, Larry's Diner, and "fifty-leven visits," is all in the name of revolutionary love. The action of the narrative practices liberation and is in sync with Bambara's ethos of representing the whole of the people and transformation cell-by-cell, block-by-block. By the end of the story the reader and apprentice learn nuances of broad-based organizing and strategizing; that it is tiring and one must be tireless. They work all day in the name of love of the people. The reward is helping folk develop political and individual consciousness. The apprentice has imbibed some very important lessons regarding self, group, and social transformation. In the end Naomi seems to succeed in making her love of revolution irresistible, positive, and productive. The narrator has learned the work and practices of liberation and the reader is introduced to the "real" of Blackness in actual fact of the lived culture of the people—their flaws, strengths, humor, and language.

During Naomi's revolutionary love talk at the end of the day at Larry's Diner, she exclaims her love of the people and it energizes the narrator to push onward. Naomi says, "I mean you work all day right? Dead on your feet and can't go on. But then a situation develops and you rise to the occasion, get your legs back, get your second wind. It's fantastic!" (37). Then she continues gleefully, "the energy that would be released if we were working for ourselves, for our neighborhoods, our children? If we owned the country?" (37). Naomi's revolutionary love banter of how "Beauuu tiii fuulll!" it would be if "worker[s] ran the shop" is such an infectious call that it evokes a spiritual response from our narrator, who unabashedly admits, "I hollered right along with her, cause I could feel the energy coming back to my feet, waking up my legs. Yeah, I could feel it" (38). She also admits that listening to Naomi's revolutionary sermonic and spending time with her has gotten her "kinda caught up in the thing [feeling revolution] myself." As the story concludes, the narrator admits to being able to: "feel the new day Naomi always lecturing about, [I] can feel it pumping through my legs. I want to be there. I am hoping to live long enough" (39).

"A Tender Man" and "Medley"

> "I am . . . more interested in the caring network that
> exists between men and women, men and men, women
> and women, children and elders."
>
> —Toni Cade Bambara

Bambara continues her reconstruction of gender politics in the stories "Medley" and "A Tender Man." In "A Tender Man" she squarely questions conventional meanings of manhood, male and female communication, and gender roles. She subverts Western definitions of masculinity and gives them new spiritual meaning. The first glimpse we have of the main male character Cliff is when he is waiting for Aisha to return to her seat, all the while "feeling preoccupied of late, off-center, anxious even" (Bambara 1977, 125). Cliff misreads his feelings as signs of being "simply nervous about the impending student takeover" (126). Aisha, for whom Cliff waits, is another of Bambara's female protagonists who serve the community in some capacity. Aisha is a nurse; she helps to heal the sick. Cliff does not know that he is among the sick in need of a cure. He impatiently waits for her to get off work at the clinic and is admittedly "uncomfortable amongst so many women and this young [child] crying" (126).

Yet, immediately after her description of Cliff, Bambara has him encounter a model of a new form of manhood. Cliff meets a father of three who has come to the clinic to fill his wife's birth control prescription, and this sets the tone for Cliff's reconstruction. The man tells him, "My ole lady says to me 'go to the clinic and pick up my pills.' Even calls me long distance to remind me she's running out" (128). Besides the ensuing commentary on institutions and how much of a "bitch" the clinic is, that it is "a crazy ass place" that wants to know everything from "your clinic number" to "[w]ho's ya mama," Bambara returns to the male grounding theme introduced in "The Organizer's Wife." She tropes the tradition of male characters running off somewhere and grounds them with the responsibility of family and nurturing. In "The Organizer's Wife" Graham returned to the community to help organize, and here, in the wife's brief absence, the father assumes the role of primary caregiver. Also, the man has an equal responsibility in the reproductive concerns, which is why he goes to the clinic to get his wife's pills. After the inhuman treatment he receives, he decides he is "goin straight to the drugstore and get me a crate of rubbers right on. I ain't putting my woman through this shit" (128). The main point is that Bambara implodes all rules of masculinity. There are no set rules; fathers must bear or share all burdens, from child rearing to reproductive responsibilities. Actually, this scene is a wonderful balance to Cliff's absent role in rearing his daughter because it displays what can and should be possible. It models for Cliff how revolutionary manhood must be performed.

Once again, Bambara's wholeness aesthetic forces her and her readers to examine the whole of Black men—good and bad—as well as the many variables surrounding Cliff's nonrelationship with his daughter. Bambara takes the reader through the events leading up to the conception and abandonment of Cliff's daughter, without making excuses for him. Through Aisha, Bambara pushes "for clarity, honesty" regarding life in general and male responsibility specifically. Cliff's description of Aisha as hard, quick, sure, yet soft at the edges explains her ability to negotiate gender tensions, to meet "him halfway" (131). Still, this negotiation does not deter Aisha from challenging him to "swear no child of [his] is starving to death" (131). Aisha's poignant query compels Cliff to honestly analyzes his own masculinity, his human vulnerability, the pressure of being a "man" and "always putting yourself out there to be rejected" (131). Bambara presents Cliff's vulnerabilities in order to provide insight into the conjured macho behavior that causes men to perform like "gorillas." She begins this excursion into his psyche to expunge or "slay" the gorilla (of masculinity), so to speak. Cliff seems to agree that, "It was silly, he told himself, these endless control games he liked to play with assertive types" (131).

At the workshop, Cliff and Aisha deal truthfully with male/female conflicts such as women's liberation, male irresponsibility, fathering, mothering, birth control, and paternity. The question of male responsibility arises and it sets off a discussion on numerous other topics. This interaction is consistent with Bambara's commitment to eradicating sexism in the movement and healing wounded relationships between Black men and women. She believed male/female healing was important if leaders of the liberation struggle expected to talk about Black subjectivity in an honest and visionary manner. Another point of the scene is to confirm that antagonistic approaches may sidetrack discussion and lead to: "Everybody talking at once, all up in each other's face" (132) but they are important. Once dealt with, this clears space to deal more effectively with a common struggle.

Amazingly, during this conflict Cliff begins "thinking about his daughter Rhea" (132), which brings forth a transformation that helps him realize that "[h]e had put off taking inventory too long, his life was adrift, unmonitored" (133). Once again Bambara reminds us that change comes from within and that inner obstacles must be cleared for a whole, new, self or spirit to emerge. In most of Bambara's stories redefinition first requires a change in spirit and creates the power to subvert language. Although Cliff is a significant figure in political organizing on campus and Aisha likes that aspect of his personality, she finds his minimalist participation in the rearing of his child counterproductive to practicing spiritual wholeness. Cliff's manhood begins to find redefinition because the traditional meaning and representation of manhood is challenged by ideas that transcend static ideas of what it means to be male and protector and provider.

What is also significant about Aisha's dilemma is that it is another example of the complexity and heterogeneity of spiritual wholeness. Aisha's critique of Cliff avoids stasis: she likes him as a person and activist, yet finds his absence as a father deplorable.

Cliff learns to look beyond Aisha's physical beauty, and although he is angry his feelings take on a complex, medley-like turn:

> He thought he might like to take her home to make love to her—no fuck her. The atmosphere kept changing, the tone, the whole quality of his feelings for her kept shifting. She kept him off balance. Yeh, he'd like to fuck her, but not cause she looked good. . . . [He] [l]ooked at her and decided he was being absurd. (142)

Cliff comes to terms with Aisha's honest critique of him and fights through his anger. His attraction to her is both physical and mental, and the type of intimacy he desires fluctuates for those two reasons. She tells him that before meeting him she had met his ex-wife (who happens to be White) and asked her, "Where's the nigger daddy who should be taking the weight" (142). This exchange between Aisha and Cliff punctuates Bambara's contention that relationships function like a medley. Although Cliff is angered by Aisha's truths, he stops to analyze himself because he realizes that Aisha, after learning this about him, continues to see him, telling him, "I'd have had to judge what kind of man you are behind your whole sense of what it means to bring a child into the world. I'm funny that way, mister" (143). Bambara's constant hope, optimism, search for truth, and insistence on female self-definition and representation produce truthful critiques of men without excluding them or subverting them to the margins. Yet, despite Aisha's patience with Cliff, her ultimate concern is for the future of the community, Cliff's child, which compels her to notify him, "Anyway, Brother . . . I'm prepared to take the child. . . . I'd do right by the little girl, Cliff" (143). While Cliff struggles to decide what type of father he will be, Aisha is ready to "do right by the little girl." Bambara is not suggesting that the child will be better off without Cliff, but that strong family is important and that the children are important and the child cannot wait for a parent like Cliff to get himself together; therefore something must be done, now. Aisha is letting Cliff know that revolution begins with the self—one cannot serve the community if one is not taking care of one's family, which is the first nation.

The impetus of Bambara's African-centered and feminist aesthetic in this exchange is honesty, unity, and the suggestion that a relationship between Cliff and Aisha is possible if Cliff can change and move toward a spiritual wholeness that makes him a strong father first. Thus, he begins his transformation with a critical self-examination of his bitterness toward Black women. He discovers that it emanates with "those Black women who had raised him," and that his problems stemmed from "his own blindness contracted from poisons he should have pumped out somehow long ago cause they weren't reasonably come by either. He was sick of his dissertation [of how bad Black women were], the arguing, the venom, even thinking about it" (145). Cliff's willingness to honestly and critically examine and learn about his own spirit is an important practice of liberation and a major step forward.

Perhaps one of the story's best examples of honestly negotiating male/female tensions, of Afrocentric and feminist aesthetics, occurs in the exchange between Cliff and Aisha after she offers to take responsibility for his child. She tells him:

On the one hand, I'm very attracted to you, Cliff. You care about the students. I mean . . . well, you have a reputation on campus for being—Well, for being one of the good guys. Plus you so sharp, ya know, and a great sense of humor. Not to mention you fine. . . . And I dig being with you.

You're comfortable, even when you're drifting off, you're comfortable to be with.

On the other hand . . . well . . . while you seem to be a principled person . . . I mean, clearly you're not a bastard or coward . . . not handling shit on campus like you been doing . . . but—

Hey look. It's like this, Cliff. I don't understand brothers who marry white girls, I really don't. And I really don't see how you can just walk away from your kid, let your child just . . . Well, damn, what is your daughter, a souvenir? (145–46)

This is a nice balance of gender tensions along the lines of community responsibility. It also expands the concept of commitment to family. The point is that manhood is a holistic venture that requires humility, honesty, and family activism. The man Cliff runs into at the clinic, although not engaged in the task of organizing the community like Cliff, is doing his part with his family in the struggle for freedom.

Throughout the story Cliff inches closer to renewal and, like the spirituals, his emotions swing rhythmically throughout the story. His slow progress is a reminder that the practice of revolution is a gradual process. At the end he manages to work the sorrows of his situation with his daughter into hope. Near the conclusion of the story, Cliff's meal with Aisha (food as a symbol of spiritual nourishment is a consistent metaphor in this collection) nourishes his spirit and helps prepare him to take "time to himself" to reassess (150) and try to settle into a reconstruction of manhood. He moves beyond his personal concerns, telling himself, "they hadn't met at the wrong time. It'd been the right time for him. The wrong time for them maybe. But what the hell" (150). Bambara maintains her insistence that male/female unity produces freedom for the greater community. Here, the focus is the community and the child that represents its future. Despite their differences and shortcomings, Aisha and Cliff commit to unifying to serve the children—the future—for community wholeness. And although it is not apparent when his transformation will be complete, we know he is moving toward reconstruction, for he answers Aisha's query "What did you want to be when you grew up?" by saying that he wants to be "a tender man" (151).

A similar dynamic emerges in the story "Medley." The male protagonist Larry Lander's stasis limits his relationship with Sweet Pea. Larry's last name, Landers, hints at his inability to play jazz music (bass) very well and is instructive, suggesting he might be land-locked or mired in old notions of what it means to be male. Larry struggles with improvising to reach new heights as a bass player and with nurturing progressive ideas regarding relationships, which dooms his relationship with Sweet Pea. Bambara immediately alerts readers that although Larry plays a wonderful medley in the shower, he cannot create new jazz music, which demands improvisation. Because his musical and masculine imagination are limited, he eventually loses Sweet Pea.

The story "Medley" continues Bambara's project of female and male reconstruction and pluralistic representation. Larry is unable to change his tune and imbibe the multidimensional spirit of jazz, which is representative of African American life and culture. As the story's title suggests, the principles of medley and jazz model practices of revolutionary male/female relationships. Bambara also tropes the "bad man" myth to convey the idea of breaking rules and approaching male/female relationships with an outlaw attitude. Instead of the work song–inspired mock sermon she employed in "A Tender Man," Bambara reconstructs the "bad man" figure mythology that limits itself to outlaw men, on the road, free, denying rules and order. Such men are fast-talking figures of action who are willing to use violence to achieve their ends and are unafraid to die. In this story Moody, the gambler, is the bad man outlaw whom Sweet Pea teams up with to form a platonic working relationship. Once again, Bambara shifts a tradition in favor of a holistic representation as she centers females in this mythology, placing Sweet Pea alongside of the traditional male bad man figure. In this story a bad woman is instrumental to the bad man's success. In fact, Bambara plays around the entire myth, humanizing her "bad man," showing him to be gentle and stable, while depicting Sweet Pea, his manicurist and accomplice, as a pivotal part of his success and as equally fearless. This story is like a jazz medley, in that it is fast paced, is filled with empty spaces that allow characters room to improvise (Moody and Sweet Pea oblige but Larry does not), and has parallel plots that overlap each other to tell a story. The first plot Bambara introduces is that of Larry and Sweet Pea. Larry is a bass player and bartender who is not good enough at the former to get gigs but is "damn" good in the shower. As Sweet Pea tells us, "He a nice man, considerate, generous, baad in the shower, and good taste in music. But he wasn't nobody's bass player. . . . Knew all the stances . . . had the choreography down" (106).

The medley that Bambara refers to in her description of Larry as bass player and performer in the shower (with Sweet Pea) is quite instructive. The medley invokes the new spirit, the polyphony, and the improvisation that is necessary for successful male/female relationships to occur and thrive. Bambara seems to be suggesting that both men and women must be willing to create their own sense of relationship—she advocates a jazz ethos. This sense that both parties should know what they want a relationship to do is important since her earlier stories stressed male and female reconstructions. Many BAM artists privileged jazz because it was in tune with notions of Blackness becoming and being; Bambara seizes upon it as a metaphor for the type of spirit that will also aid in the creation and practice of revolutionary gender relationships. The names of the two key male characters (Moody and Landers) suggest one is prone to change while the other might be more static.

The character Moody is a blues and jazz man who represents the type of free or flexible spirit Larry needs in order to play jazz music and cultivate a progressive relationship with Sweet Pea. Moody is in the trickster, gambler, hustler tradition of African American literature and culture. He is fast moving and slick. His hands are so skillful that "[t]hem cards move around so fast in his hands, he can actually tell me he is about to deal from the bottom in the next three moves and I miss it" (113). However, Bambara, soon after introducing him to us, alerts us that this mythical figure is not limited to males. As I mentioned earlier, Sweet Pea joins the "bad man" tradition too. We learn that she is a "bad woman," for she informs readers that she and her ex spent "three good years on the circuit [burglary]. . . . Then choke-and-grab muggers killed the whole tradition" (114). Without removing Moody, Bambara adds Sweet Pea to the bad man tradition to create narrative balance along gender lines. She even teams them up to work together when Sweet Pea becomes Moody's regular manicurist, and she is so good that he invites her to go on the road with him for two weeks, where she braves the dangers of hustling and gambling. He treats her as an equal and has high expectations.

The working relationship between Moody and Sweet Pea is one of mutual respect for each other's talents. This sense of mutual respect, which simulates riffing, is something that Larry fails to learn, which is evident when he asks her: "Why don't you quit? You think I am dumb?" (115). To this she responds, "I expect some kind of respect for my work, which is better than good . . . he was insulting my work" (115). Larry's linear approach to life and relationships hinders his ability to accept the improvisational working relationship between Sweet Pea and Moody, and it perhaps also hinders his ability to play bass.

Rather than launching into an anti-male diatribe, Sweet Pea practices patience with Larry and is able to negotiate tensions because she "realized he wasn't really jealous. He was just going through one of them obligatory male numbers, all symbolic, no depth" (115). Larry is jealous; he cannot fathom a platonic working relationship and feels vulnerable, but his machismo causes him to deny it, which strains their relationship. Sweet Pea realizes Larry's vulnerability, and is sympathetic, which is why she rationalizes his behavior, confiding to the reader that: "men are like that. Gorillas, if you know what I mean" (116). While she is critical of his shortcomings and empathetic regarding his insecurities, she is unwilling to endure his abuse or obtuse masculine performance. As Sweet Pea says about Larry's stasis, "I figure it ain't my place to try to develop them so they can make the leap from gorilla to human . . . it ain't my weight. I got my own weight. I'm a mother" (117). Sweet Pea practices a form of feminism that is even more nuanced than that of the characters in previous Bambara stories. This evolution allows her to express understanding but will not allow Larry's insecurity to impede her "woman stride." She confides to the reader, "Some things I'll go off on. Some things I'll hold my silence and wait it out. Some things I just bump off, cause the best solution to some problems is to just abandon them" (117). This unique philosophy is improvisational; it plays around a theme or melody of unified relationship and female self-determination and power without acquiescing to static masculine ideas; Sweet Pea is jazz while Larry is stuck repeating medleys.

Sweet Pea's posture is very much jazz influenced. Her flexible antistasis is very much driven by a spiritual wholeness aesthetic that is akin to the cosmic nature of Native American culture.[8] Although Sweet Pea's willingness to abandon Larry seems to contradict Bambara's recurring theme of unity and family, the truth is she is abandoning a situation that will not produce a cohesive family unit anyway. Sweet Pea recognizes that "Larry Landers wasn't ready to deal with no woman full grown," and this stifles any fruitful relationship (117). Larry wants family or at least "Half grumbling, half proposing, he hinted around that [he and Sweet Pea] should live at his place like a family" (118). She explains that she avoids answering Larry for three reasons: (1) she has hit her woman stride, (2) he offers a "nonproposed proposal," and (3) her two previous marriages. Her "woman stride" arms Sweet Pea with self-confidence and a sophisticated perspective. She explains that: "Marriage just ain't one of the things on my mind no more," and that she "Got no regrets or bad feelings about them husbands neither" (119). She is not against men or against marriage but she is not bound by a traditional notion of a relationship. Instead she is pro-self, and like the spirituals her mantra is one of flexibility and hope. Larry's limited thinking leaves her with no choice but to end their relationship, which, like the cold shower, has run its course. The point here is that stasis impedes progressive reimagination and spiritual wholeness.

"Xmas Eve at Johnson's Drugs N Goods"

"It perhaps takes less heart to pick up the gun than to
face the task of creating a new identity, a new self, perhaps an androgynous self, via commitment to struggle."

Toni Cade Bambara

Practices of revolutionary love take a unique twist in "Xmas Eve at
Johnson's Drugs N Goods," which also happens to be the final story
in the collection. Strategically positioned as the final story, it is Bambara's final statement on the importance of embracing Black customs,
culture, and beliefs; self-determination; self-love; self-development;
and Black socioeconomic self-reliance. In this story practices of liberation are deliberately extended via Kawaida principles: unity (*Umoja*),
self-determination (*Kujichagulia*), collective work and responsibility
(*Ujima*), cooperative economics (*Ujamaa*), purpose (*Nia*), creativity
(*Kuumba*), and faith (*Imani*). Bambara suggests that these alternative
values could guide the young protagonist, Candy, who is struggling to
define self and womanhood on her own terms. Candy grapples with
what kind of woman she will be as she struggles with the impending
divorce of her parents during the Christmas season. She lives with her
mother, a traveling singer, and her father comes to visit often, but
her new womanhood is shaped by several female and male influences.

While writing this collection of stories Bambara was writer in
residence at NAC, a Black arts center in Atlanta where Kwanzaa celebrations were not uncommon aspects of the community center's pro-
gramming.[9] This is one of several stories in this collection that feature
a Black culture or Black arts center. The alternative organizing system
Candy encounters complements the spiritual wholeness aesthetic that
permeates Bambara's fiction. It aligns with healthy practices of family,
faith, feeling, and freedom. The spiritual wholeness and the Kawaida
value system present an alternative route to self-determination and self-
definition, change, and liberation.

The story balances the community dynamics of Candy's job at Johnson's Drugs N Goods, a Black-owned drugstore, and family dynamics and struggles with self-determination, or what Bambara calls getting right "with the self." The beauty of this story is its focus on the minutia of spiritual wholeness practices, such as role models, Black economics, self-determination, self-respect, creativity, parenting, and strong examples of the Black feminine.

Johnson's Drugs N Goods is a space where prescriptions for healing medicine are filled, and the store is also a symbol of socioeconomic self-determination and collective work and responsibility. The colorful sundry of characters assembled represents a diverse and capacious Black community. Some of the characters are nice and progressive, while others are not so nice, and Candy is tasked with sifting through them all to figure out the appropriate advice and behavior to model as she determines her own vision of womanhood. Ironically, her father is the figure charged with challenging her, and he instructs her to "decide what kind of woman you're going to be" (196). One might think her mother would assume this role, but her mother is too busy attending to her singing career. Once again, Bambara flips gender convention on its head. Candy heeds her father's advice and studies different women at home and work (her mother, Aunt Harriet, Miz Della, her sister Madeen, and Mrs. Johnson) and those that visit the store (specifically two older women). Those women, Ethel and Fur Coat, become the focus of the theme of new womanhood and cultural practices of liberation. Candy's father encourages her to shape a new womanhood, and he does not place restrictions on what it might look like, which is not uncommon in Bambara's narratives that negotiate male/female relationships. Candy's connection with her dad, who visits during the Christmas holiday, leads to his heart-to-heart with her about proper behavior. He informs her, "it's [womanhood] not about looks" and "it ain't always about attracting some man either" (198). So Candy heeds his advice to contemplate the type of "woman [she is] going to be" (198). While she is not quite clear about what her new womanhood will be, she *is* certain what it will not be:

I'll look like Mama but don't wanna be no singer. Was named after Grandma Candestine but don't wanna be no fussy old woman. . . . Can't see myself turning into Aunt Harriet either; doing crossword puzzles all day. . . . I look over at Madeen, all sprawled out in her bed, tangled up in the sheets like the alcoholic she trying to be these days . . . I don't wanna be stumbling down the street with my boobs out . . . and all. (198)

Candy is at least clear that any type of revolution, whether feminist or cultural, "without transformation is half-assed" (200). This wisdom is important, and ironically it comes from another male figure, "the new dude in Drugs" whom she jokingly calls "Ali Baba" (200) although his real name is Obatale. This is significant because in Bambara's spiritual wholeness, mentorship is not gender specific. Indeed, for Bambara the main criteria is social consciousness and truth, which Obatale possesses. He is someone Candy "listened real hard [to] whenever he opened his mouth . . . [a]nd [she] jotted down the titles of the books" (200) she spied him reading.

The first step to discerning and becoming the type of woman she will be begins with her intellectual self-development on her own terms, and her father and Obatale help her shape her own direction. Obatale's name is similar to the name of a Yourba deity, Obatala, an Orisha, known as the creator of human bodies or the shaper of human beings. He helps Candy take the shape she desires without being overbearing. The revolutionary love he extends to Candy is similar to what Aisha extends to Cliff in "A Tender Man" and Naomi extends to the narrator and Dexter in "The Apprentice." Unlike Candy's father, who intends well but comes off as giving a decree, Obatala extends alternative principles and patient revolutionary love; the friendship is not intimate in the traditional sense, and it allows Candy to move at her own pace and independently craft the direction of her budding revolutionary womanhood.

Initially the two older women who enter the store, Ethel and Helen (Candy renames Helen "Fur Coat"), fascinate Candy and emerge as ideal models of womanhood "cause they shopping the right way, having fun . . . [a]nd they got plenty of style" (203). But upon closer examination of these women, Candy discovers that they lack character and the values that are spiritual wholeness. However, before she makes this discovery she is transfixed by them, specifically Fur Coat, who enters the store backward, "shoving hard against the turnstile folks supposed to exit through" (189). Yet their behavior soon reveals serious flaws. The values they practice are void of joy, love, and respect, which leads her to realize they are "not nice people" (206).

She gleans this from their mean treatment of both of the male salesmen, which disappoints Candy. Her first realization that they are not what they appear surfaces after Piper displays the spirit of creativity when he plays an imaginary shell game with them, a con game that he allows them to win. But despite his best efforts he is rudely rebuked—no sale. However, the turning point for Candy's epiphany occurs when they mistreat Obatale, who, going against the commercialism of Christmas, does not try to sell them anything except respect, love, and intellect, and he is treated the worst. Fur Coat attempts to give Obatale a small box of condoms as a Christmas gift in an "icy tone" to insult him for outsmarting her, but the positivity of his Kawaida value system flusters the older woman. He politely rejects her gift, explaining to her that he does not celebrate Christmas: "But I do accept Kwanza presents at the feast" (206). He solidifies his place as Candy's role model when he explains to Helen and Ethel that he can only accept a gift "If it is given with love and respect," to which Ethel replies: "He gotcha. . . . Give the boy credit" (207). In addition, to Ali Baba's actions, their rudeness and selfishness allow Candy to grasp "that Fur Coat (Helen) is fun, dazzling, witty, but not nice" (206), unlike Obatale, who deals with their insulting behavior with class. Obatala, she surmises, is "nice people" (206) and the older women are not worthy of emulation. Here Bambara demonstrates the power of the alternative value system like Kawaida, which respects all people, but stifles those who are rude just for the sake of being rude, even if the culprits are hip older women.

Indeed, Bambara introduces Kawaida as an alternative value system to supplement or replace the Western values that produce people who behave like Helen and Ethel. She seems to be suggesting that strong, independent Black womanhood can be powerful, fun, and dynamic without exhibiting vitriol or rude and nasty behavior. Bambara's introduction of Kwanzaa and its Kawaida principles as the alternative value system for Black people is an effective practice or framework for positive and productive self-definition and revolutionary love. The seven principles frame the story, providing holistic alternatives that privilege unity, self-determination, cooperative economics, creativity, collective work and responsibility, and purpose. The middle-class strivers Helen and Ethel, who are mean-spirited, represent an old framework for womanhood. Candy decides that "nice people" Obatale, with his Kawaida infused spirit, offers a better value system upon which to model and build her new womanhood because it teaches the power of love and respect of others.

Because Bambara is a self-proclaimed "feminist/Black Nationalist," she allows Obatale to have the strongest influence on young Candy. She makes the point that the search for new womanhood will look like this if it is in the best interest of the person. Candy decides that her womanhood will not resemble the two women who prove to be disruptive and unfriendly forces in the store community. Furthermore, it is no coincidence that the person she gravitates to the most has a name similar to the Yoruba deity Obatala, an Orisha known as the sky father and creator of human bodies, the shaper of human beings.

In this story the Black-owned store, Kwanzaa, and Bambara's iteration of Kawaida represent the new rules and reality that Black Power demanded. This story is Bambara's response to the Black Power movement call for Blacks as a group to find "new ways to relate to one another and to determine their own goals and activities" (Glasgow 1981, 166). Obatale and Candy model the behavior of new man and woman coming together to share revolutionary love. Bambara conjures a new political posturing and a psychological metamorphosis using Kawaida. In addition, the positive new indigenous viewpoint ensconced in Kwanzaa purports far from second-class status and promises Candy a new foundation upon which to build her budding womanhood. Candy, who has not spent much time with her mom or dad pre-Christmas, opens up these possibilities when she remarks: "Maybe there's something joyous about this [Kwanzaa] celebration he's talking about. Cause Lord knows Christmas is a drag" (Bambara 1977, 207). The phraseology "Lord knows" emphasizes the spiritual truth that she has lost faith and that the traditional holiday has failed to meet her expectations. As Candy considers Obatale's invitation to attend Kwanzaa, she remembers that she received a similar invitation from "The sister who taught [her] how to wrap gele" (207). This is important, for Bambara is committed to proffering healthy gender-balanced solutions and role models. Furthermore, similar to other stories in this collection (namely "Broken Field Running" and "A Girl's Story"), in this story a Black community center offers an oasis (a liberation zone) for young men and women like Candy trying to shape who they will become.

The story's conclusion is significant, powerful, undetermined, and filled with hope. Not only is its discussion of Kwanzaa a recitation on Black people loving and respecting one another but it also invokes Kawaida as a viable practice of liberation for Candy, a budding feminist and nationalist. Moreover, the formation of a friendship or mentorship between a man and woman that is not romantic is significant. In fact, it is one of the most important practices of liberation and a reminder that revolutionary love comes in all shapes, sizes, and genders.

It is also fitting that the last story in the collection celebrates feminism, Black Nationalism, and an alternative value system in the guise of the Kawaida. In seeking alternatives in the spirit of the BAM, Bambara rejects vertical hierarchy and ends with a story that suggests something new might be considered. The art of this final story is a wonderful example of second-wave BAM because it models being "a breath of the future" as it tries to fashion the "new way," or what Baraka in *Kawaida*

Studies: New Nationalism called a pathway toward "National Liberation and the new consciousness of the million year old African personality" (Baraka 1972, 25). This final story, and *The Sea Birds* collection in general, artfully practices and performs "National Liberation" and a "new consciousness" (25) whereby Black men and women complement each other, create the environment together, and are equally responsible for inspiring and raising the spirits of the people to defend and develop "this new consciousness."

Writing in *The Black Collegian* in 1980 in an essay titled "What It Means to Be a Black Woman," Bambara says the conditions Black people were struggling against were as follows: "relentless racist oppression, the orchestrated . . . antagonisms between sisters and brothers, the insidious manipulation of our token class and the persistent downpressing of mass folks, and the trivializing and commercializing of our artistic endeavors" (Bambara 1980b, 133–35). Given these challenges, she believed it was her duty to make revolution irresistible. It is only fitting that I end with Bambara's words, as they shape my theoretical paradigm and guide my thinking about her fiction. I return to *The Black Collegian* essay, where she explains that

> oppression is not our only reality. It is not even our paramount reality. It is definitely not our permanent reality. Struggle is. And community is. And imagination is. The struggle against all constraints and imposed limitations on the body, mind, psyche, spirit, vision of real community principled and potent relationships with our selves, each other, other communities and with all the forces of the universe—that is our history. That is still the challenge. And in that challenge our opportunity individually and collectively. (134–35)

Now that, to me, is irresistible love—of self and the people. This is what Bambara conjures in some form or fashion in her fiction. Her art lovingly and irresistibly tells truths, celebrates struggle, and fights to cultivate a feeling of commitment to family, faith, and freedom.

4

SPIRITUAL WHOLENESS IN *THE SALT EATERS*

> What I strive to do in my writing, and in general . . . is to examine philosophical, historical, political, metaphysical truths, or rather assumptions. I try to trace them through various contexts to see if they work.
>
> Toni Cade Bambara

> [W]e are at war, and that war is not simply a hot debate between the capitalist camp and socialist camp over which economic/political/social arrangement will have hegemony in the world. . . . The war is being fought over truth: what is the truth about human nature, about human potential? My responsibility to myself, my neighbors, my family and the human family is to try to tell the truth . . . the truth works . . . it releases the Spirit and that is a joyous thing.
>
> Toni Cade Bambara

Toni Cade Bambara's *The Salt Eaters* (1980a) is a difficult yet masterful example of her experiential skills as a writer and commitment as an activist to improve the world and achieve freedom for herself and Black people. Like her earlier collections of short fiction, *Gorilla, My Love* (1972) and *The Seabirds Are Still Alive* (1977), her first novel was an equally significant contribution to African American literature and feminism. Prominently on display is a spiritual wholeness aesthetic that moves the protagonist Velma toward liberation. This spiritual wholeness contains what Donald H. Matthews in *Honoring the Ancestors: An African Cultural Interpretation of Black Religion and Literature* (1998) calls the "Four Fs" (family, faith, feeling, and freedom). It is a conflation of African spirituality with Black religion and culture that produces a multidimensional representation of the complexity and diversity of Black life. The spiritual wholeness aesthetic I am reading here transcends the provinciality of any single interpretive method and relies on African spiritual ethics and spirituals as a narrative device. Approaching the spirituals as a practice of liberation privileges renewal of cultural and individual purpose.[1] *The Salt Eaters* represents a conjuration of a spirituality that acknowledges the existence and power of the human spirit, which has held African people together through slavery. Here I examine how spiritual and cultural practices reconnect characters to a holistic self that can become free and centered. This examination continues my exploration of Bambara's polyphonic negotiation of gender tensions, only here I emphasize that these negotiations renew faith in the power of African spirituality and that the spirituals are within a spiritual wholeness aesthetic that demands a search for truth via roots from the past for renewal of individual and cultural purpose. Spiritual wholeness here focuses on the psychological, political, and cultural desires and concerns of Africans in America. *The Salt Eaters* is a strong example of liberation practices that balance present and future with roots firmly planted in the past (African and African American) and taps into the power of conversions, healing, and conjuring derived from African and African American religions and cosmology.[2]

Practicing the Spirituals and Spiritual Wholeness

The Black aesthetic–influenced quest for a lost spiritual quality is evident in Bambara's fiction, particularly *The Salt Eaters*.[3] It draws from a tradition of African American spirituality indebted to African philosophy, namely traditional West African religious practices that privilege nature worship and ancestor reverence. The unique thing about spirituality in the African diaspora is the emphasis on being centered in a consciousness of divinity all the time, a sense that Donna Marimba Richards calls "a spirituality that gives force and energy to matter. Thus, humans are divine; the spirits manifest themselves in us (spirit possession) in the height of religious experience."[4] The spirituals' variations around a theme and emphasis on improvisation is driven by syncopation (a temporary modification of regular metrical accent in music) and polyrhythm (simultaneous combination of contrasting rhythms), which have ancient African roots. These theological and musical features are prominent forces that drive the ethos and ideology in much of Bambara's fiction, especially *The Salt Eaters*, where multiple voices converge in a nonhierarchical conjuring chorus and convey collective truth.

Spirituals, like the African religions by which they are influenced, are pluralistic and replete with creativity that ceaselessly attempts to reconstruct their own history. John S. Mbiti explains that for African peoples, there is "no formal distinction between the sacred and the secular, between the religious and non-religious, between the spiritual and the material areas of life. Wherever the African is, there is his religion" (Mbiti 1970, 3).[5] Throughout Bambara's fiction we see cases where a character holds some infinitely small portion of a large, collective truth. This is definitely true in *The Salt Eaters*, which honors the collective contributions of Velma, Minnie, Fred, Doc Serge, and several other characters. The lens used here is one that recognizes Bambara's feminist agenda within the context of a spiritual thrust that emphasized a new education for Blacks and used Africa for revitalization and roots. Spiritual or traditional African religion, according to Mbiti, values the community over the individual. Africans believe that "to be human is to belong to the whole community," and therefore "[a] person cannot detach himself from the religion of his group, for to do so is to be severed from his roots, his foundation, his context of security" (1970, 3–4). Velma's attempted suicide is merely the final physical stage of her detachment, and to survive she must evoke notions of communal creativity, interaction, and solidarity. For Velma to achieve spiritual wholeness requires, similar to Paule Marshall's Avey in *Praisesong for the Widow*, reattachment to African traditions and ideas. Such reattachment is critical if Velma hopes to occupy the "whole person" and the "whole" of her life without limiting what that means. For Bambara and other BAM participants, the idea of reattachment to Africa for revitalization and negotiation of individual and communal was important. Although this idea functions to varying degrees in Bambara's early stories, it is most pronounced in her novels *The Salt Eaters* and *Those Bones Are Not My Child* (I discuss the latter novel in the next chapter).

Donald H. Matthews explains that spirituals are a cultural style by which Africans in America express their deepest joys and sorrows. As living entities within the African American community, they take sorrow and work with it until it becomes a shout of joy, and are able to create praise from pain. Matthews, suggests that the spirituals are equally about rebellion, militancy, and freedom, and serve an important function in most, if not all, African American narratives and culture (Matthews 1998, 137). In fact, the African heritage of boundless creativity (such as antiphony, polyrhythms, syncopation, and repetitions) is the foundation of contemporary musical forms such as jazz, blues, rap, reggae, and "Go Go" dance funk.[6] Thus I explore the points of convergence between the spirituals in *The Salt Eaters*, which revives and conflates African spirituality, heritage, female self-definition, and folk myth into feelings of wholeness for Velma and Obie. I am intrigued with the possibilities a spiritual wholeness aesthetic creates for Velma's healing and conversion. This convergence is also a symbolic representation of healing sordid notions of gender relationships and a conduit toward wholeness for Black communities in post–civil rights and Black Power America. *The Salt Eaters* features a liberation impulse that revolves around individuals' and the Black community's ability to renew, recover, and improve via these radical reorienting practices. At the core of these practices of liberation is an embrace of the interrelated roles of ancestral intelligence and political activism to sustain unity of community, self, and social change.

The plot of *The Salt Eaters* involves the attempted suicide and recovery of Velma Henry, who is a political activist beleaguered by the problems she faces with her son, her husband, and the overwhelming political corruption she witnesses. Velma is part of the fragmented Black society, and Minnie Ransom, the faith healer, starts her on a spiritual journey that will release her from her coma. She must pay a small ransom (of introspection) to replenish her spiritual energy. It is not coincidental that the name of the person who directs Velma's search for balance recovery, and to become a whole mother, political activist, and wife, is named Minnie Ransom. Her name is a tongue-in-cheek pun. Velma's journey is quite similar to Avey's search for her own place in *Praisesong for the Widow*.[7] Similarly, in *The Salt Eaters* Velma reconnects with what "one's own people" had taught, and for Velma those teachings include the slave narratives, the fables, the songs, DuBois, Garvey, her parents, Malcolm, Contrane, the poets, her comrades, her godmother, and her neighbors. Without a doubt, for Velma, wholeness requires knowing herself and understanding that she is tied to this assembly of ancestral knowledge.

African and African American Spirituality

Ever mindful of the historical power of ancestral knowledge, Bambara utilizes African spirituality and invokes the strength of the diviner, the healer, the juju and hoodoo man (or woman) as a medium or guide to spiritual and cultural recovery and wholeness. Bambara's spiritual wholeness is similar to the Neo-HooDoo that Ishmael Reed describes in his poem, "Neo-HooDoo Manifesto," a concept he describes as language, rhythm, thought patterns, feelings, and spirituality of African American culture put into words.[8] In the spirit of "Neo-HooDoo" Bambara utilizes the ethos of Christian influences, as well as African American and African cultural concepts such as mediums, ghosts, and priests to guide her characters to wholeness.

Velma's suicide attempt slips her into a state of meditation, and with the help of Minnie and Old Wife, representatives of African cosmology and the African American Christian spirit, she learns the importance of adhering to the practice of forgetting those things that are in the past and reaching toward the now and the future. As she does this she conjures spirits and ghosts, witches, "hags, hants and conjurers," which, according to Mary Berry and John Blassingame in their insightful essay, "Africa, Slavery, and the Roots of Contemporary Black Culture" occupied a place of significance "in traditional African society . . . and . . . in the slave quarters" (Berry and Blassingame 1979, 247–48). Berry and Blassingame explain that "Ghosts played a more prominent role in African religions and cosmology" because of their power to "retain an interest in the affairs of the living and punish or frighten them for misdeeds, aid descendants . . . and sometimes inhabit the body of newly born infants" (248). Africans revered ghosts as integral to the process of honoring ancestors, and ghosts functioned to preserve the social order. Finally, the African priest or medicine man functioned as a "mediator between the living and the dead, a discoverer of witchcraft, and a physician" (248). His roles were multifaceted. The presence of medicine women is not unique to African American women writers but in *The Salt Eaters* Bambara draws on the African cultural memory of the medicine woman as a medium to restore faith in individuals, family, and community.

Velma might be viewed as a warning or a model for what the post–civil rights generation might consider healthy practices that will lead to a healthy self, family, feeling, and freedom. Velma acknowledges as much:

Thought she knew how to build resistance, make the journey to the center of the circle, stay poised and centered in the work and not fly off, stay centered in the best of her people's traditions and not be available to the madness, not become intoxicated by the heady brew of degrees and career and congratulations for nothing done, not become anesthetized by dazzling performances with somebody else's anesthetic, not go under. . . . Thought the vaccine offered by all the theorists and activists and clear thinkers and doers of the warrior clan would take. But amnesia had set in anyhow. (Bambara 1980a, 258)

Bambara makes wonderful use of the conjurer figures Minnie and Old Wife as mediators who conjure and drive the spirituals' themes of faith, family, feeling, and freedom to center Velma's renewal within the context of African and African American traditions.

To achieve this Minnie is solicited to function as the medium that guides Velma, or as Minnie says, throws her the "life line" to recovery (42). With the assistance of Old Wife (a spirit guide), Minnie helps to correct wrongs; they attend to Velma's spiritual and cultural wounds and try to reshape the Claiborne community in the best of its traditions. Minnie and Old Wife are at the center of her recovery, using the vernacular of blues and the jazz of "Charlie Parker playing 'Now is the Time' . . . to restore Velma's socio-psychological balance and wholeness" (262–63). Indeed, Minnie Ransom and Old Wife represent Black Christian faith and African cosmology working in tandem as agents of healing and unity in the Black community to make the people whole again. Bambara recognizes that perhaps one of the shortcomings of Black Power proponents was to separate Black Christian faith from the larger Black Power struggle. Here Bambara makes the case that the spirituals are an essential form of resistance and that they must work together. The interchangeable nature of the two is important for Black peoples' struggle for faith, feeling, and freedom. Bambara says as much when the narrator medium tells the reader, "all the systems were the same at base—voodoo, thermodynamics, I Ching, astrology, numerology, alchemy, metaphysics, everybody's ancient myths—they were interchangeable, not at all separate much less conflicting. They were the same . . . their origins survived detractors and perverters" (211).

Bambara includes and experiments with several of the aforementioned vernacular voices—ancient and present seeking sustained spiritual wholeness. As Bernard Bell points out, "Bambara deploys interrelated transcultural belief systems, faith healing rituals, ancestral presences, and grassroots political organization" (1987, 173). She produces a freedom impulse that emphasizes a wonderfully balanced freedom of the individual that is not separated from the group but focused on psychological and cultural revolution that are essential practices that must be adhered to if a larger, more whole social revolution is to take place. Bambara explained her perspective of the spiritual to Zala Chandler, telling her: "Through time, I have come to realize that, for many people, there is a division between the religious or the sacred and the secular. For me it is all sacred. I've become recently aware of, however, that there need to be statements made about the spiritual and the political . . . the need for the two to join hands" (Lewis 2012, 90).

The spiritual transformations of her protagonists are grounded in the religious spirit of Africa and in the traditions of African American culture. This religious spirit is evident in *The Salt Eaters* where Velma's spiritual transformations emerge with the assistance of the elders. The healing process involves Velma and how she prevails with the assistance of spiritual healers in reorienting both herself and the fragmented Black society that has fallen prey to misdirected ideas and failed to look inward for the proper guides to wholeness. As Minnie explains, "looks like we clean forgot what we have come to do, what we been learning through all them trials and tribulations to do" (Bambara 1980a, 46). A similar reorientation is the focus of *Those Bones Are Not My Child* (1999), where Zala and her family and the community must prevail by looking within for truth and justice. Indeed, a primary practice of liberation obliges inward reflection that shifts responsibility from the individual to the collective individuals within the community.

My reading of *The Salt Eaters* is comparable to Joyce A. Joyce's discussion in *Warriors, Conjurers and Priests* that "spiritual elements are natural to Black American consciousness and daily living" (1994, 166). However, I contend that Bambara culls aspects of Black culture, from African spirituality to folk culture and jazz, to expose possibilities for wholeness. Bambara's mixture of African and African American spiritualism, her circular structures, improvisational jazz/spiritual aesthetic, and the multiple storytellers in her novel belie her commitment to African and African American traditions. This explains why Minnie openly utilizes music to convey her message that wholeness requires memory and direction: "Wish I had some music to get it out there. These crazy folks need some saying-it to music" (Bambara 1980a, 47). Like Zora Neale Hurston's tales, Bambara's narratives are holistic—they synthesize many forces (the Black aesthetic and jazz and blues forms, mixed with her own brand of spirituality) to create different energy relationships and provide a more whole representation. *The Salt Eaters*, with its jazz structure and African spiritual influences, revives and conflates African spirituality, heritage, female self-definition, and folk myth with a feeling of wholeness.

The spirituality inherent in Bambara's fiction displays reverence for elders and memory. While Bambara's interpretive framework may strive for the freedom "to go anywhere in the universe" (Holmes and Wall 2008, 60), freedom requires memory and forward movement with the help of the past. For the characters in this novel, spiritual wholeness mandates a healing process that begins with knowing and using one's own history and mythology, followed by an understanding of how Black identity connects to that history. *The Salt Eaters* suggests that healing requires a conflation of history and mythology with female self-definition, spirituality, and commitment to community. Velma's suicide attempt clearly suggests she has lost this connection, but it leaves her in a state of meditation that prepares her to regain faith and passion in the resurrection of the struggle for liberation or freedom.

Community Healing

Bernard Bell, in *The Contemporary African American Novel*, correctly contends that writers like Bambara commit their "life and art to exploring the limitations and possibilities of political and cultural agency in improving social conditions and gender relationships in African American communities" (Bell 2004, 168). In *The Salt Eaters*, the proponents of spiritual wholeness seek not "a solution" but instead are interested in "improving social conditions" that provoke "spiritual" death in Black communities. Bambara crafts *The Salt Eaters* to capture a new spiritual quality and to renew the lost spiritual quality of the community and individual families. In *The Salt Eaters*, the possibilities of political and cultural agency are conjured via the spirituals. Velma's and the community's sorrows are worked into hopes: "New possibilities in formation . . . [become] a new configuration to move with. A flood one moment in time could drown the earth, next create fish farms and deserts" (Bambara 1980a, 293). To regain agency and spiritual qualities lost through poor education, lack of responsibility, and an inability to look inward, Velma relies on her cultural roots in the form of the conjurers Minnie and Old Wife.

The structure of the novel resembles Bambara's belief in individual and community healing as vital practices of liberation. Community members' spirits and the general spirit of the community must become whole for sustained liberation to be possible. First, the infirmary is the place where sick members of the community come to be healed and made whole at the hands of African spirituality–inspired conjurer Minnie. The spiritual memory of Porter haunts Fred into wholeness. Further, the collective stories of Fred, Obie, the Brotherhood, and the Seven Sisters stress that healing is a process that requires the entire community to be spiritually whole. Along with Velma being healed, Obie must also be healed for the community to successfully move toward spiritual wholeness. Near of the end of the novel during the Spring Carnival Velma ritualistically recovers her mental and spiritual balance, recalling her ancestral lessons, triggered by the sound of the vernacular of blues while in the prayer circle. These are practices of liberation. Bambara is committed to a spiritual wholeness aesthetic that is inspired by BAM aesthetic practices of ancestral or ancient past and present with an eye toward the future. Thus, Velma's liberation lies in "the truth that was in one's own people, and the key was to be centered in the best of one's own traditions" (Bambara 1980a, 169). The individual and cultural revolutions spark and sustain the social revolution, hence Velma's revolution begins with the self and her *own* cultural traditions.

Bambara is critical of the implications of community and the responsibility of individuals to find self before trying to serve the wider community. Therefore, Velma must first achieve a state of self-awareness before she can participate in healing the community with her newfound knowledge that each individual in the community is an essential part of the whole and is responsible for what happens to the community, as much as an individual is responsible to the community. For example, when Sophie sees Velma on the brink of being healed, she thinks to herself, "Once Minnie brought Velma through perhaps the girl at last would be ready for training. . . . Once Minnie opened her up and welcomed her back anew, renewed" (293–94). There is hope that eventually Velma will take her place and assume responsibility in the community as a healer too.

James Coleman makes a similar point in his informative essay, "The Quest for Wholeness in Toni Morrison's *Tar Baby*." Wholeness, he explains, is not achieved in Morrison's earlier novels *The Bluest Eye* and *Sula* because of "individual, family, and community fragmentation, blight and disruption" (Coleman 1986, 63). However, in *The Salt Eaters*, spiritual wholeness unifies individual, family, and community; it is essential to renewing the characters' faith in self and the struggle for liberation. Indeed, *The Salt Eaters* models the importance of a united community, a harmonious and cohesive individual and family. It also stresses the importance of African cosmology and the spirituals, as Velma's and the community's recovery revolves around the themes of family, faith, freedom, and feeling. For Bambara, conversion differs from the traditional notion of conversion. Thus, characters and the community in *The Salt Eaters* contend with Black life and death based on the African religious belief in the here and now.[9] The reverence for the here and now in *The Salt Eaters* keeps Velma from suicide and acknowledges the influences of Black religion and African American culture in the present form of Minnie and Old Wife.

To be sure, Bambara is not the only novelist to show positive portrayals of a community healing. For example, Morrison's *Song of Solomon* (1977) portrays the community positively and shows a "realization of heritage, folk myth, folk and primitive ambiance, and folk character on the part of the major characters, Pilate and Milkman" (Coleman 1986, 63–64). Milkman, Coleman explains, is "energized by a feeling of wholeness as he touches the live roots of his past on a trip . . . to Virginia" where he "learns to love, absorbs folk myth, identifies with Black folks and effaces himself in the wholesome ambiance of folk/primitive/ natural world of Shalimar, Virginia" (64). It is this feeling of wholeness that is exhibited in Velma, Obie, and Fred through healers, conjurers, ghosts, and priests in *The Salt Eaters*.

The concept of a ghostly medium functions on multiple levels in the novel. Constantly moving forward, Bambara conflates the African traditions she conjures with Christianity. One example of this occurs when Old Wife explains to Minnie that she is not a ghost but "a servant of the Lord" because "[t]here is no death in spirit" (62). In Bambara's iteration of Minnie as African witch/priest as mediator she reconstructs this witch/priest to manifest as good, a unifying force, who heals rather than brings harm to the community. Further, as a conjurer Minnie's role is, as Old Wife explains, to

> churn up all them bones we dropped from the old ships, churn up all
> that brine from the salty deep where our tears sank, and you grab them
> chirren by the neck and bop'm a good one and drag'm back to shore and
> fling'm down and jump to it, pumping and cussing, fussing and cracking

they ribs if ya have to to let'm live, Min. Cause love won't let you let'm go. (61)

Bambara has made the witch a sort of good priest. Further, she complicates the idea of ghost as medium, since there are several layers of medium in the story: Bambara the narrator is a medium who uses Minnie as medium, who uses Old Wife to help her heal Velma, who has tried to heal the community but has given up. By reviving Velma, then, Minnie indirectly extends healing to the entire community.

In *The Salt Eaters*, healing and conjuring figure prominently as routes to spiritual wholeness, and a large part of the conjuring in the novel manifests through the narrator as a medium who works through Minnie and Old Wife. The narrator does not claim to be omniscient but does function as a medium or griot through which others reflect inward to tell their stories. Bambara's approach to healing via a divine spirit within can be seen in her contemporaries like Morrison, Walker, and Marshall. However, the spirituality in Bambara's literature sustains both Black women and men. We see this in Obie and Fred's salvation, which is as important to the health of the community as is Velma's health. The relationship between healers and patients includes considerations of preventive measures rather than mere remedy. An integral part of Velma's healing entails a spiritual quest that conjures Afrocentric and feminist traditions that rely on African and African American cultural productions.

Bambara's characters cull memory, traditions, and spirituality as part of the process of becoming whole. Thus, Minnie Ransom, says Bambara, "calls people to something higher. . . . She is a healer trying to find out from her patients if they are interested in being whole and healthy. . . . [S]he is an orderer of chaos of sorts."[10] *The Salt Eaters* breaks the mold of Black novels that show Black characters successfully integrating and living by clearly defined folk values in the context of a White world. As I have argued throughout, Bambara's wholeness aesthetic explores many dimensions of African American culture and spirituality as healthy practices of liberation. Among the most important of those dimensions are knowledge and use of one's own history and mythology to understand how Black identity connects to that history. Hence, *The Salt Eaters* presents the healing practices that guide individuals toward understanding how as an individual they are responsible to the community, just as they are responsible to self.

Negotiating Gender Tensions

The spiritual conjuring in Bambara's fiction values what Joyce A. Joyce calls "true liberation," which arises "only when we recognize that a breakdown in communication between African-American men and women destroys the African communal system"; it is a system that understands that "nothing is separate, isolated or detached" (Joyce 1994, 37). One reason Bambara successfully negotiates gender tensions seems to lie in her belief that Black men have got to develop some heart and some sound analysis to realize that when Black women get passionate about themselves and their direction, it does not mean they are trying to belittle men. Most important, male/female superiority is never an issue in her work. Wholeness, as practiced in her fiction, requires harmony and balance between male and female characters. Hence, for Bambara, there is never a need to place men on the margins. Unity is a requirement in her fiction, as spiritual wholeness produces feelings of faith in family and freedom. Therefore, her female characters constantly display heart and sound analysis so they can resist the temptation of buying peace with self-sacrifice and posturing. To paraphrase Bambara, the job, then, regarding "roles" is to submerge all breezy definitions of manhood and womanhood, or reject them out of hand, until realistic definitions emerge through a commitment to Blackhood (Bambara 1970, 109). Zora Neale Hurston's *Their Eyes Were Watching God* is also a good example of the type of holistic vision Bambara produces. For Bambara, the community and culture are strong and whole only if women are strong and whole, but not at the expense of their men.

In *The Salt Eaters* the very presence of Minnie Ransom and Doc Serge as healers upholds Bambara's belief that both females and males have an important responsibility in the healing process of the community. By situating both characters in prominent positions in the infirmary, Bambara negotiates tensions without displacing males or diminishing the prominence of females. In *The Salt Eaters*, Minnie Ransom is the central healer. Bambara repeatedly inserts females to play a central role in individual and community conversion. However, she does this without ignoring males like Doc Serge or the male minister. In all of her fiction, from "Raymond's Run" and "The Organizer's Wife" to *Those Bones Are Not My Child*, she negotiates an honest gender balance in the name of liberation. Bambara's male and female characters seek to share their recovery with the larger community; the self-recovery experienced in her spiritual wholeness aesthetic is not limited to charting new journeys for Black women; such recovery, she suggests, is incomplete.

Conversions

To better emphasize how conversions work in this novel, I briefly turn to C. Eric Lincoln and Lawrence H. Mamiya's study, *The Black Church in the African American Experience*, which contends that "at the center of the black sacred cosmos African deities and spiritual forces play prominent roles in the rituals and worship of the people . . . which requires a deep regenerating experience, a spiritual journey, that requires critical self-examination and ends with salvation through the Holy Spirit" (1990, 2–4). Donald Matthews makes a similar argument in *Honoring the Ancestors* (1998), claiming that Black culture is replete with the spirit of improvisation and that playfulness within African cultures. Indeed, *The Salt Eaters* is grounded in this spirit and a continuum of the spiritual's four themes: faith, family, feeling, and freedom, which, according to Matthews, "comprise the matrix of African American religion and culture" (1998, 119).

Velma's reorientation in *The Salt Eaters* mirrors Zora Neale Hurston's description of African American religious practices and spiritual conversions in her study *The Sanctified Church*.[11] According to Hurston, a typical religious service is filled with spontaneous chants and hums that have a definite time and place; they "bear up the speaker" (respond to speaker) in response to emotion or songs (Hurston 1981, 83). As Hurston asserts, "the vision is a very definite part of [Black] religion. It almost always accompanies conversion" and "the call to preach" (85). To become converted, first an individual must become conscious of his or her guilt. Next, the individual must go somewhere (usually a place that has an emotional effect upon the seeker) to fast and pray (this three-day period is called "lyin"), which induces the vision. Then, the supplicant gives in under the threat of eternal damnation. Finally, the individual flees into an open acknowledgement of salvation and he or she is converted and ready to preach and convert others (86).

During a typical African American sermon there is an introduction to prayer, the actual prayer, a "Bearing up"—rhythmic breaks throughout prayer during which the church responds—then the body of prayer is presented, and finally the closing—here people can join in the final amen. As Hurston explains, a refusal of the calling is met with God punishing the refuser "by every kind of misfortune until he finally acknowledges himself beaten and makes known the call" (86). Yet what is interesting about *The Salt Eaters* is that Velma's reorientation is somewhat different from the "bearing up" process described by Hurston. Bambara constructs and actualizes spiritual conversion as only she can, and she explains that the dominant metaphor of *The Salt Eaters* is dialectic: salt is both facilitating and debilitating and connects to the myth of the flying African. She goes on to explain how "according to old folks we got grounded because we ate too much salt; others say we got grounded because we opened ourselves to horror."[12] *The Salt Eaters* plays around various myths and aspects of the African flying myth that have to do with salt. A central aspect of the conversion process, according to Bambara, requires remembering myths and traditions "whose roots had been driven far under ground" (Bambara 1980a, 292). For example, the time Velma takes "to finish fasting and the silences" (294) transforms the myth into something different.

Perhaps this is why the number seven figures prominently in the text, and the seven sisters are elements of harvest that yield a new spiritual energy. It is well known that seven is a sacred spiritual number that represents the energy of the mystics, and one could argue they symbolize the novel's attempt to make spiritual connection to the earth and ancestors, which is essential to Velma's renewal and perhaps represents holistic renewal of the people. Also, "Seven Sisters" and the fictional "7 Arts Academy" could be viewed as symbolic of coalition and the many activist groups seeking social change. Just as Obie's unfaithfulness to Velma threatens their union, many of the activists who cheat the struggle for change with avarice and personal gains jeopardize the people's liberation. Bambara plays with myths, numbers, and the conversion tradition to emphasize the need to go "underground" to roots of African spirituality in order to move toward spiritual wholeness. Yet because Bambara believes liberation begins in the self with the self, Minnie can take Velma only so far. It is Velma's responsibility to finish the process. As she says, "No need for Minnie's hands now so the healer withdraws them . . . just as Velma, rising on steady legs, throws off the shawl . . . a burst cocoon" (295).

On full display in *The Salt Eaters* is Bambara's nuanced ability to embrace diverse worldviews and voices of African American cultural representation, as well as her ability to expand meanings and expressions of Blackness and feminism. The driving force behind Bambara's creative approach extends from her New York City "bebop heaven" beginnings to her experiences as an adult in Atlanta.[13] These environments, she says, taught her "about what can be communicated, can be taught through structure, tone, metronomic sense, and just sheer holy boldness. . . . [T]he voice of my work is bop . . . and since moving South, I've expanded my repertoire to include a bit of the gospel idiom."[14]

Throughout *The Salt Eaters* Bambara evokes spiritual improvisations and themes that embrace and express the spectrum of Black cultural expression. Velma's spiritual journey navigates an Afrocentric feminism that elevates the nationalist search for new spiritual quality to great heights while healing wounds and recapturing elements of an old spiritual quality, lost and buried in an African past. The novel conjures African American cultural representations to construct notions of spiritual wholeness. The spirituals' themes of family, faith, feeling, and freedom that Donald Matthews contends are dominant narrative structure in African American literature hold true in Bambara's fiction. Bambara achieves her goal

> to celebrate struggle, to applaud the tradition of struggle in our community, to bring to center stage all those characters, just ordinary folks on the block, who've been waiting in the wings, characters we thought we had to ignore because they weren't pimp-flashy or hustler-slick or because they didn't fit easily into previously acceptable modes or stock types. I want to lift up some usable truths—like the fact that . . . staying centered in the best of one's own cultural tradition is hip, is sane, is perfectly fine despite all claims to universality-through-Anglo-Saxonizing and other madnesses. (Tate 1983, 18)

Without doubt, *The Salt Eaters* is true to Bambara's goal of staying centered in the best of African and American traditions such as spirituals, jazz, African religion, Black feminism, and other elements. Velma's recovery negotiates these elements using spiritual wholeness.

The Salt Eaters expands Bambara's discourse around intersections between spirituals and Afrocentric and feminist ideologies, because they strive for healing and spiritual wholeness via multiple voices, perspectives, and traditions derived from African and African American culture. The novel upholds and transcends the Black aesthetic goal of redefinition of identity. Velma achieves a personal spiritual rebirth, while her husband Obie, nears his own. The novel amplifies a spiritual voice of wholeness (for both men and women) that functions as a spiritual voice of community, nationalism, and feminism.

What is wonderful and refreshing is that the novel achieves this while skirting a traditional linear narrative. In fact, the oral and the griot tradition on display allow the characters to convey their tales without the narrator disrupting their stories. Indeed, the multiple narratives from the community that converge in *The Salt Eaters* function like a jam session to tell a story. Velma's narrative revives a formerly "closed" discourse, inundating readers with divergent elements that make the notion of liberation holistic. Moreover, the reader is treated to Velma's memory while the narrative also entertains the memory of male characters like Fred, Doc Serge, and Obie. Still, the focus of spiritual reclamation is on Velma and the community. The array of cultural forces deployed in the novel disrupts familiar conceptual determinations of oral narratives and the use of communal frames. This jazz jam session moves different characters into the forefront with solo fragments of a story that complete *the whole* story.

The Salt Eaters is also unique because it neutralizes the negative effects of racism and patriarchal oppression, while propagating a feminist perspective and African spiritualism. The narrative is a discontinuous reflection on Velma's healing session but her breakdown from fatigue and overwork is a palimpsest for the Black post–civil rights struggle that lost momentum in the 1970s amidst some small gains. Reading spiritual wholeness as an examination of philosophical, historical, political, and metaphysical truths and assumptions expands the limits of African American literature. What separates Bambara from other Black women writers is her consistent attachment to a communal frame without splitting the Black community along gender lines. Indeed, while she joins other Black women writers in interrogating unilateral notions of liberation and a unilateral definition of what "blackness" is, her search encompasses a new spiritual quality that emphasizes and gains power from utilizing African cosmology as well as the narrative structure and themes associated with spirituals. Velma transcends;

she does not merely endure or prevail but rather emerges more aware of her personal identity and potential for self-actualization. She becomes a linchpin for the nation's awareness and liberation with the assistance of spiritual healers who reorient her, and in effect she reorients or reshapes the larger Black community of Claiborne.

The changes that Bambara's characters and community undergo are rooted in distinct religious traditions in African American culture. As an artist and cultural worker she is in tune with the spiritual universe and works from "a distinct Black literature with very particular kinds of traditions . . . [that confront] what is particular or peculiar about this country" (Lewis 2012). Indeed, *The Salt Eaters* undeniably embraces the notion of spiritual wholeness, and it expands the scope of African American narrative and cultural representations by negotiating gender tensions and clearing the way for multidimensional perspectives. Bambara opens the third eye of the people, raising conscience and consciousness.

Finally, *The Salt Eaters* is a novel that is a sort of gospel of renewal—individual, communal, spiritual, and cultural. As a practice of liberation art it recaptures the community and liberation spirit that was cultivated during the Black Arts Movement. As such, it exemplifies Bambara's ability to convey the fundamental human reality in the everyday motion of Black people and the role of Black women in the struggle for equality during the Civil Rights and Black Power movements of the 1960s and 1970s. Viewed in this way the novel is an extension of ideas broached in *The Black Woman* regarding the emancipation of Black women being tied to the emancipation of Black men in a manner that required a different approach to masculinity. Ultimately, *The Salt Eaters* advocates and models spiritual wholeness practices of family, faith, feeling, and freedom that were necessary for mobilizing Black communities (the people) in the post–civil rights and Black liberation struggle. That "work," as Obie begins to realize, requires men and "Women for Action" working together "to build, to consolidate and escalate" (Bambara 1980a, 93) their salient struggle for freedom and liberation.

5

REMEMBERING THE COVENANT

Summoning Choral Spirits in
Those Bones Are Not My Child

The question I raise from "Gorilla" to "Sea Birds" to *Salt*
to "Faith of the Bather" is, is it natural (sane, healthy,
whole-some, in our interest) to violate the contracts/
covenants we have with our ancestors, each other, our
children, ourselves and God?

Toni Cade Bambara

Those Bones Are Not My Child (1999) upholds and transcends the Black
aesthetic goal of redefinition of identity. Using traces of Black sermon
and the metaphor of the gospel choir, the novel is a reminder that Black
people should not "violate the contracts/covenants we have with our
ancestors, each other, our children, ourselves" (Bambara 1984, 47).
Indeed, the novel is a call to recover and trust one's own traditions,
impulses, and agenda. A common motif in Bambara's art is the panoramic presence of a multivoiced collective chorus that champions the
causes of Black people, encouraging them toward liberation practices
that allow them to define their own realities. Her posthumous novel

Those Bones Are Not My Child continues this trajectory and extends her practice of producing art with the political function of social change for Black people in the United States. Indeed, it extends her concern with practices of liberation that "offer usable truth . . . to document the many truths or realisms that make up the black woman's experience" (Lewis 2012, 8) and the Black experience. This liberation impulse includes a belief "in transformation politics or transformation psychology" (121) that privileges "responsibility to self and to history" (121). The primary focus is "[t]o be whole—politically, psychically, spiritually, culturally, intellectually, aesthetically, physically, and economically whole" (91). The novel convalesces the covenant with ancestors, family, faith, and feeling, literally embracing a mission to teach or to sing the gospel of African-centered practices of liberation. Indeed, *Those Bones Are Not My Child* harkens Black communities to see the Atlanta child murders as a cautionary reminder of the importance of a liberation impulse that privileges personal sacrifice and commitment to family, faith, feeling, spirituality, African ancestry, and choice.

Those Bones Are Not My Child, edited and posthumously published by Bambara's friend and former editor, Toni Morrison, is entrenched in the idea of "resurrecting" and connecting "ties" to covenants that are intended make Black people "politically, psychically, spiritually, culturally . . . and aesthetically" whole (Lewis 2012, 91). Set in Atlanta, the novel, which began as journal entries, engages this process by resurrecting and recovering the Atlanta child murders that were never adequately resolved. The Atlanta child murders took place between 1979 and 1981 and resulted in the unsolved murder of more than twenty Black children and young adults. The murders stopped once twenty-three-year-old Wayne Williams was apprehended and charged with the murder of two people. Authorities tried to tie many of the other murders to Williams. Bambara, who resided in Atlanta during this period, was very much involved as a community member writing articles and organizing to get answers to solve the case. The novel is an outgrowth of her journal notes, and this fictional telling of the events parallels real events. This factual retelling reveals the humanity and private pains of the parents who endured the tragedy. Not only has the Atlanta community failed to protect its greatest liberation asset, its children, but Atlanta is symbolic of post–civil rights Black Americans' failure or shirking of their covenantal duty, which is to continue to engage in practices of liberation by staying attuned to faith, feeling, and family and defining their own reality. Bambara deems herself equally culpable of this offense (she lived in Atlanta during the murders), which is why when the novel opens she is the first person critiqued for shirking the covenantal duty of protecting the children. The novel is an act of redefinition of the "official" narrative that Wayne Williams was the culprit and points fingers at all of the suspects she deemed culpable.

The opening entry of the epilogue is Bambara's nonfiction explication of the murders and the literature produced about it. Pulling directly from her journal notes, Bambara lays out for the reader everything that has been said before she provides us with her fictional retelling that personalizes, humanizes, and fills unsolved gaps. This neo-realism is a unique iteration of a gospel of resistance and redemption that calls for a return to "the way" that had forced significant change in the 1950s, 1960s, and early 1970s via a Black Power emphasis on redefinition and Black self-determination. While the novel is expansive, the primary focus of this essay is to examine Bambara's iteration of the myth or legend of what allegedly happened to the children. *Those Bones* is a retelling of the Atlanta child murders that is infused with a gospel aesthetic that uncovers "truths" that were buried in the dominant narrative. The gospel-infused aesthetic utilized here is similar to what we find in gospel music. Fictional character Marzala (Zala) Rawls exhibits an improvised recitative (declamation) speech and melisma (singing of multiple pitches or notes per syllable) that is infused with an extraordinarily expressive delivery that personalizes and humanizes the events. The neorealist tale of Zala's recovery of her child, Sonny (when no missing children were actually found), ritualistically reroutes the people to lost or forgotten values and practices from the civil rights era that privileged children as the promise for a future liberation.

Those Bones, like most of Bambara's fiction, answers then extends the Black Arts movement's call for art with the political function of liberating the minds of Black people in the United States. *Those Bones* models a recommitment to the covenants and practices of liberation: family, faith, feeling (African cosmology and African American spirituality), and freedom. The motif of redefinition and identity is central to this novel, which is entrenched in the sermonic tradition of challenge and change. The panoramic Black cultural traditions on display continue her tradition of featuring an organic multivoiced collective narrative structure that challenges readers to locate conditions behind the alleged facts and discover and consider *other* truths. Bambara's main muse is a constant thread of African and African American culture that embraces the spiritual power of the people past and present. The prominent cultural thread is gospel music, which has roots in the Black oral tradition and typically utilizes a great deal of repetition and "call and response" designed to achieve an altered state of consciousness and to strengthen communal bonds. Bambara utilizes this element of Black vernacular along with realism and modernism to recover the spiritual wholeness aesthetic: family, faith, feeling, and freedom. These principles deemphasize personal gain in favor of values such as social justice, moral conscience, social consciousness, and resisting sexism, racism, poverty, and corruption. The novel is a call for Black people to the edicts of Black Power, which encouraged them to unite, to define their own goals, to recognize their heritage, to reject racist institutions, to lead and support their own organizations, and to build a sense of community that allows new values to flourish.

For scholars interested in a contemporary literature exploring how social, historical, and political conditions have framed production, *Those Bones Are Not My Child* is a great example. Hence, the novel is representative of the impetus of Bambara's art, which focused on recuperating varied spectrums of African and African American culture, spirituality, and religion. This novel is ever mindful of evoking resistance and self-determination; because it challenges the "official" media version of what happened in Atlanta. Bambara's retelling offers hope. It is also a gospel that validates the contributions of spirituality, religion, and Christianity as core building blocks of a successful struggle for strong Black communities, liberation, and revolution.

On one level a focal point of this novel, the disappearance and recovery of Zala's eldest child, Sonny, is symbolic of the need for Black folk to recover African cosmology and African American spirituality as core weapons in the battle for liberation. This neorealist narrative is, in many ways, a lament over the how the post–civil rights movement got lost and how the people were led astray by avarice and token progress. Yet it is also an effort to urge people to return to healthy practices of liberation—it is a road map home to privilege family and faith. Bambara's choral call seeks to return the people to consciousness, conscience, social criticism, and a tradition of protest. Similar to her previous work, *Those Bones Are Not My Child* blends feminist, Black Nationalist, and activist social protest for freedom. This unique conjuration of fact and fiction makes creative use of the African American sermonic tradition and Black spirituality as only she can—both inside and outside of convention. Indeed, her version, while attacking a racist city and government (which boasts its first Black mayor), displays unswerving faith in the community's redemption and fulfillment of the justice goals that the civil rights movement sought. Throughout the entire novel Bambara and her protagonist, Zala, lead the imperiled Black community of Atlanta (the imperiled people of God) toward truths about the murders and toward refocusing on fulfilling their destiny or promise. However, her narrative structure allows Zala, Spencer, and their child, Sonny, as well as the Black community of Atlanta—the American city of God—to be instruments of their own salvation.

For Zala, the healing process lies in the spirit of the Black gospel and sermon as she and the imperiled Black community of Atlanta seek healing, recuperation, and revival and the fulfillment of finding the truth. Bambara relies on a bevy of traditions past and present to reclaim cultural space and conjure using a spiritual wholeness aesthetic. The spiritual wholeness in *Those Bones Are Not My Child* is not to be confused with spiritual redemption, as Bambara's concern is with earthly matters; the wholeness at work here for Zala and the Black Atlanta community is a search for integrity within a wider framework of reclamation and memory. Emphasis is placed on the interior of Zala and her family and the unwritten or undocumented lives of Black Atlanta, which suffered during this period of terror. In doing so Bambara constructs a sermonic of sorts that conjures healing connections to African religion as a bridge to Zala's and the community's return to practices of liberation that lead to spiritual fulfillment and the Black Power mission and promise of freedom for the Black nation.

Two other prominent motifs that anchor *Those Bones* are its sermonic structure and the influence of African and African American spirituality. This unique gospel discourse intersects spiritual, Afrocentric, and feminist ideologies that transform the spirit and social consciousness of her characters. The gospel is useful for harnessing pain, healing and spiritual wholeness and tapping the multitude of voices excluded in mainstream media during the Atlanta travesty. The people become their own instruments of Providence. In addition to this, Bambara's iteration of African and African American spirituality compels characters' lives or spirits holistically and generates new power where it previously did not exist through the subjugated knowledge of foremothers and fathers. By positioning herself as narrator as medium, the author panoramically interfaces the political, metaphysical, and artistic for an unobstructed view of what she terms "old powers lying dormant" that need to be wrested from those who have it.[1] Spirituality in her novels is not limited to fallible human institutions, or worship on Sundays, but is about presence, a motion and a spirit, a journey that culls intuitive senses and an "inner guide" (Anthony 2007, 11–12).

While Bambara's pen is certainly panoramic, her supreme achievement is her unique ability to nestle the gospel and sermonic within the Black aesthetic challenge of *tradition* and search for Black artistic reformation via recovering an African spiritual ancestry. As this novel suggests, Atlanta and post–civil rights America were supposed to promise Black folk a new reality because of Atlanta's new Black mayor and expansive economic development. Yet the cost of this economic success was sacrificing a tradition of community, family, faith, and local and ancient ancestral knowledge that previously served the people well. Thus the conflation of these goals and the practices and rites of recovery makes *Those Bones* a uniquely fascinating work of fiction. It is a fine example of why Bambara's fiction exemplifies the apex of what the Black Arts Movement and Black feminism strove to achieve. The novel embraces a holistic spectrum of Black expressive culture, representing the roots of the rich humus of Black culture.

The fictional tale of Zala Spencer and her family spurs a call for reclamation of the liberation impulse that changed the world in the 1950s and 1960s. Through Zala and her family we see Bambara's self-proclaimed interest in "approaching the complexity of ourselves in a fearless way" and vestiges of what Bambara calls "an aspect of black spirit, of inherent black nature that we have not addressed: the tension, the power that is latent, still colonized, still frozen and untapped, in some 27 million black people" (Lewis 2012, 8–9). Zala's search for her missing son unlocks the tension and power of liberation practices inculcated in aspects of the spirituals, namely the themes of family, faith, freedom, and feeling, in a powerful manner.

At the very beginning of *Those Bones Are Not My Child* it is clear that a covenant has been broken and recovery is necessary. For Bambara, the first step toward liberation and recovery lie within. Fittingly, the prologue begins with Bambara the narrator critiquing herself for the catastrophe that recently befell the community. She reveals her own inadequacies and vulnerabilities as a parent. Bambara's self-reproach in the opening prologue not only conveys that "the way" has been lost but shifts her narrative status from omnipotent to medium narrator who is as flawed as the characters in her story. This prologue that situates her among the people begins on November 16, 1981, at 3:51 p.m., after the killings have ended and the killer has been apprehended. Bambara reveals herself anxiously awaiting the arrival home from school of her daughter, who is late, and she is growing more fearful by the minute.

In the prologue Bambara also reveals the promise from the "authorities" that the murders are over: "The terror is over, the authorities say. The horror is past, they repeat every day. There've been no new cases of kidnap and murder since the arrest back in June" (Bambara 1999, 1). Yet, unconvinced, the narrator (Bambara) calls the school, then rushes to school "trying to keep [her] mind off the murders committed since the arrest in June, cases that match the six patterns devised by community instigators" (7). Her version of truth doubts the "authorities" and places faith in the truths and wisdom of "community investigators." Once she arrives at the school, Bambara informs us that she, too, is guilty of breaking a promise, and her daughter chastises her for forgetting her promise to meet her on this day to sign a form to allow her to go swimming. Another woman standing nearby, watching the incident, also chastises her for her negligence in lieu of the recent atrocities. The woman chides her: "Some mother. . . . Leaving your girl to wait on the corner. . . . This is Atlanta, honey, where is your mind?" (14). Bambara, whose mantra is that liberation "begins with the self," begins her narrative with a painful self-critique for being guilty of also failing to uphold a covenant with her daughter. The prologue immediately forces readers to acknowledge the murdered children, while reproaching those who allowed it to happen—the community (parents, including the author), the local government, White supremacists, and the federal government and its agencies. Bambara blames or suspects all of these entities as culprits in the crime (20).

Besides the questionable promise that the murders are over, Bambara makes clear that the children are the promise, as is the city of Atlanta and its first Black mayor, Maynard Jackson, who "ushered in, folks were prone to say, the Second Reconstruction" (16). Atlanta was supposed to be the promise of a new day for Black America; the reward for all that had been endured before and during the civil rights movement. It was considered the "Black Mecca of the South; the Second Reconstruction City, the home of a bulk of Fortune 500 companies, the scheduled host of the World's Fair in the year 2000, the proposed cite of World University, slated to make the Top Ten of the world's great financial centers" (18). This initial revelation of the retrogressions of parents, community, government, and the city of Atlanta to uphold their covenant sets Bambara's iteration of spiritual wholeness in motion. The retrogression is clear, and the reader immediately learns that the narrator is not convinced by the governor's announcement after a three-week investigation of Georgia Klans that they have a "[c]lean bill of health" (21). She is suspicious of everyone.

Bambara's frank and accusatory opening reflections from her journal, which she says she began "in September 1979 with nothing particular in mind . . . [b]ut [she] recorded the fact that [her] mailman had rapped on [her] screen back in the summer to ask if [she had] heard about the kidnappings reported in the McDaniel-Glenn area" (15), is both a lament of the promise and a critique of the present declension from the promise, without being self-righteous. In interviews, Bambara discusses how this book began as journal entries, and thus it is appropriate that the opening scene derives directly from the first two halves of her personal journal. She gains readers' trust because she bears her own shortcomings. This authenticates her perspective of the present declension upon which the reader is about to embark. The reader immediately pays attention when she laments that no one seems to remember anymore that "prior to the arrest, a member of the Atlanta City Council, not totally persuaded by the Task Force version of the case(s), requested Lee Brown to submit by June 30 a list of all unsolved homicides in Atlanta. Suspect Wayne Williams was formally charged on June 22 making the report moot. . . . Meanwhile, the slaughter continues" (21). Indeed, her frank contention that "the slaughter continues" despite the governor's assertion that the travesty has ended is where the story begins. For Bambara the resolving prophesy is unsettled and the promise is unredeemed as she begins her fictional account of the Atlanta events. However, there is a hint of optimism at the end of the prologue. If one reads closely the scene of her daughter playing dead in the pool, there is assurance that Bambara "will find [her] voice before [her daughter] climbs out of the pool" (21) and that the declension is temporary and there will be a rebirth.

Much like this opening prologue, the narrative that ensues mixes fact with Bambara's fictional retelling of the Atlanta child murders. The fictional Zala, who loses and miraculously regains her son during the murders, is at the center of the retelling of a story sorely in need of truthful closure—a new ending that might bring a new beginning. The fictional account unfolds the loss and recovery of Zala's family and renders the lives of children that had been lost and minimized much more significant. Because the case is framed in fiction, readers become acutely aware of the humanity and the loss of the actual families involved. As Sonny's family frantically searches for him the reader learns details of the family, the promise, and retrogression from the promise (on behalf of the parents, the government, and the Black leadership). The fictional narrative creates empathy and reveals that the promise of love, protection, and communal progress (mantras of the civil rights movement) has been broken or forgotten in the scramble for avarice and personal gain.

The declension becomes personal when Sonny disappears while on a camping trip. Yet his absence also ignites the family's path to healing. While searching for their son both Zala and Spencer become spiritually introspective, recommitting themselves to their marriage, as they examine the impact of their separation on their family, specifically the child Sonny. Furthermore, when Sonny mysteriously reappears they discover that his spirit (part of the promise) is damaged; he is always silent, jumpy, afraid, lifeless—in desperate need of redemption. Sonny's return home from the "dead" intensifies his family's attempt to redeem the promise of happiness, hope, unity, and safety. This leads them further south, home to Zala's roots, where her mother, Lovey, helps them all heal, especially Sonny.

While the spiritual revival of the Atlanta community is a clear focus of the novel, so is Zala and Spencer's quest to recover the promise of their union as husband and wife and their promise as parents to their children. The path they seek to complete this journey is to their personal roots, Zala's home place deep in the South. Zala and Spencer find Lovey's home to be the perfect environment in which to heal the wounds of their separation and strengthen their family's future. In a rural region, far from urban Atlanta, the pastoral natural setting encourages Zala and Spencer to revive the passion of their relationship. Away from the confines of urban Atlanta, they recapture the passion that brought them together: looking "up at the moon [and turning] to the fields behind them, the cabin's chimney gleaming in the night, [they] exchanged sly smiles, increasing their pressure on each other's hands" (Bambara 1999, 554). Recovering the promise of marriage and family are essential to being able to heal their son and aid the community in its quest to find the abductors and recover its lost children. Spencer and Zala's relationship is a linchpin to the family's renewal, as well as the community's. However, the community, Zala, Spencer, and their son all have to undergo a reorientation of faith, family, and communal values to complete the process of fulfilling the promise of freedom.

This reorientation leads Zala to confront a generation and community void of appreciation for the historical struggle for basic civic rights and freedom, as well as the cultural traditions that made this struggle successful. Zala assumes a leading role in reorienting the community toward the former power of the revivalist religion. The post–civil rights generations strayed from these roots, deeming this tradition less effective than a more confrontational posture and philosophy. *Bones* reveals what happens to the children of a generation that has lost faith in and abandoned history and tradition (in the form of revivalist religion) as liberation practices and lost focus on the promise amid *some* progress. Zala explains to community members how her son was lost but that she was fortunate to have recovered him. She inspires hope that others will be found if they have faith without chastising.

Zala is a choir member, and the pulpit that she preaches from stages a revival of spirit, a sense of community and consciousness. It is not uncommon for sermons to be accompanied by the choir. Indeed, the voice of the Black gospel preacher is commonly affected by Black secular performers and vice versa. The choir features the extremes of female vocal range in call-and-response counterpoint with the preacher's sermon. However, Bambara's multifaceted approach alters this ritual and alternates Zala between being a choir member and in the pulpit as a catalyst for the congregation's recovery of the promise. Furthermore, most important, the effectiveness of her presence stems from the fact that gender hierarchies are absent. Zala's presence alongside of Reverend Thomas to address the community is consistent with Bambara's spiritual wholeness, which demands that men and women perform equally important roles in fulfillment of the promise of liberation. The preacher and choir member collaborate on an equal platform to renew the community's spirit and refocus on the promise.

Bambara makes fantastic use of the raw materials of the Christian revivalist tradition while engaging the issue of the post–civil rights failed promise. She does so using a spiritual twist more attuned to the dictates of the Black aesthetic and some components of African spirituality. Her unique twist incorporates the Black aesthetic quest for art that is political, about liberation, and pragmatic, but without negating the power of Christian spiritual revivalist traditions. Moreover, the memory of the dead Atlanta children and Sonny's presumed death and rebirth harken what Donald Matthews eloquently explained in *Honoring the Ancestors* as "psychological adjustment . . . [that] is intricately tied to an understanding that a person's mental well-being is tied to the person's relationship with the divine. The greatest source of support for African Americans has been the church and other religious philosophies" (1998, 30). Here Zala's revival-style sermon is reminiscent of the place where the civil rights movement gained its strongest footing, the church.

Bambara does not reject the power of Christianity or African cosmology, or any other aspect of Black spirituality in *Bones*. In fact, Zala's spiritual transformation emanates from it. Indeed, it aids Zala's personal spiritual transformation; the pulpit (the divine) assists the psychological adjustment of the rest of the community. In *Bones* the significance of the Black church and other religious philosophies conflate to evoke an organic iteration of Black cultural traditions. Bambara truly believes that "[t]o be whole—politically, psychically, spiritually, culturally, intellectually, aesthetically, physically, and economically . . . is of profound significance. There is a responsibility to self and to history that is developed once you are whole, once you are well, once you acknowledge our powers" (Chandler 1979, 348). Given this philosophy, it is not surprising that Zala uses the spiritual power of a church gathering to unite and make the community whole and also challenge the community to uphold its responsibility or promise to protect its children. In fact, Bambara suggests that the parents and community perform equal roles as Orisha of sorts for the children to make amends for failing to protect the youth of the community—the hope and promise for the future.

The fictional recreation of the Atlanta child murders is meant to haunt the reader in the same way the strange reappearance of Sonny haunts his family and the community in the narrative for being silent. Like the reader, they are challenged to partake of the practice of challenging authority. Indeed, the novel is a sort of ghost or manifestation of the spirit or soul of the Black liberation spirit that had lost its way and been murdered. Moreover, the return of Sonny suggests that redemption is possible; it is a manifestation of all the Atlanta children's souls and the hopeful recovery of the 1970s liberation impulse. The narrative, the pain of Zala and her family, and Sonny's otherworldly reappearance all are projections of a reality that runs parallel to the "official" facts of the child murder case. The message here is to recapture the spirit and practices of the covenant.

Just as a preacher or sermon conjures a message in African religions and cosmology, ghosts play prominent roles as conjurers or those who deliver messages. They have enormous power and are integral to the process of honoring ancestors and preserving social order. African "medicine men and women" functioned as mediators between the living and the dead in a multifaceted role. The fictional Sonny who reappears out of nowhere is the ghost that haunts us in this story. As Mary Berry and John Blassingame explain in their essay, "Africa, Slavery, and the Roots of Contemporary Black Culture" in the transfer to America the roles of witches, ghosts and medicine men were inverted and conflated (1979, 248). Witches lost some of their malevolence, while ghosts retained many of the features of African cosmology and the conjurer. Ghosts combined "the malevolence of the witch with the benevolence of the medicine man and priest," becoming "the medium [for the enslaved] for redressing wrongs committed by his master or fellows and served as druggist, physician, faith healer, psychologist and fortune teller" (248). Sonny's miraculously reemergence is a declaration of hope and an attempt to redress the wrongs committed against the Black Atlanta community that witnessed a gross negligence during the murders.

Mediators, conjurors, and ghosts driven by the spirituals' themes of faith, family, feeling, and freedom conflate with a narrative structure influenced by rhythmic complexity and the call and response of the spirituals and jazz to produce a narrative that is a quest for spiritual renewal. For example, in *The Salt Eaters* Minnie Ransom is the medium that guides her protagonist Velma, or, as Minnie says, throws the "life line" to recovery (Bambara 1980a, 42). Bambara tropes and follows the tradition of the ghost in the form of Old Wife who helps to correct wrongs and assists Minnie as she attends to Velma's and the community's spiritual and cultural wounds. In fact, the concept of a ghostly medium functions on multiple levels. Minnie is a witch/priest who is good and unites and heals rather than bringing harm to the community.

However, the medium concept in *Those Bones* functions a little differently. In this story notions of family, faith, and freedom have significant influence. For instance, when Zala reminds the community of its promise of spiritual renewal, Bambara eschews the structure of disclaimer, the statement of theme, and the articulation of social and personal conditions, followed by an answer and a closing statement. On the contrary, Bambara's Reverend Thomas jumps right into the statement of theme (have the strength to be accountable and courageous). He uncharacteristically jumps to the point, telling the crowd, "If people are to win victories over their worst terrors, the noblest traits in them must be appealed to" (Bambara 1999, 657). Next, Thomas moves to set the context. He informs the congregation, "We have all been favored before with articles and talks that point up the . . . untruths. . . . But many of us are still unwilling to dismantle the authorities' myth. . . . Let us bow our heads and pray for the strength to overcome our own fearlessness . . . the strength to become more accountable to the generations to come . . . to make this city responsible to the people's need for truth, so that our children will not grow up cynical and warped by our failures of courage" (657). Reverend Thomas's declension is a brief sermon of sorts that articulates the promise, the critiques, and the mission to redeem the promise. He concludes with a disclaimer of sorts, calling upon "Father, Mother, God, Spirit," then asking that "the tongues of the speakers be touched with the light" (658).

Among the most prominent "tongues . . . touched with light" is that of Zala, a choir member, when she is temporarily thrust into the role of preacher or medium, using the power of sermon to reach beyond the church. Bambara, always a humorist, toys with the notion of "preaching to the choir" by having a choir member preach to the congregation. In this iteration Thomas, the preacher, frames the message that Zala, the choir member, delivers to the community. Always committed to the power of women and the common folk (silent voices), Bambara reverses the sermonic structure completely, trusting that Zala's appeal as mother will humanize the loss and touch souls more deeply. The decision to reposition Reverend Thomas to work alongside a member of the choir instead of the traditional hierarchy of role of the choir in call-and-response counterpoint with the preacher's sermon also moves the community closer to the covenant.

The interaction between Reverend Thomas and Zala is important because both are situated as mediums trying to heal the community and make them whole. Thomas uses his spiritual power as a preacher, while Zala, the gospel choir member, relies on the sentimental spirit of the gospel music vernacular and the spirit of her rediscovered son to move the people (the community of parents) toward reconnecting with the practices and faith necessary to find the killers and perhaps other missing children. In fact, the gospel motif Zala represents is even more significant because the songs represent testimony, persuasion, religious exhortation, or warning. Zala's speech is a testimony about the return of her son; she repeatedly warns and engages the community in "call and response" to persuade them to lead their own investigation to find the rest of the children, or at least the culprits. It is important that the muse for the recovery of the covenants of liberation is a gospel choir member because gospel music entails all the elements necessary for rousing the liberatory spirit of the people. It is sentimental and, at its core, a call-and-response chant whose inspiration is social problems and is filled with warnings, testimony, and persuasion. Indeed, gospel music effectively integrates elements in African music to achieve an altered state of consciousness. As a member of the gospel choir, Zala embodies this spirit to strengthen communal bonds. If truth be told, Bambara's novel is a call to Black communities everywhere to be conscious, to be courageous, to challenge authority, and to recommit to faith based in African cosmology and African American religion. It is not a coincidence that Zala repeats the challenge to "question authority" and refuse to remain silent. Zala's contention that the people refuse to be silent or obedient is also in line with Black gospel music's tendency for syncopating hymns and recasting them rhythmically by accentuating normally weak beats. Here the "hymn" being recast is the authorities' version of the truth, and the weak beats being accentuated are the voices of the community, the people whom Zala challenges to speak out and be heard.

I want to focus a bit more on the collective sermon of Reverend Thomas and Zala because it is unique and consistent with Bambara's interest in a feminism that unites Black men and women in a struggle for national liberation. Her unique feminist, gospel-infused sermon becomes a locus for articulation of a holistic Black voice that conveys the substance of Black life. As the preacher and a gospel choir member synchronize their messages their listeners get to bear witness to the practice of gender-neutral leadership and self-determination. Historically the sermon stands at the center of the Christian apprehension of a sacred self both as text and worldview, which is important. (For more on this see Dolan Hubbard's 1994 work on the Black sermon.) Bambara's trademark Black Nationalist and feminist ethos is on full display when the male preacher, the typical voice of the community, surrenders the podium to Zala, a mother and a voice that is normally silent but equally important. This is consistent with gospel music's tendency to accentuate the silent, and it is not uncommon for choirs to feature the extremes of female vocal range in call-and-response counterpoint with the preacher's sermon. The difference here is that Zala's vocal range is sermon or message and singer. Indeed, an impetus of the novel is to hear the silent. It is significant that Zala, a mother and choir member, embodies a strong Black feminism as she represents the voices of common folk. Zala's collaboration with Reverend Thomas, her husband, and the community activists reflects Bambara's belief in the possibility of a strong feminism that does not equate, isolate, or ostracize Black men. Black men and women refocus and reunite to work together to achieve truth and justice for the people. Bambara's vision of a new Black man is akin to Spencer and Reverend Thomas—men willing to work as equals with Zala to defeat the real enemy. Thus, Thomas and Zala collectively deliver the message because Thomas recognizes Zala's value and respects her standing as a leader in the community.

Not only does Bambara alter the pace and order of the sermon but her decision to invert the role of choir member and preacher, playing with the cliché "preaching to the choir" masterfully speaks to Bambara's panoramic vision that is committed to a whole community voice. It is a voice that speaks to men and women who work together to achieve a common goal. Placing a choir member in the role of preacher is an ingenious shift of the sermonic. It is also a move that is consistent with Bambara's belief in a panoramic vision of liberation that requires holistic contributions from the *whole* of the community. The collective voices make healing possible and move the people toward reachable practices of liberation.

While Zala's sermonic call for a return to practices of liberation is in line with Reverend Thomas's theme of "question authority" and "speak out," her words call for the people to respond by becoming activists. She exhorts the congregation to "demand answers from the people who run the city" (Bambara 1999, 661). While the term "gospel" means "good news" and it is the church's mission to teach, reveal, or preach the gospel, this is not your traditional gospel. While it definitely is concerned with teaching and revealing truth, it also comments on Black life and offers the community much-needed psychic relief, but not an escape from the reality of the unsolved Atlanta child murders. In this unique gospel-infused sermon Reverend Thomas departs from his usual invocation. After telling the community to "pray for the strength to become more accountable to the generations to come, and for the strength to make [Atlanta] responsible to the people's need for the truth" (657), Thomas calls on "Father, Mother, God, spirits" (658). This holistic embrace of African American Christianity, African cosmology, and feminism, punctuated by his absorption of Zala's voice and message, which is about truth, is an improvised recitative, a melisma, and an example of expressive delivery. While the good news Zala shares is not about God, her challenge for the community to "question authority" and show "courage," resist silence, and practice self-determination is a unique spirit-filled message. Indeed, in the true spirit of gospel choir music and the Black sermon, she calls the community of parents to respond by ignoring the authorities and calling "the witnesses and [asking] the questions" themselves. Zala's sermonic and gospel choir improvisation reinterprets the past, setting the tone for future transformation (Williams 2005, 10). The spirit of the folk preacher is perhaps one of the most improvisational voices in the African American cultural tradition of reinvention.

In *Bones* the dead children haunt Zala, her family, and the community. The punishment is knowing they failed to protect the children from harm, or failed to act to resolve the situation and usher forth satisfactory protection and resolution. Their failure is that they became complacent. Bambara's fictional story haunts readers who are forced to relive the horrifying events in Atlanta. The reader is reminded and informed of several versions of the awful reality. They also learn that the murders happened and that justice did not prevail because the people strayed from the ultimate promise: staying focused on preparing and protecting the next generation for reaping the fruits of liberation struggle. Thus, just as Lovey applies herbal medicine, mother wit, and ancient wisdom to straighten out her family, the fictional story functions similarly as a medicine to readers in real life about necessary practices of liberation.

Christian spirituality and African spirituality are effective narrative strategies in this novel. What emerges is a complex picture of a female character deftly negotiating a Black Art–influenced adherence to Black artistic reformation that seeks to recover an African spiritual ancestry without rejecting the Christian spirituality and revivalism that was key to sparking the civil rights movement. The iteration of spiritual wholeness at work here also embraces Black aesthetic impulses without denying the importance of the Black church, particularly its women. In an interview with Zala Chandler, Bambara confirms that the church and women are prominently artistic influences:

> [W]omen who moved me were the sanctified church women, members of
> the Women's Departments of various sanctified churches. These women

frequently spoke on Speakers Corner. They were significant because they were the historians of the church, and, as such, they always insured that the contributions of women in the church were "lifted up." They taught women how to be speakers, to be historians, to be researchers, to be bibliophiles . . . and to monitor each other's development. (Chandler 1979, 346)

Unlike the Black radicalism that might have eschewed the church for being passive or representing a link to the shackles of European influences that had hampered Black literature and arts, Bambara appreciated, acknowledged, even embraced the importance of these spiritual cultural traditions. While critiques were leveled at the revivalist forms and tendencies of the civil rights movement that always believed in miracles, emotional conversions, public testimony, and region-wide enthusiasm for charismatic preachers because they were vital to the political movement, here Bambara relies on this very thing to sway the community. We might also consider Sonny's reappearance and Zala's charisma as Bambara's message to her contemporaries that Black political movements have religious dimensions and significant female presence. Bambara has an appreciation for the historical role of the church as the backdrop for nearly every significant social, cultural, political, and historical experience witnessed and performed by the Black community. Indeed, Bambara knows the power of the church, for Zala tells her daughter that she is unafraid when addressing the crowd because she knows "the old folks in the choir would hum [her] along" (Bambara 1999, 661).

Here, as in much of Bambara's work, the spiritual transformation of her protagonist is grounded in the spiritual energy of an elder figure. In *Bones* that figure is Lovey. Whole spiritual recovery for Zala and her family is grounded in the love and spiritual healing and traditions of African American culture via Zala's mother, Lovey. She is an elder and is a close link to African spirituality. Lovey represents culture, roots, and knowledge or rememory of who Zala and her family are. For Sonny, who is now lost, her presence, love, touch, and folk wisdom are just what he needs. Lovey helps them heal: "Lovey applied glutinous poultices to [his] wounds, and Sonny was nodding in recognition" (554). After attending to his physical wounds, Lovey turns her attention to cleansing his spirit, renewing his damaged faith and feeling. She alerts him of his role in fulfilling his promise: "Think it don't make me shame to know what you've become in this lost year? You need to see about yourself, little Spencer. Just so much other people can do for a person" (565). Here Lovey represents a challenge and unconditional love in her embrace of the return of the lost grandson. Yet, for Bambara, redemption, consciousness, and liberation are organic processes. The burden is placed upon Black people to redeem the promise themselves, and thus Lovey challenges her grandson to participate in his redemption. Zala and her family reconnect with a healing process that mandates knowing and using one's own history and mythology and understanding how Black identity connects to that history. Furthermore, as Joyce Ann Joyce suggests in *Warriors, Conjurers and Priests*, this idea is prevalent in the fiction of Margaret Walker's *Jubilee*, Toni Morrison's *Song of Solomon* and *Beloved*, and the poetry of June Jordan and Sonia Sanchez (Joyce 1994, 159).

Bambara also uses her novel to confront the dilemma of a generation whose faith and focus have waned, particularly regarding the influence of revivalist religion. She seems to feel that post–civil rights Atlanta with its Black mayor and promise of becoming America's greatest city lost a connection to Black identity and that history. *Those Bones* reveals what happens to the children of a generation that has lost faith and abandoned faith revivalist religious traditions, Black history, and identity. This helps to explain why, in *Those Bones*, Zala plays such a pivotal role in the revival of spirit, community, and consciousness. Yet the beauty of Bambara's panoramic vision is that recovery is multifaceted, and revival occurs among ancestors, both immediate and distant, and even among community activists outside the church. However, the most impressive aspect of Bambara's vision is that men and women play equally important roles in the struggle for justice.

To be sure, Zala's role as choir member conjures spiritual twists attuned to the dictates of Black aesthetic and African spirituality. Zala, Spencer, Sonny, and their family endure a conversion that involves a life-and-death process that makes them new people with the Orisha as their core foundation.[2] Thus, the salvation of the people in *Those Bones* is tied to the spiritual power of the church and other religious philosophies. Bambara acknowledges this about Black culture, which is why Zala is a member of the choir and why her plea to the community to reclaim an activist tradition transpires in a church. Bambara creatively conflates African American church and African cosmology in her work to emerge with her own organic representation that negotiates Black aesthetic ideology and Black feminism and offers holistic practices of liberation. As Bambara herself has said,

> To be whole—politically, psychically, spiritually, culturally, intellectu-
> ally, aesthetically, physically, and economically whole—is of profound
> significance. It is significant because there is a correlative to this. There
> is a responsibility to self and to history that is developed once you are
> whole, once you are well, once you acknowledge your powers. (Chandler
> 1979, 348)

Zala's sermon/speech/gospel endeavors to get the community to become "whole" and acknowledge its powers and solve the murders independently of the authorities' version of the truth.

Indeed, it is only natural that Zala makes her appeal for the community to respond to the covenant of self-determination, self-love, and responsibility to family, faith, feeling, and freedom in order to uphold its responsibility to protect its children in a church. Bambara, a feminist and Black Nationalist, embraces this rich aspect of the history of Black struggle (not all Black Power and Black Arts participants fully embraced this history and power) to transform the communities' values.

The Reverend Thomas challenges the community to return to values that once gave them courage, reminding them,

We have all been favored before with articles and talks that point up the . . . untruths. . . . But many of us are still unwilling to dismantle the authorities' myth. . . . Let us bow our heads and pray for the strength to overcome our own fearfulness . . . the strength to become more accountable to the generations to come . . . so that our children will not grow up cynical and warped by our failure of courage. (Bambara 1999, 657)

The covenant that both Zala and Reverend Thomas privilege here is in tune with the Black Power mantra of self-determination, accountability, and truth. Zala's lament is not a call for prayer but rather a call for action, a call for the untapped and latent power frozen in millions of Black people yet to be unleashed. Furthermore, although she stands on the pulpit with the preacher, Zala rejects any high moral ground. In Bambara's novel, no one is free from blame; Zala confides to the community that she, too, lost her way and allowed her son to be a victim. This is why the novel continues long after Sonny has returned. The remainder of the novel entails efforts to get the larger community to also reclaim what it means to honor ancestors and elders without shame. The story cannot end when Sonny returns because his return merely signals the beginning of a process of looking inward for truth and justice and returning to practices that lead to upholding the covenant of liberation. Zala's choral sermonic encourages the congregation to reflect inward and shifts responsibility from the individual to the collective community. Moreover, she leads the process of bearing up when she informs the congregation that: "Death happened to [children]. Because we allow it. We allow ourselves to be manipulated . . . we silence ourselves because we are afraid of being called names like traitor to the race. We swallow the line that security means secrecy and silence" (660). Bambara uses Zala to speak what she thinks is the unspoken truth, the facts as told by the voice of the people to solve what Reverend Thomas calls the "untruths concerning the Atlanta Missing and Murdered Children's case" (657). The novel cannot end because the people and children must endure and understand the process for getting change to occur.

In many ways the act of writing *Those Bones* was a gesture meant to expose an oppressive political system that failed to bring truth and justice to the families that lost their children. In addition to exposing truth(s), the novel is also a call to Black communities to remember the spirit of family and faith, and the importance of a liberation impulse unafraid to challenge authority. This novel addresses not only truth and facts but also the community within the novel and the reader. Zala, prods her community to consider whether, as Bambara questioned in "Salvation Is the Issue," it is "natural (sane, healthy, wholesome, in our interest) to violate the contracts/covenants we have with our ancestors, each other, our children, ourselves and God?" (Bambara 1984, 47).

On another level Sonny is allegorical and the murdered children of Atlanta are a symbol of the horrors that befall a community that forgets or ignores its covenant with ancestors and self. The story is also an allegory of the majority of the folk who were forgotten and silenced in the post–civil rights moment. Yet the neorealist rendition of the unsolved Atlanta child murders is also the wake-up call; the character Sonny and the novel itself are mediums for change that lead the community on a path to recuperate subjugated knowledge and a neglected promise. *Those Bones* is a call to the tradition of indicting mainstream hypocrisy and prophesizing retribution, a salvation that emerges through adherence to an unwavering commitment to practices of liberation.

Those Bones is a panoramic embrace of the spectrum of Black expressive culture without omitting the voices of common folk who represent the roots of the rich humus of the culture. The novel is a call to return to practices of liberation that will protect the community: family, feeling, faith, and freedom. This liberation impulse gives voice to the silenced Black community through the fictional story of Marzala Rawls and her family. The most powerful and consistent motif is a cultural tradition of spiritual wholeness, conveyed via the silent voice of average folk, offering a contrapuntal vision and version of the truth. Zala is the female medium that not only makes a choral plea but also trumpets the sermon that calls the community to remember and respond to the covenant.

Bambara's fiction makes it easy for twenty-first-century scholars of African American literature to engage in the business of preserving and revitalizing African American traditions, because she self-consciously uses important beliefs and values to drive her narratives.[3] Throughout *Bones* she embraces ancestral wisdom and uses African and African American religious and cultural forms to launch a story of recovery and hope. Bambara conjures a narrative that echoes the Black Power concepts of self-determination and nationhood and the Black feminist emphasis on a new Black womanhood and manhood that creates room for whole and united families. *Those Bones* speaks directly to the needs and aspirations of Black Americans who have lost "the way" and, in the process, endangered their greatest revolutionary asset—children. In fact, the return of Sonny is conflated with the memory of the other lost children to spur people to adhere to the contract with ancestors, children, themselves, and God. Sonny's silence upon his return compels the reader to want to hear from him to find out what really happened to this forgotten child—which is precisely the effect Bambara seeks!

The novel reflects a soul-searching and activist fiction in tune with the covenant of relying on the African American cultural tradition of reinvention and transformation. Zala and Spencer lose their son because they are fractured, and the consequence is an allegory for Black communities. Once Spencer embraces a neomasculine construction, their unity becomes a force that helps the larger community assume control to find out the true culprits of the crimes. Their success is also tied to Zala's assertion of a reality of new Black womanhood that is not dependent on Spencer first defining his manhood. In fact, as Zala moves forward in her new womanhood, Spencer is forced to get himself together and catch up. Then, as a united force, Zala and Spencer lead the community to move autonomously and take matters into their own hands to get justice.

In the end the people trust their own voices, facts, feeling, traditions, and family and thus put faith in themselves to discover truth and strive to bring the murderers to justice. Bambara once claimed in an interview that "for many people there is a division between the religious or the sacred and the secular. For me it is all sacred. . . . [T]here need to be statements made about the spiritual and the political . . . the need for the two to join hands" (Chandler 1979, 347). Indeed, in *Those Bones*, the two join hands to fulfill the promise of a fundamental change for the people. Bambara cleverly balances the role of the spiritual in the historical struggle for change for African Americans in *Those Bones Are Not My Child*. What she manages to conjure, with the assistance of African American sermonic tradition and African spirituality, is a narrative mindful of the covenant, practices, and process of recuperation, healing, and freedom—a process of spiritual wholeness.

CONCLUSION

Liberation Art for the People

I'm a nationalist; I'm a feminist, at least that. That's clear,
I'm sure, in the work.

Toni Cade Bambara

To be whole—politically, psychologically, spiritually,
culturally, intellectually, aesthetically, physically and
economically whole—is of profound significance.

Toni Cade Bambara

In her essay, "Toni Cade Bambara: Free to Be Any Where in the Universe," Farah Jasmine Griffin explains that Bambara's legacy of social vision and social struggle challenges us upon every re-reading and "proves what we have always known—that the writing can be both beautiful and political" (1996, 229). As someone who has spent many years examining Bambara's papers and interviews, I would concur that Bambara's writing is not only beautiful but has had a significant impact on contemporary literary theory. Not only does Bambara's work capture a full range of African American tradition but it also champions unique and common experiences. It absorbs the many aspects of a collective truth that conjure the intricate web of African and African

American cultural influences, from folklore, myth, political history, and literary histories to memory and female perspectives. The spiritual wholeness aesthetic that I contend dominates her fiction acknowledges an ancestral past while simultaneously looking inward and forward.

Bambara's vision and contributions to twentieth-century Black feminism and African American literary tradition and culture are significant. Furthermore, although her artistic contributions have been somewhat undervalued, she is an important component of a tradition of writers that interrogated race, class, and sex. The Harlem Renaissance (1919–39) produced the likes of Nella Larson, Jacques Garvey, and Zora Neale Hurston. The Realism and Modernism era (1940–60) produced writers such as Gwendolyn Brooks (Pulitzer Prize winner in 1950), Lorraine Hansberry, and Dorothy West, who documented the struggles of Black women and Black people and reached a wide sector of Americans through work that combined activist and feminist concerns. I believe that among 1960s and 1970s Black women issuing calls for a transformative Black feminism that interrogated the nature of Black women's political, social, and economic roles, Bambara is one of the most important figures. Two works at the helm of this call were, of course, Bambara's 1970 anthology *The Black Woman*, followed a decade later by Barbara Smith's 1983 anthology *Home Girls*.

Critics have pointed out elements of Black Nationalism, feminism, community, and the focus on language in Bambara's work but early criticism completely failed to highlight Bambara's wonderful utilization of the Black aesthetic, intersectionality, and nonlinear thinking. Often overlooked is how adroitly she took these forms to their limit, using a blues, jazz, gospel, or spirituals ethos to drive her fiction toward new political and artistic frontiers. As I have previously mentioned, her first two collections of short stories broke new ground, as did the narrative strategy on display in her 1980 novel *The Salt Eaters*.[1] Bambara's work embodies a spiritual wholeness aesthetic that merged political folk with the spiritual community. It introduced a liberation impulse that demands that readers have a sense of justice and injustice and be willing to reimagine America. Bambara best explained what she is exploring during an interview with Beverly Guy-Sheftall: "The major question that corners me at this moment is what constitutes development for the systematically underdeveloped" (Lewis 2012, 19).

The literature produced during the 1960s was trying to answer this question with rounded, smart, useful, and careful portraits of Black people. My reading of Bambara's fiction here pays close attention to how fluidly she incorporated an adherence to feminism, Black Nationalism, and even aspects of Kawaida and the Black aesthetic focus on spiritual recovery. She also incorporates elements such as the spirituals, African religions and cosmology, folklore, jazz, blues, and other cultural products, and my analysis of her work addresses these ideas as part of a liberation impulse. Her practice of incorporating the aforementioned elements into her art not only taught "valuable lessons of life . . . [but also offered] characters who are rounded and who give dimension" (Lewis 2012, 6).

During the early 1970s and 1980s, Bambara led the way in presenting us with literature that reflected varied ideological, cultural, and literary perspectives because she rejected monolithic or homogeneous Black feminism or cultural theory. The practices of liberation via family, faith, feeling, and freedom that comprise the framework I term spiritual wholeness empowers her narratives to embrace a balanced, diverse, and multifaceted reality. From *Gorilla, My Love* to *Those Bones Are Not My Child*, her characters and narratives engage these practices. First they build the self and the family, and then they focus on building the inner then outer nation, and then freedom. A constant goal is a search for truth and self-determination, and to revitalize from the ancient to the future. Finally, the practices of spiritual wholeness involve embracing multidimensional perspectives and producing flexible cultural liberation zones with women and men leading the way, so that the voices of all of the people can be heard.

Too often Bambara is mistakenly characterized as a writer for young people. Those ignoring her BAM roots fail to realize that she was practicing nation building in her art. The BAM believed strong nation building required building strong future generations (youth), organizations, and institutions. Thus, building communities of resistance (liberation zones) is an important practice in Bambara's fiction. The spiritual wholeness aesthetic I utilize to read her fiction is a polycentric model that promises sustainable liberation because it demands specific practices of spiritual wholeness, namely family, faith, feeling, and freedom.

Using multiple approaches, she conjures in the time and space of her fiction mechanisms for adjudicating conflicts and practices for striving toward freedom or sustainable practices of liberation. In essence I am reading with one eye on African American literature, another eye perched on feminism, and my third eye on a spiritual and holistic approach to avoid what Barbara Christian calls the urge to invent a theory of how we ought to read (1988, 75). What I have tried to articulate throughout this study is that Bambara's practices of liberation that comprise a spiritual wholeness aesthetic follow the tenants Darlene Clarke Hine points out in "A Black Studies Manifesto" (2014). According to Hine, there are five characteristics that are ideal for work in Black Studies: (1) Intersectionality; (2) nonlinear thinking; (3) diasporic perspectives and comparative analysis; (4) oppression and resistance; and (5) solidarity (Hine 2014, 12).

I am hopeful that this study will increase appreciation for the paths that Bambara's fiction blazed, as she conjured and unearthed a way for contemporary Black feminism and African American literature to strike a healthy accord. Hopefully better appreciation of Bambara as a pioneering voice of race and gender whose work relies heavily on the presence and strength of the ancestors, as well as the energy and power of African cosmology and spirituals, is forthcoming. Through spiritual wholeness she negotiates gender and cultural tensions and embraces a holistic spirit of Black culture that extrapolates from the Black aesthetic, feminism, and spirituals. My examination of Toni Cade Bambara's fiction culls from Black feminist and Black aesthetic theory, as well as African and African American cultural products, to unearth

Bambara's unique conjure motif and draw connections along gender and generational lines that privilege multiple perspectives. There is no question that Bambara is an important literary figure because she effectively confronted both a woman question and a race problem and produced art that was a model for Black Studies. Joyce Ann Joyce in her insightful essay "Toni Cade Bambara's *Those Bones Are My Child* as a Model for Black Studies," lauds Bambara for crafting art that has a "symbiotic relationship" between "The Black artist/community activist and the creative performance of the university professor" that has "the mutual goal of . . . transformation politics" (2006, 193).

One of the critiques of the 1960s BAM was that they "lacked ideological clarity, political skills, and the effective power and answers" (Glasgow 1981, 163–64). Bambara seemed to be aware of this critique and crafted stories that responded to this. Thus she answered this critique with stories that often modeled pragmatic political skills, ideology, and self-empowerment. Her first two collections of short stories were filled with tight narratives that began with self-love and community love, followed by self-determination and solutions that existed beyond the norms of society but within the Black community. This spiritual wholeness aesthetic also transcends existing values and culls futuristic or androgynous realities. The people in her narratives are either confronted with or challenged to avoid being what she calls a limited "four."[2] There is no mistaking what she is doing in stories like "The Lesson," "The Organizer's Wife," "The Apprentice," "Broken Field Running," "Christmas Eve at Johnson's Drugs N Goods," or her novels *The Salt Eaters* and *Those Bones Are Not My Child*. She consistently modeled protagonists courageous enough to seek alternative ideologies and value systems.

Toni Cade Bambara's women and men escape the confines of explicit spatial and temporal parameters of liberation. Characters individually interpellate Euro cultural models and extend the diversity of Blackness outside of the linearity of space-time. What she produces are healthy paradoxes that enhance the liberation discourse. In her two novels she collapses linear space-time parameters and stepped outside the limits of Euro and patriarchal space-time in favor of holistic family and leadership, truth, and liberation. For her, truth is an essential liberation practice. This strategy creates space for cogent liberation narratives to take shape that reflect a healthy community identity that is capacious and complex. Bambara rejected labels and the limits of vertical hierarchy in thought or action. Her fearless critique of any linear limitations within Black Nationalist and feminist ideology and behavior resonates most effectively in the narrative structure in *The Salt Eaters* and *Those Bones Are Not My Child*.

Bambara's quest to separate from linear cultural parameters gave her fiction space to develop and explore alternative views of feminism, Blackness, nationalism, Marxism, and liberation in general. This was on par with the BAM, which was imbued with a spirit of spontaneity and a discourse that raised complicated questions about the relation of individual performance (especially for women) to the collective performance or struggle for liberation in a world that was not yet prepared for such ideas. Bambara simultaneously simplified and complicated the relationship between feminism and Black Nationalism, all the while keeping the focus on practices of spiritual wholeness that would produce liberation for the people. Thus, her fiction dismisses a binary between the past (ancestors) and the present (youth) in favor of a structure that privileges interrelations and interactions with myriad people. A Black Nationalist or feminist dichotomy is absent in the spatial Bambara constructs. For her there is a symbiotic relationship between these entities that allows her to use an ancestral past to lift toward and seize a better future for the people or the nation. Her fiction is the manifestation of and exceeds what the BAM theorized a Black aesthetic could be; she conjured art that reimagined Black life. The stories she produced are filled with characters that openly speculate the parameters of gender, brighter futures, and a different present that is grounded in the past.

Rather than allow White supremacy, oppression, or sexism to limit her communities, in the spatial fiction she constructs she produces communities of people capable of speaking to one another in nuanced and progressive practices of liberation that lead to sustained change. In the spirit of the BAM she rejects inhibiting analytical frames that privilege linear space-time in favor of communities that create space to *become*. Bambara progressively critiques limited notions of liberation, of being, and of Blackness. The liberation strategy in her fiction is multidimensional and pushes back against vertical and hierarchal assumptions. Bambara's novels *The Salt Eaters* and *Those Bones Are Not My Child* precede what Alondra Nelson calls "post-future visions" (2000, 34). These novels best exemplify her ability to reflect on "African diasporic past and renderings of our possible futures," and transform individual's spaces of alienation into forms of "creative potential" to lodge space for "new ideas about politics and new visions of black life: new icons, new heroes, new futures" (35).

Not only does she achieve this in her aforementioned novels but in her earlier collections of short stories, *Gorilla, My Love* and *The Sea Birds Are Still Alive*. She is at her best at this in her novels where she masters the art of abandoning linear time—"the past, present and future as chronological, epiphenomenal time" in favor of "spacetime: the moment of the now, through which we imagine the past and also move into future possibilities."[3] As these texts focus on youth, women, and elders, hierarchy and chronology are absent in favor of a *now* through which she moves into future possibilities—they are the future possibilities. Even in her second collection, *The Sea Birds*, she harvests several stories whereby characters practicing liberation *now* pave the way for future possibilities of liberation. In *Salt Eaters* she reconstructs the past in the *now* to move Velma and Obie and members of the community like Fred into healthy future possibilities. This reconfiguration of time and cultural models was a common impulse among BAM artists. It is an ethos that, for them, was an essential liberatory practice. On display in Bambara's fiction are characters that either seek to or manage to locate the self when and where one is in the now. This is a primary practice of Bambara's liberation impulse that begins with the self. No other practices can be carried out before this is accomplished. Therefore Bambara's characters often grapple with establishing and locating the self in the now, which frees them to practice spiritual wholeness and achieve or move toward liberation.

Because liberation is the ultimate goal, women in her fiction inhabit communities as leaders or they work alongside males to create sustained change. Her spiritual wholeness aesthetic impulse rarely cast men aside or situated them as enemies. Furthermore, it kept women from being marginalized. It encouraged family and healthy male/female relationships and discarded traditional notions of roles or patriarchal hierarchy. Within a spiritual wholeness aesthetic the enemy is any man or woman that is a threat to the goal of liberation.

The practice of liberation in Bambara's fiction breaks boundaries of traditional and patriarchal family structures as well as established Black linear—and some not so linear—progress and value systems. Indeed, as Toni Morrison suggests, Bambara "Gently but pointedly . . . challenges us to rethink art and public space . . . her insights are multiple, her textures layered and her narrative trajectory implacable" (1996, ix). Her iterations of feminism and Black Nationalism are not commonplace. She hewed both doctrines in her constant search for truth and spiritually whole liberation practices that would serve the people. Spiritual wholeness is multidimensional because it subverts linear notions of liberation and Blackness to get at the whole of the spirit of the people in order to produce sustainable liberation.

This is also why revolutionary visions that are futuristic and forward thinking abound in Bambara's art. Her narratives did not elide and reduce because her panoramic vision emphasized an organic, multivoiced collective of women, men, and children. It is no coincidence that in her fiction the primary characters are mothers, social workers, teachers, and youth workers. While much of her fiction champions the causes of Black people, women of all races and ethnicities were encouraged to define their own realities. She extended the call for art with a political function of social change for Black women and Black people. In addition, she challenged men to reach new heights of gender consciousness. I would agree with Courtney Thorsson's assessment that "Bambara uses the literary negotiation of difference she inherits from the Black arts writers to respond to the same alienation from national belonging that motivates black nationalist leaders" (2014, 19). Many of Bambara's stories conjure rebellious feminism and freedom that transcend the provinciality of any single interpretive method of issues that preoccupy members of the critical community at a given historical moment.

Viewed in this manner it is easy to position Bambara as an early adherent of what Alondra Nelson terms: "Afrodiasporic cultural production" (Nelson 2000, 37) and future vision. In fact, the ancient ancestral and future focus of the BAM certainly fits the futurism description, and the spiritual wholeness aesthetic vision her work displays was a pioneering force. One might make an argument that the spiritual wholeness aesthetic in Bambara's fiction was an early example of the tenets of Afrofuturism, "a new and improved and dispersed 'blackness' free of the weight of the historical past" (Nelson 2000, 37) but always grounded in knowledge of self and in one's own history and cultural traditions. Bambara's aesthetic vision routinely stepped outside the four corners of the box to discover alternative realities.

How unique for an author to produce fiction that was entrenched in social realism that protested inequalities while also venturing toward speculation, experimentation, and abstraction. Her two novels *The Salt Eaters* and *Those Bones Are Not My Child* are evidence of the nimbleness of her pen. Bambara's "speculative cultural production" in both of these novels was about real events and issues. She fearlessly explored notions of future as a hybrid of times and places. In other words, she successfully transcended the limits of conventions—be it feminism, the Black aesthetic, fiction, or narrative. There are shades of this in her second collection of fiction, but her two novels clearly experiment with what science fiction writer and theorist Samuel R. Delany terms "images of tomorrow" (Nelson 2000, 37). Indeed, it is only logical that a writer whose aesthetic direction is anchored by a commitment to: "liberation from the exploited and dehumanizing system of racism . . .

[and] liberation from the constrictive norms of 'mainstream' culture" (Bambara 1970, 126) would dare to craft "images of tomorrow" fiction that celebrates and encourages progress now and a brave new world for Black women and Black people in general free from the constraints or pretensions of gender, race, or class bias.

Bambara's Afrocentric and feminist fiction embraces a holistic spiritual essence that culls dissimilar elements of Black culture and moves women from the margins of discourse to a central position. Bambara's feminist and Black Nationalist fiction stresses male/female collaboration as comrades for change.[4] Put simply, Bambara settles on a spirituality of wholeness that is first and foremost focused on representations of African American culture crucial for liberation. Unfortunately, many critics have failed to examine the full value of her progressive negotiation of the competing strains of feminism and Black Nationalism to heal divergence and the binaries that raged during and after the civil rights movement. More attention needs to be paid to how her fiction defies patriarchal, cultural, and even feminist hierarchies in favor of an equalitarian notion of gender that is global in perspective and is a sharp model of social reflection.

In this expansive view of the practices of liberation in fiction Bambara produced I hope to have revealed an author who embraces an Afrocentric and feminist-leaning agenda that deconstructs limited Afrocentric or rigid feminist views in favor of truth. I hope to have given nuanced insights into a writer who was revolutionary beyond her time—and beyond time as we know and understand it. One constant tangible in Bambara's work was an extraordinary ability to convey the full reality that represents the Black community. Few writers have done a more effective job of pushing back against rigid depictions of Black art, community, Black Nationalism, or Black womanhood to honestly explore inner and outer identity. What she achieves are fluid narratives that are always about the *business* of Black people searching for and grappling with "the tension, the power that is latent, still colonized, still frozen and untapped, in some 27 million black people . . . because we have been so long on the defensive and have invested a great deal of time and energy posturing and trying to prove that indeed, we are as clean as they are" (Lewis 2012, 8).

This mindset compelled her to craft multivalent identities and diverse sources of knowledge that produced narratives so diffuse that they erased limited notions of nationalism, Black women, or Black consciousness and cultural expression. She was concerned with liberating Black people, period. What she sought was "A national black women's union and . . . a national strategy for organizing . . . [with] solid enough analysis . . . [to] equip us to respond in a positive and constructive way to the fear in the community from black men as well as others who said that women organizing as women is divisive" (Lewis 2012, 9). This is the legacy and the model that she left behind in the life she lived and the art she produced. It is a model that embodies specific and decipherable practices of liberation for African American individuals, culture, and the nation. The impetus of the spiritual wholeness aesthetic in her fiction was, according to Bambara: "in the caring network that exists between men and women, men and men, women and women, children and elders."[5] The body of work she left behind, from her screenplays to her short stories and essays, is infused with her uncompromising insistence that we tell the truth about ourselves; it is a primary practice of liberation in her fiction—the first step toward spiritual wholeness.

To be sure, her art successfully models the consistent message that the healthy spirit of the whole of the people is essential to generating the power necessary for effective and sustained social change. Indeed, there is no singular savior, and no one person can be part of the solution unless they first get basic with themselves and liberate the inner self. I concur with Bambara when she said "No black women or children or elders or men or any other sector of the community has any monopoly on that kind of wisdom [how to deal with the complexity of black experience], a grasp on that new way to prepare for the future" (Lewis 2012, 9). Bambara, adverse to hierarchies, functioned as a sort of conjurer author or medium who created stories alongside the people occupying the same space, while at the same time creating space for the people to speak for themselves.

Notes

Introduction

1   Toni Cade Bambara, "Working at It in Five Parts," Toni Cade Bambara Papers; Part I, Box 4, Spelman Archives.

2   Bambara's interviews with Kay Bonetti and Louis Massiah reveal her reasons for relocation. See *Conversations with Toni Cade Bambara* (Lewis, 2012).

3   Deborah McDowell (1994) outlines how some women writers were trapped in essentialism or subordinate gender differences as their work sought to celebrate the people. Many of these works, McDowell claims, stumbled into inauthentic representations, stereotypes, and pathology. Also, Madhu Dubey's *Black Women Novelists & the Nationalist Aesthetic* makes a strong claim that "black women novelists of the 1970s insist upon a communal call and response perspective that seriously unsettles the category of the individual subject" (1994, 154). She is correct that they affirm a collective vision via "formal models derived from black music" (154), but she does not include Bambara among those prominently featuring this in their work (at a minimum Bambara's novel *The Salt Eaters* should be included). While Bambara's work is not mentioned, she also invokes the communal call and response structure of Black musical forms. Yet what make her unique is her ability to posit her work in a self-sufficient individuality that applies to women and men and youth in a manner that practices a complex and complicated communal sensibility whereby characters critique self, men, and women.

4   See her comments in "Realizing the Dream of a Black University and Other Writings, Part I" (Lavan and Reed 2017, 16). Bambara's dissatisfaction with the American university stemmed from her belief that it failed to take seriously the "variety of purposes, teachers, students, administrators" and chose "to merely study and perpetuate the idea of our cultural heritage . . . only the mainstream culture" (Lavan and Reed 2017, 14). Also, in *Conversations*

with Toni Cade Bambara (Lewis 2012), the author discusses her decision to relocate to Atlanta.

5   For more about this see Linda Holmes's (2014) biography of Bambara, where she reveals Bambara's disappointment upon her arrival in Atlanta is that the Black colleges were not much better. In fact, in Holmes's biography there is a wonderful but sad story of Bambara teaching a Black women's writers course from her home—for free—because Spelman University canceled the course at the last minute and Bambara was committed to the work of teaching.

6   Compared to such notable contemporaries as Alice Walker and Toni Morrison, Bambara does not receive the attention she should. Some of this is due to her preference for the short story, which was not as marketable in the 1970s. Despite her works being published by mainstream presses, and her close association with Walker, Morrison, and other popular fiction writers, she is an understudied figure. This is troubling given her productivity and the fact that she was responsible for the important and popular anthology *The Black Woman* (1970), which catapulted Black women's literature forward during this era. Too many critics categorized her fiction as children's literature and failed to realize her focus on youth and elders was central to her spiritual wholeness aesthetic. Furthermore, her two novels are daunting narrative constructions that many critics find too difficult to engage.

7   I am thinking of Natalie Margo Bryant's *Black Post-Blackness: The Black Arts Movement and Twenty-First Century Aesthetics* (2017). Also, what comes to mind is Howard Rambsy's discussion of black arts discourse in *The Black Arts Enterprise and the Production of African American Poetry* (2011) for more about writers of this era and topics surrounding "black aesthetics." Here he discusses the intentionality of the art and criticism and publishing.

8   For a more complete understanding see Rambsy's discussion of this in *The Black Arts Enterprise* (2011, 11–12).

9   In *"Realizing the Dream of a Black University" and Other Writings, Part I* and *"Realizing the Dream of a Black University" and Other Writings, Part II*, editors Makeba Lavan and Conor Tomas Reed offer an insightful explanation of Bambara's extensive trail of how to navigate the complexities of family, motherhood, social movements, and creative process.

10   There have been several useful essays, such as Carole Anne Taylor's "Post-Modern Disconnection and the Archive of Bones: Toni Cade Bambara's Last Work" (2002), Janet Ruth Heller's "The Lesson," (2003), Katy M. Wright's "The Role of Dialect Representation in Speaking from the Margins" (2008), Elizabeth Muther's "Bambara's Feisty Girls: Resistance Narratives in *Gorilla, My Love*" (2002), Sheila Smith-McKoy's "The Perfect Future: Reframing

Ancient Spirituality in Toni Cade Bambara's *The Salt Eaters*" (2011), Sala-mishah Tillet's "Make Revolution Irresistible: The Role of the Cultural Worker in the Twenty-First Century" (2015), and Kelly Wagner's essay "Telling Run Away: Novel Testimony in Toni Cade Bambara's *Those Bones Are Not My Child*" (2016).

11   Madhu Dubey is to be applauded for her wonderful examination in *Black Women Novelist and the Nationalist Aesthetic* (1994) of the power of Black cultural nationalism and its literary program that catalyzed the formal experimentation of the 1960s and 1970s, and how Black women's literature rose to "supplement and restructure the ideological program of black cultural nationalism" (Dubey 1994, 1). In this study Dubey effectively interrogates and illuminates the racial discourse of nationalism and the manner in which three writers in particular (Toni Morrison, Alice Walker, and Gayl Jones) negotiate the ideological and formal priorities of Black feminist criticism. Notably absent from her study, however, is Toni Cade Bambara, whose anthology *The Black Woman* was at the helm of catalyzing the shift in Black women's writing of this era.

12   See Madu Dubey, *Black Women Novelists and the Nationalist Aesthetic* (Bloomington: Indiana University Press, 1994). Dubey situates Bambara among her contemporaries like Shange, Walker, Naylor, and Morrison in her discussion of Black Women's fiction of the 1970s.

13   The Black aesthetic freed Black artists from the proscriptive trap that con-formed to particular definitions—of other men, that were irrelevant to their art and life. It also allowed writers of the Black aesthetic to create outside of the White-imposed social and cultural symbols of Black inferiority and to correct the concepts of Black art and culture as inferior. As literary critic Addison Gayle Jr. reminds us, the early tradition of English literature, from Shakespeare's *Othello* and *The Tempest* to Daniel Defoe's Friday in *Robinson Crusoe*, is filled with symbols of evil "dark" influences, and White aesthetic values and cultural chauvinism have hampered the development of Black art. What is clear is that the White aesthetic of writers like Shakespeare and Defoe effectively strangled the cultures of other nations. "The extent of the cultural strangulation of Black literature by white critics has been the extent to which they have been allowed to define the terms in which the Black artist will deal with his own experience" (Gayle Jr. 1971, 42–45).

14   See Joyce A. Joyce's discussion of Black studies and humanity studies (2005) for more on this.

15   In *Black Fire* Larry Neal's essay "And Shine Swam On" outlines and stresses the importance of Blacks leaving behind a sinking *Titanic* of ideas and deriving and relying on new ideas and aesthetics that reflect Black life, cul-ture, and realities. See discussion on pages (Barak and Neal 2007, 646–48).

16 Morrison talks about this in the anthology *Savoring the Salt* (Holmes and Wall 2008) and Bambara mentions her commitment to the political in her art in *Conversations with Toni Cade Bambara* (Lewis 2012, vii).

17 This contrasts with a novel like *The Bluest Eye* that, as Madhu Dubey in *Black Women Novelists and the Nationalist Aesthetic* points out, suffers some limitations because it deploys "the grotesque mode [that is] not quite commensurate with Black Aesthetic intentions [and offers] contradictory representation of black femininity" (Dubey 1994, 145). A multitude of voices participate in these works; the sheer force of these voices renders an alternative representation of black femininity, community, and liberation. Bambara's fiction pushes back against the notion that Black aesthetic ideology precludes a full rendering of black femininity. Dubey discusses this in detail (147–50).

18 In *Conversations with Toni Cade Bambara* (Lewis 2012), Bambara positions herself as Marxist, feminist, and Black Nationalist. This was a distinctive ideological position that was not replicated by any of her peers.

19 Amiri Baraka is Neal's coeditor for this important early anthology that attempted to theorize Black aesthetics for the BAM artists.

20 Her second collection of short fiction, *The Sea Birds*, is Bambara at the top of her game producing fiction that opens new formal possibilities for contemporary Black women's fiction. Also see Madhu Dubey's discussion in *Black Women Novelists* (1994) of how her contemporaries were producing new possibilities. The spiritual wholeness aesthetic lens I use to examine Bambara reveals why she is able to avoid engaging in contradictory terms of Black Nationalist discourse.

21 Julian Mayfield articulates the notion of a new Black spiritual quality that must draw on African roots with a forward vision in *The Black Aesthetic* (Mayfield 1971, 28).

22 Bambara's anthology, *The Black Woman*, is an early example of the discontent of Black women. Also, see Giddings's *When and Where I Enter* (1984), which details the historical omission of Black women during the civil rights movement. Bambara adheres to Black feminist goals and Black aesthetic tenets without suffering stasis. Her revisionist spiritual wholeness aesthetic pushes and restructures feminism and Black cultural nationalism ideologically, as well as pushing America to adhere to an authentic and pluralist democracy.

23 Joyce A. Joyce has a wonderful essay, "Toni Cade Bambara's *Those Bones Are Not My Child* as a Model for Black Studies," that appears in *A Companion to African American Studies* (2006). Joyce points out that the novel is a continuum of the material values from slaves, and she sees this novel as a model for understanding the psychic dynamics and phobias of Black people. Joyce

applauds Bambara's willingness to give voice to female characters and the Black community. This is a common motif in Bambara's work.

24 As Komla Messan Nubukpo contends in "Through Their Sisters' Eyes," "Toni Cade Bambara's fiction posits that the black man's aspirations in the context of American society cannot materialize until he decides to acknowledge the black woman's contribution towards their common future. . . . Toni Cade Bambara writes against the background of a psychology of blackness that stresses the common destiny underneath the various individual choices made by each member of the black community. . . . Bambara does not allow the individual choices to irremediably work against the cohesion of the community" (1987, iv).

25 In the anthology *SOS* (Bracey, Sanchez, and Smethurst 2014) Traylor offers a detailed explanation of Black Arts fiction.

26 Bambara made these comments during an interview published in the *University of Washington Daily* on November 2, 1971. She was outlining the corpus of her fiction with Black women's liberation as a movement that included women, young, and old working together to comprehend a salient direction.

27 November 2, 1971, interview in the *University of Washington Daily*.

28 Many are aware of Alice Walker's Womanism but the review of Bambara's essays in *The Black Woman* and the scope of this project will reveal Bambara's early influence on Walker's Womanism, which proposes an alternative ideological frame that transforms and extends radical elements of Black Nationalism and the creation of a new Black femininity. Like Womanism, Bambara's spiritual wholeness aesthetic seeks to fill gaps and absences, and her primary goal is correction, improvement, self-knowledge, and liberation via a multivalent, whole Black identity.

Chapter 1

1 This framework draws from Donald Matthews's important book *Honoring the Ancestors* (1990), which outlines the "Four Fs" and the power of the spirituals in Black literature and culture.

2 For more about the influence of the Black aesthetic and literature, see Margo Crawford in "What Was IS" (2015, 22–25).

3 In *The Black Woman* (Bambara 1970), Bambara's mother lists her name as Helen Cade Brehon in her essay "Looking Back." In *Savoring the Salt: The Legacy of Toni Cade Bambara* (Holmes and Wall 2008), the authors give her mother's name as Helen Henderson (Brehon) Cade, and her father's name as Walter Cade II.

4 Thabiti Lewis interview with Walter Cade at Medgar Evers College, March 2014.

5   See her interview with Louis Massiah. Also similar ground is also covered in "Toni Cade Bambara: Voices from the Gaps" (Curtright and Schirack 2004).

6   Bambara discusses her Harlem childhood with Claudia Tate in *Conversations with Toni Cade Bambara* (Lewis 2012).

7   In a 1982 interview with Deborah Jackson, she reveals to readers that *The Salt Eaters* "is structured as a jazz suite—with the gospel and blues voice(s) and characters." She also credits her move south in 1974 with helping her to absorb "the particular pitch, pace, and voice."

8   See her interview with Louis Massiah (Lewis 2012). Similar ground is also covered in "Toni Cade Bambara: Voices from the Gaps" (Curtright and Schirack 2004).

9   Bambara discusses why she shifted her major to English in "Working at It in Five Parts" in *Realizing the Dream of a Black University, Part II* (Lavan and Reed 2017).

10 The Settlement Houses have a unique history. New York City was known for having many Settlement Houses, which emerged beginning in the 1880s. The settlement movement was a reformist social movement that peaked around the 1920s in England and the United States. Its primary goal was getting the rich and poor in society to live more closely together in an interdependent community.

11 Bambara talked about this in 1969 in an essay in *Realizing the Dream of a Black University, Part II* (Lavan and Reed 2017, 15).

12 Bambara acknowledged the power of writing as an activist vocation during her 1980 interview with Kalamu Ya Salaam in *First World*. A few years after this she relocated to Philadelphia and began to work with film, which she felt afforded her more room to express herself.

13 Interview with Walter Cade, March 2014, at Medgar Evers College Black Writers program honoring Toni Cade Bambara. Walter claimed he was not aware of a trunk bearing their grandmother's name. He said he thought Toni made the story up.

14 In her 1980 essay "Working at it in Five Parts" that is published in *Realizing the Dream of a Black University, Part I* (Lavan and Reed 2017), Bambara discusses her appreciation for and knowledge of several languages. Here she includes phonetic Bambara and Kiswahili as the languages with which she is preoccupied. I find her mention of phonetic Bambara to be insightful, given this community's appreciation for family, gender equity, and community.

15 See "Toni Cade Bambara: Voices from the Gaps" (Curtright and Schirack 2004, 2–3).

16 See James D. Hart and Philip Leininger's entry about Bambara in *The Oxford Companion to American Literature* (1995).

17 Deborah Jackson Interview, 1982.

18 Bambara talks about being in this group, which led to her Vietnam invitation in *Conversations with Toni Cade Bambara* (Lewis 2012, 130) (Holmes and Wall 2008, 105–7).

19 For more of Bambara's "Vietnam Notebook," see *Savoring the Salt* (Holmes and Wall 2008, 105–7).

20 Conversation with Eleanor Traylor in New Orleans in April 2014 at CLA Convention.

21 For more about her views on this topic, see *Savoring the Salt* (Holmes and Wall 2008, 117).

22 In *Conversations with Toni Cade Bambara* (Lewis 2012, 19), Bambara launches into a detailed discussion about her disdain for colonialism and celebration of liberation struggles worldwide.

23 Bambara's papers at Spelman College reveal an enormous number of letters that confirm her interaction with many, many organizations in Black communities across the United States throughout the 1970s and 1990s. In a letter from the Archive of American Minority Cultures they thank her for participating in a workshop titled "Crime Against Black Women." In another letter Micheal Lomax thanks her for supporting his campaign for Fulton County Commission.

24 This information taken from an advertisement Bambara submitted to Spelman's *Spotlight*. It included a long, short, and medium version of her news release.

25 Bambara mentions the reason for her shift and the importance of film for her as a medium during her dialogue with Akasha Hull in 1987 at San Francisco State University. She also discusses the writer as new medium notion in her interviews with Kalamu Ya Salaam (1980) and Kay Bonetti (Bambara 1982).

26 Thabiti Lewis interview with Massiah at his home in Philadelphia, 2003.

27 Interview with Gloria Hull at San Francisco State University. In *Conversations with Toni Cade Bambara* (Lewis, 2012).

28 Interview with Gloria Hull at San Francisco State University (Lewis 2012), where Bambara goes on to discuss how eventually the form or shape of the novel presents itself to her. She also explains how the novel *The Salt Eaters* emerged and announced itself to her. This project stemmed from essays she initially intended to write about the murders that were taking place in Atlanta when she lived there.

29 This is part of Bambara's wonderful 1980 essay "Working at It in Five Parts" published in *Realizing the Dream of a Black University and Other Writings, Part I* (Lavan and Reed 2017, 30).

Chapter 3

1   In the same interview with Guy-Sheftall Bambara laments that the opportunity was missed in the 1970s for a coalition among people of color: "Namely . . . Afro-American, Afro-Hispanic, Indo-Hispanic, and so forth," whom she felt shared not only "a common condition but also . . . a common vision about the future" in *Conversations with Toni Cade Bambara* (Lewis 2012, 10).

2   See Linda Holmes, *A Joyous Revolt* (2014, 82). She details Bambara's notes about what she learned from the women in Vietnam.

3   In her powerful essay "Deep Sightings and Rescue Mission" in the book of the same title Bambara talks about writing as revolutionary activism (Bambara 1996, 149).

4   April 2014 discussion with Eleanor Traylor in New Orleans about what Bambara was doing in her fiction. Traylor explained to me that Bambara's work was about creating "liberation zones." Kalamu Ya Salaam was also there and concurred with Traylor's assertion.

5   See Bambara's interview with Louis Massiah in *Conversations with Toni Cade Bambara* (Lewis 2012).

6   Bambara offers a wonderfully progressive paradigm regarding gender in this essay in *The Black Woman* (1970, 109). Her first collection of fiction nibbled at these ideas but *The Sea Birds* takes a full bite, beginning with the story "The Organizer's Wife."

7   See Stuart Hall's discussion in "New Ethnicities" about building "those forms of solidarity and identification which make common struggle and resistance possible but without suppressing the real heterogeneity of interests and identities, and which can effectively draw the political boundary lines without which political contestation is impossible, without fixing those boundaries for eternity" (1995, 166).

8   For more about the cosmic nature of Native American culture see Paula Gunn Allen's discussion in her informative study of Native American spirituality, *The Sacred Hoop (1986)*.

9   In Bambara's papers at Spelman among the many events held at NAC and in the Atlanta community, including Kwanzaa celebrations.

Chapter 4

1   I mention Donald Matthews's discussion of the spirituals and the "Four Fs": family, faith, freedom, and feeling in the introduction and earlier chapters. Matthews articulates the power of the spirituals in his book, *Honoring the Ancestors* (1998).

2   My analysis of *The Salt Eaters* is also influenced and reinforced by two of Bambara's essays, "On the Issue of Roles" (1970) and "Realizing the Dream of a Black University" (Lavan and Reed 2018). It is important to note that other women writers utilize aspects of the spirituals and spirituality, but their use differs from what Bambara does here. I refer the reader to Alice Walker's *The Color Purple*, Toni Morrison's *Beloved* (1987), and Paule Marshall's *Praisesong for the Widow* (1983).

3   Cultural critic and theorist Maulana Karenga outlined the nationalist struggle as being divided into three tendencies or thrusts: "(1) the religious thrusts; (2) the cultural thrust; and (3) the political thrust" (see Karenga 1993, 172). In this essay I focus on Bambara's feminist agenda within the context of the spiritual thrust, which emphasized a new education for Blacks that used Africa for revitalization and roots. Such a thrust accepted Blackness and searched for an Afrocentric perspective that was what Karenga called "functional, collective, and committing" (173).

4   For more on African spirituality and possession, see Donna Marimba's wonderful essay, "Let the Circle Be Unbroken" (1979, 210–11). Other helpful studies of African spirituality are John S. Mbiti's *Introduction to African Religion*, Stephen D. Glazier's *The Encylopedia of African and African American Religions* (2001) and Jacob K. Olupona's *African Traditional Religions in Contemporary Society* (1991).

5   See John S. Mbiti, *African Religions and Philosophy*. As John Mbiti explains, each "African [people (tribe)] . . . has its own religious system" (1969, 1–2). Mbiti's pioneering work guides my examination of Bambara's deployment of African-inspired spirituality.

6   Black cultural elements such as music, spirituality, and signifying, specifically the simulation of Coltrane and Sun Ra's jazz sounds signifying, provide a solid creative framework that promised freedom and exploration.

7   For more on this see "Ritualistic Process and the Structure of Paule Marshall's *Praisesong for the Widow*" in Barbara Christian's *Black Feminist Criticism (1985)*.

8   Berry and Blassingame explain, "the traditional African witch was a . . . malevolent and frightful reality. . . . [W]itches were persons possessed by demons" who caused harms such as "sores, incurable diseases, sterility, impotence, [and] adultery," and "[p]ersons proven to be witches were killed" (1979, 247).

9   John Mbiti discusses Black life and death based on the African religious belief in the here and now. See *African Religion and Philosophy* (Mbiti 1969, 6–7).

10   For more of Bambara's explanation of what she is trying to accomplish in this novel see her interview with Kay Bonetti in *Conversations with Toni Cade Bambara* (Lewis 2012).

11   Also, for information about Zora Neale Hurston and her negotiation of gender tensions, see Michael S. Harper's "Gayl Jones: Interview" in *Chants of Saints* (1979).

12   Bambara discusses her first novel in a 1982 audio interview with Kay Bonetti that is published in *Conversations with Toni Cade Bambara* (Lewis 2012).

13   Toni Cade Bambara in *Black Women Writers at Work* (1983, 29).

14   This interview was originally published in *Black Women Writers at Work* (Lewis 1983). She discusses the influence of living in New York City and in the South on the pitch and tone of her fiction. This interview is reprinted in *Conversations with Toni Cade Bambara* (Lewis 2012).

Chapter 5

1   Dolan Hubbard's study, *The Sermon and the African American Literary Imagination* (1994) provides a wonderful explanation of the sermon as the locus for articulation of an authentic Black voice, an expressive and creative medium that conveys the substance of Black life in literature. Hubbard sees the sermon as inspirational and artistic. He details how writers utilize sermons to probe the heart and soul of African American ethos.

2   For more about Orisha, see Susan Blier, *African Vodun: Art, Psychology, and Power* (1998).

3   In *Yearning*, bell hooks lists Avey in Paule Marshall's novel, *Praisesong for the Widow*, Celie in *The Color Purple*, and Baby Suggs in *Beloved* as characters that exemplify Christian faith and African Caribbean religious traditions, and who in some cases must break with Christianity so that a new spirituality can emerge (1990, 342).

Conclusion

1   Elliott Butler-Evans was among the first to explore the fictive discourse in her stories and in her novel, and of course, one of the earliest critics to articulate the many dimensions of Black community in her work was Eleanor Traylor, whose memorable essay "Music as Themes" outlines a jazz impulse in *Salt* and as a central metaphor for Bambara's approach to community in her fiction.

2   During her interview with Kalamu Ya Salaam she laments that Black folk all too often box themselves into limited possibilities.

3   For more on "spacetime," read Michelle Wright's *Physics of Blackness* (2015, 145).

4   In fact, Bambara precedes Alice Walker's Womanism and Shirley Anne Williams's call for literary creations that are about community and dialogue and can promote the enlargement of both.

5   In *Conversations with Toni Cade Bambara* (Lewis 2012, 16), Bambara explains to Guy-Sheftall her approach to negotiating feminism and nationalism and that the ultimate goal is liberation of the people. She tells Guy-Sheftall that her "head is somewhere else" and that place is the larger liberation struggle for Black folk.

Works Cited

Allen, Paula Gunn. 1986. *The Sacred Hoop: Recovering the Feminine in American Indian Traditions*. Boston: Beacon Press.

Anthony, Booker T. 2007. "Religion and Spirituality in Literature." *CLA Journal* 51, no. 1: 1–13.

Awkward, Michael. 1994. "Appropriative Gestures: Theory and Afro-American Literary Criticism." In *Within the Circle: An Anthology of African American Literary Criticism from the Harlem Renaissance to the Present*, edited by Angelyn Mitchell, 360–67. Durham: Duke University Press.

———. 1995. *Negotiating Difference: Race, Gender, and the Politics of Positionality*. Chicago: University of Chicago Press.

Bambara, Toni Cade. 1970. *The Black Woman: An Anthology*. Edited by Toni Cade Bambara. New York: New American Library.

———. 1971. *Tales and Stories for Black Folk*. Edited by Toni Cade Bambara. Zenith Books.

———. 1972. *Gorilla, My Love*. New York: Random House.

———. 1977. *The Sea Birds Are Still Alive: Collected Stories*. New York: Vintage.

———. 1979. "Commitment: Toni Cade Bambara Speaks." Interview by Beverly Guy-Sheftall. In *Sturdy Black Bridges: Visions of Black Women in Literature*, edited by Roseann P. Bell, Bettye J. Parker and Beverly Guy-Sheftall. Garden City, NY: Anchor Books.

———. 1980a. *The Salt Eaters*. New York: Vintage.

———. 1980b. "What It Means to Be a Black Woman." *Black Collegian*, vol. 35: 34–35.

———. 2015. Foreword to *This Bridge Called My Back: Writings by Radical Women of Color*, edited by Cherrie Moraga and Gloria Anzaldua, xxix–xxxiii. Albany: SUNY Press.

———. 1981. "Some Forward Remarks." In *The Sanctified Church*, edited by Zora Neale Hurston. New York: Marlowe and Company.

———. 1982. Interview with Kay Bonetti. American Audio Prose Library. February.

———. 1984. "Salvation Is the Issue." In *Black Women Writers (1950–1980): A Critical Evaluation*, edited by Mari Evans, 41–71. Garden City, NY: Anchor/ Doubleday.

———. 1986. "The Bombing of Osage Avenue." WHYY-TV, Philadelphia.

———. 1996. *Deep Sightings and Rescue Missions: Fiction, Essays, and Conversations*. Edited by Toni Morrison. New York: Pantheon.

———. 1999. *Those Bones Are Not My Child*. New York: Random House.

———. "Working at It in Five Parts," Toni Cade Bambara Papers; Part I, Box 4, Spelman Archives.

———. 2017. *Realizing the Dream of a Black University & Other Writings*, Part I, edited by Makeba Lavan and Conor Thomas Reed. New York: Lost & Found: The CUNY Poetics Document Initiative.

Baraka, Amiri. 1972. *Kawaida Studies: The New Nationalism*. Chicago: Third World Press.

———. 2008. "Toni." In *Savoring the Salt: The Legacy of Toni Cade Bambara*, edited by Janet Holmes and Cheryl A. Wall, 109–12. Philadelphia: Temple University Press.

Baraka, Amiri, and Larry Neal, ed. 1968. *Black Fire: An Anthology of Afro-American Writing*. New York: William Morrow, 1968.

Bell, Bernard W. 1987. *The Afro-American Novel and Its Tradition*. Amherst: University of Massachusetts Press.

———. *The Contemporary African American Novel: Its Roots and Modern Literary Branches*. 2004. Amherst: University of Massachusetts Press.

Berry, Mary F., and John W. Blassingame. "Africa, Slavery, and the Roots of Contemporary Black Culture." In *Chants of Saints: A Gathering of Afro-American Literature, Art, and Scholarship*, edited by Michael S. Harper and Robert B. Stepto, 241–56. Urbana: University of Illinois Press.

Blier, Susan. 1998. *African Vodun: Art, Psychology, and Power*. Chicago: University of Chicago Press.

Bracey, John, Sonia Sanchez, and James Smethurst, eds. 2014. *SOS–Calling All Black People: A Black Arts Movement Reader*. Amherst: University of Massachusetts Press.

Butler-Evans, Elliot. 1989. *Race, Gender, and Desire: Narrative Strategies in the Fiction of Toni Cade Bambara, Toni Morrison, and Alice Walker*. Philadelphia. Temple University Press.

Chandler, Zala. 1979. "Interview with Bambara and Sanchez." In *Chants of Saints: A Gathering of Afro-American Literature, Art, and Scholarship*. Urbana: University of Illinois Press.

Christian, Barbara. 1985. "Ritualistic Process and the Structure of Paule Marshall's *Praisesong for the Widow*." In *Black Feminist Criticism*, 149–58. New York: Pergamon.

————. 1988. "The Race for Theory." *Feminist Studies* 14, no. 1: 67–79.

Coleman, James. "The Quest for Wholeness in Toni Morrison's Tar Baby." *African American Review* 20, nos. 1/2: 1986.

Collins, Lisa Gail, and Margo Natalie Crawford, eds. *New Thoughts on the Black Arts Movement.* New Brunswick, NJ: Rutgers University Press, 2006. *JSTOR,* www.jstor.org/stable/j.ctt5hj474.

Crawford, Margo. 2015. "What Was IS: The Time and Space of Entanglement Erased by Post-Blackness." In *The Trouble with Post-Blackness,* edited by Houston A. Baker Jr. and K. Merinda Simmons. New York: Columbia University Press.

————. 2017. *Black Post-Blackness: The Black Arts Movement and the Twenty-First-Century Aesthetics.* Bloomington: University of Indiana Press.

Curtright, Lauren, and Maureen Schirack. 2004. "Toni Cade Bambara: Voices from the Gaps." http://voices.cla.umn.edu/artistpages/bambaraToni.php.

Deck, Alice. 1999. "Deep Sightings and Rescue Missions: Fictions, Essays and Conversations." *African American Review* 33, no. 1: 170–72.

Dubey, Madhu. 1994. *Black Women Novelists & the Nationalist Aesthetic.* Bloomington: Indiana University Press.

Gayle, Addison Jr. 1971. *The Black Aesthetic.* Garden City, NY: Doubleday.

Giddings, Paula. 1984. *When and Where I Enter.* New York: William Morrow.

Glasgow, Douglas. 1981. *The Black Underclass: Poverty, Unemployment and Entrapment of Ghetto Youth.* New York: Vintage.

Glazier, Stephen, ed. 2001. *The Encyclopedia of African and African American Religions.* New York: Routledge.

Griffin, Farah Jasmine. 1996. "Toni Cade Bambara: Free to Be Anywhere in the Universe." *Callaloo* 19, no. 2: 229–31.

Guy-Sheftall, Beverly. 1979. "Commitment: Toni Cade Speaks." In *Sturdy Black Bridges: Visions of Black Women in Literature,* 230–49. Garden City, NY: Doubleday.

————. 1995. "Introduction: Evolution of Feminist Consciousness among African American Women." In *Words of Fire: An Anthology of African-American Feminist Thought,* 1–22. New York: The New Press.

Hall, Stuart. 1995. "New Ethnicities." In *The Post-Colonial Reader,* edited by Bill Ashcroft, Gareth Griffith, and Helen Tiffin. London: Routledge.

Harper, Michael, S. 1979. "Gayl Jones: An Interview." In *Chants of Saints: A Gathering of Afro-American Literature, Art, and Scholarship,* edited by Michael S. Harper and Robert B. Stepto. Urbana: University of Illinois Press.

Hart, James D., and Philip Leininger. 1995. "Bambara, Toni Cade." In *The Oxford Companion to American Literature.* Oxford: Oxford University Press.

Heller, Ruth. 2003. "The Lesson." *Style* 37, no. 3: 279–87.

Hine, Darlene Clark. 1992. "The Black Studies Movement: Afrocentric-Traditionalist-Feminist Paradigms for the Next Stage." *Black Scholar* 22, no. 3: 11–18.

———. 2014. "A Black Studies Manifesto: Characteristics of a Black Studies Mind." *The Black Scholar* 44, no. 2: 11–15.

Holmes, Linda Janet. 2014. *A Joyous Revolt: Toni Cade Bambara, Writer and Activist*. Santa Barbara, CA: Praeger.

Holmes, Linda Janet, and Cheryl A. Wall, eds. 2008. *Savoring the Salt: The Legacy of Toni Cade Bambara*. Philadelphia: Temple University Press. *JSTOR*, www.jstor.org/stable/j.ctt14bt0dw.

hooks, bell. 1990. *Yearning: Race, Gender, and Cultural Politics*. Boston: South End Press.

———. 1995. "Challenging Sexism in Black Life." In *Killing Rage: Ending Racism*, 62–76. New York: Henry Holt.

Hubbard, Dolan. 1994. *The Sermon and the African American Literary Imagination*. Columbia: University of Missouri Press.

Hurston, Zora Neale. 1981. *The Sanctified Church*. Berkeley, CA: Turtle Island.

Jackson, Deborah. 1982. "An Interview with Toni Cade Bambara." *Drum Magazine* (Spring).

Joyce, Joyce Ann. 1994. *Warriors, Conjurers and Priests: Defining African-Centered Literary Criticism*. Chicago: Third World Press.

———. 2005. *Black Studies as Human Studies: Critical Essays and Interviews*. New York: SUNY Press.

———. 2006. "Toni Cade Bambara's Those Bones Are Not My Child as a Model for Black Studies." In *A Companion to African American Studies*, edited by Lewis R. Gordon and Jane Gordon, 192–208. Hoboken, NJ: John Wiley.

Karenga, Maulana. 1993. *Introduction to Black Studies*. Los Angeles: University of Sankore Press.

Korenman, Joan S. 1994. "African-American Women Writers, Black Nationalism, and the Matrilineal Heritage." *College Language Association Journal* 38, no. 2: 143–61.

Lavan, Makeba, and Tomas Reed, eds. 2017. *Realizing the Dream of a Black University and Other Writings, Part I and Part II*. New York: Lost and Found: The CUNY Poetics Document Initiative.

Lewis, Thabiti. 2003. "Philadelphia Interview/Conversation with Massiah," June.

———, ed. 2012. *Conversations with Toni Cade Bambara*. Jackson: University Press of Mississippi.

Lincoln, C. Eric, and Lawrence H. Mamiya. 1990. *The Black Church in the African American Experience*. Durham: Duke University Press.

Marimba, Donna. 1979. "Let the Circle Be Unbroken." In *Chants of Saints: A Gathering of Afro-American Literature, Art, and Scholarship*, edited by Michael S. Harper and Robert B. Stepto. Urbana: University of Illinois Press.

Marshall, Paule. 1983. *Praisesong for the Widow*. New York: Putnam.

Matthews, Donald H. 1998. *Honoring the Ancestors: An African Cultural Interpretation of Black Religion and Literature*. New York: Oxford University Press.

Mayfield, Julian. 1971. "You Touch My Black Aesthetic and I'll Touch Yours." In *The Black Aesthetic*, edited by Addison Gayle Jr. Garden City, NY: Doubleday.

Mbiti, John S. 1969. *African Religions and Philosophy*. Garden City, NY: Anchor Books.

McDowell, Deborah E. 1994. "New Directions for Black Feminist Criticism." In *Within the Circle: An Anthology of African American Literary Criticism from the Harlem Renaissance to the Present*, edited by Angelyn Mitchell, 428–41. Durham: Duke University Press.

Morrison, Toni. 1970. *The Bluest Eye*. New York: Knopf.

———. 1973. *Sula*. New York: Knopf.

———. 1977. *Song of Solomon*. New York: Knopf.

———. 1981. *Tar Baby*. New York: Knopf.

———. 1987. *Beloved*. New York: Knopf.

———. 1996. "Preface." In *Deep Sightings and Rescue Missions: Fiction, Essays, and Conversations*, edited by Toni Morrison, vii–xi. New York: Pantheon.

Muther, Elizabeth. 2002. "Bambara's Feisty Girls: Resistance Narratives in *Gorilla, My Love*" *African American Review* 36, no. 3: 447.

Naylor, Gloria. 1988. *Mama Day*. New York: Random House.

Nelson, Alondra. 2000. "Afrofuturism—Past-Future Visions." *Color Lines* (Spring 2000): 34–37.

Nubukpo, Komla Messan. 1987. "Through Their Sisters' Eyes: The Representation of Black Men in the novels of Toni Morrison, Alice Walker, and Toni Cade Bambara." PhD diss., Boston University.

Olupona, Jacob, K. 1991. *African Traditional Religions in Contemporary Society*. New York: International Religious Foundation.

Rambsy, Howard. 2011. *The Black Arts Enterprise and the Production of African American Poetry*. Ann Arbor: University of Michigan Press.

Scheuer, Jeffery. 1985. *Legacy of Light: University Settlement's First Century*. New York: University Settlement Society.

Shange, Ntozake. 1982. *Sassafrass, Cypress & Indigo*. New York: Picador.

Shockley, Evie. 2011. *Renegade Poetics: Black Aesthetics and Formal Innovation in African American Poetry*. Iowa City: University of Iowa Press.

Smethurst, James. 2005. *The Black Arts Movement: Literary Nationalism in the 1960s and 1970s*. Chapel Hill: University of North Carolina Press.

Smith-McKoy, Sheila. 2011. "The Perfect Future: Reframing Ancient Spirituality in Toni Cade Bambara's *The Salt Eaters*." *Journal of Ethnic American Literature* 1 (January): 111.

Tate, Claudia, ed. 1983. "Toni Cade Bambara (an interview)." In *Black Women Writers at Work*, 12–38. New York: Continuum.

Taylor, Carole Anne. 2002. "Post-Modern Disconnection and the Archive of Bones: Toni Cade Bambara's Last Work." *Novel: A Forum on Fiction* 35, nos. 2/3: 258–80.

Thorsson, Courtney. 2014. *Women's Work*. Charlottesville: University of Virginia Press.

Tillet, Salamishah. 2015. "Make Revolution Irresistible: The Role of the Cultural Worker in the Twenty-First Century." *PMLA* 130, no. 2: 481.

Traylor, Eleanor W. 1984. "Music as Theme: The Jazz Mode in the Works of Toni Cade Bambara." In *Black Women Writers (1950–1980): A Critical Evaluation*, edited by Mari Evans, 58–70. Garden City, NY: Anchor/Doubleday.

———. 2005. "Recalling the Black Woman." In *The Black Woman: An Anthology*, edited by Toni Cade Bambara. New York: Washington Square Press.

Vertreace, Martha M. 1989. "Toni Cade Bambara: The Dance of Character and Community." In *American Women Writing Fiction: Memory, Identity, Family, Space*, edited by Mickey Pearlman. Lexington: University Press of Kentucky.

Wagner, Kelly. 2016. "Telling Run Away: Novel Testimony in Toni Cade Bambara's *Those Bones Are Not My Child*." *Studies in the Novel* 48, no. 2.

Walker, Alice. 1976. *Meridian*. New York: Harcourt Brace Jovanovich.

Williams, Dana. 2005. *In the Light of Likeness—Transformed: The Literary Art of Leon Forest*. Columbus: Ohio State University Press.

Williams, Delores S. 1995. "Sources of Black Female Spirituality: The Ways of 'the Old Folks' and Women Writers." In *My Soul is a Witness: African-American Women's Spirituality*, edited by Gloria Wade-Gayles, 187–91. Boston: Beacon Press.

Williams, Sherley Anne. 1994. "Some Implications of Womanist Theory." In *Within the Circle: An Anthology of African American Literary Criticism from the Harlem Renaissance to the Present*, edited by Angelyn Mitchell. Durham: Duke University Press.

Wright, Katy M. 2008. "The Role of Dialect Representation in Speaking from the Margins." *Style* 42, no. 1: 73–84.

Wright, Michelle. 2015. *The Physics of Blackness: Beyond the Middle Passage Epistemology*. Minneapolis: University of Minnesota Press.

Ya Salaam, Kalamu. 1980. "Searching for the Mother Tongue." *First World* 2, no. 4: 48–53.

INDEX

Wife" and, 110; *The Salt Eaters* and, 162

Black Panthers, 31, 34, 118, 119

"Black People Are My Business," choice of title, 2, 12–13

"Black people are my business." *See* people business

Black Power movement, 30, 84, 102, 109, 120, 143, 152, 165, 171, 188, 190

Black Studies, 3, 29, 195, 196

Black vernacular, 56, 163. *See also* dialect/dialectics

The Black Woman (anthology), 7, 11, 12, 20, 204n6, 206n22, 207n28; Bambara's mother contributing to, 24; critical reception of, 47–48; gender relations in Black community and, 165; impact of, 35, 48, 193; liberation and activism in, 118; relationship of *The Salt Eaters* to, 165; support for publication of, 28; Traylor's introduction to, 48; womanist theory in, 55, 210n6; women's oppression and, 33–34

Black women's literature, 4, 5, 7, 22, 164, 205n11, 206n20

Blassingame, John: "Africa, Slavery, and the Roots of Contemporary Black Culture" (with Berry), 151, 179, 211n8

The Bombing of Osage Avenue (documentary film), 41

Bonetti, Kay, 42, 211n10, 212n12

Bracey, Steven, 16; *SOS–Calling All Black People: A BAM Reader* (with Sanchez and Smethurst), 3

Brooks, Gwendolyn, 193

Brown, Lee, 174

Bryant, Natalie Margo, 204n7

business of the people. *See* people business

Butler-Evans, Elliot, 118, 212n1 (Conclusion)

Cade, Helen Brent-Henderson (Brehon) (mother), 22–24; "Looking Back," 24, 207n3; name of, 207n3

Cade, Walter, II (father), 22, 47, 207n3

Cade, Walter, III (brother), 22–23, 29

call and response, 51, 59, 107, 123, 124, 126, 161, 169, 177, 179, 181–82, 203n3

capitalism, 13, 15, 24, 74, 105, 116

Chandler, Zala, 153, 184–85

children. *See* contracts and covenants; youth and children

Christian, Barbara, 20, 28, 33, 195; *Black Feminist Criticism*, 50, 211n7

Christianity and Christian influences, 10, 151, 170, 194; African American Christianity embracing African cosmology, 183, 187; revivalist tradition and, 177, 186. *See also* Jesus; religion

church. *See* religion

civil rights movement, 29, 31, 33, 73, 114–15, 165, 169, 175, 184–85

classism, 46, 47, 96, 98, 99

Coleman, James, 157; "The Quest for Wholeness in Toni Morrison's *Tar Baby*," 156

colonialism, 38, 105, 209n22

communalism, 8, 70, 86, 109, 126, 181, 199

community: Bambara's commitment to and love for, 18, 86, 98, 118, 170, 181, 193, 196, 201, 213n4; Bambara's critique of,

ghetto stylizations, 53–54. *See also* dialect/dialectics

ghosts, 151–52, 157–58, 178–79

Giddings, Paula, 206n22

Giovanni, Nikki, 20, 33

goodness of individuals, 87, 88, 101, 118, 142–43, 179

Gorilla, My Love, 7, 11, 14, 23, 25, 28, 32, 46–96, 194; abandoning linear time in favor of future spacetime, 198; activism in, 48; Bambara's life experiences reflected in, 48–49, 96; Black feminism and, 52, 106; Blackness and, 52, 85, 87–88, 95; contracts with past and future generations in, 49, 50, 55–63, 75, 78; critical reception of, 35; cross-generational conflicts in, 83–90; following on from *The Black Woman*, 47; impact of, 147; liberation and, 46–47, 54–55; rejecting gender restrictions in, 33, 63–71; resistance in, 47–50, 52–54, 56, 63–64, 66–69, 71–81, 88; self-definition and redefinition of sexual borders in, 65, 85; transformation in, 49–50, 52–53; stories: "Gorilla, My Love," 7, 13, 35, 42, 49, 53, 90–96, 166; "The Hammer Man," 8, 25, 32, 42, 48, 59–60, 78–83, 119, 120; "Happy Birthday," 60–63, 84; "Johnson Girls," 57–60; "The Lesson," 7, 13, 26, 32, 42, 48, 71–78, 88, 196; "Mississippi Ham Rider," 25; "My Man Bovanne," 35, 53, 59, 83–90; "Playin with Punjab," 48; "Raymond's Run," 32, 35, 48, 53, 63–71, 82, 160;

"Sweet Town," 25, 55–57; "Talkin 'Bout Sonny," 79

"Gorilla, My Love," 7, 13, 35, 42

Gramsci, Antonio, 74

grassroots representation, 52, 87, 88, 153. *See also* community

Griffin, Farah Jasmine: "Toni Cade Bambara: Free to Be Any Where in the Universe," 192

guerilla consciousness training tactics, 73

Guinea-Bissau, 105

Guy-Sheftall, Beverly, 9, 98, 194, 210n1, 213n4

Hall, Stuart: "New Ethnicities," 120, 210n7

Hansberry, Lorraine, 193

Harlem, 22–23, 27, 47, 51, 208n6

Harlem Renaissance, 193

healing: of Black communities, 14, 16, 150, 152, 153, 155–60, 178–80, 183, 201; Black gospel and sermon offering, 170–71; both genders' responsibility for, 160; conflation of history and mythology in, 154; faith healing, 153; of family, 175–76, 186; in gender relationships, 103, 131, 150

heterogeneity, 120, 126, 210n7. *See also* pluralism

Hine, Darlene Clarke: "A Black Studies Manifesto," 195

historically Black colleges and universities (HBCU), 2, 204n5

holistic discourse, 3, 11, 128, 134, 135, 143, 147, 154, 159, 164, 171, 172, 182, 183, 197

Holmes, Linda Janet, 16, 33, 204n5; *A Joyous Revolt: Toni Cade Bambara, Writer and Activist,*

spiritual wholeness, 2, 5, 7; "The
    Apprentice" and, 117–18,
    123–24; Atlanta's promise as
    new day for Black America
    and, 173–74; Baraka and,
    102; Black femininity and,
    8, 9, 18; components of, 6,
    15, 21, 61, 100, 111, 178,
    192, 194; consequences of,
    105–6, 164–65, 196, 207n28;
    essential to reading Bambara's
    work, 13–14, 18, 45, 193,
    195, 200–201; four themes of
    African American religion
    as aesthetic for, 7, 160, 169,
    179, 189, 195; gender equality
    and politics and, 43, 199,
    202; healing and conjuring
    as conduits for, 158–59;
    heterogeneity and, 120, 126;
    individualism and, 124;
    liberation and, 2, 9, 16, 18,
    46–47, 87, 98, 121, 197, 199;
    male connection with, 124–25;
    metaphor of compost heap and,
    112–13; "On the Issue of Roles"
    and, 35; "The Organizer's
    Wife" and, 106, 110, 116;
    restructuring of feminism and
    Black Nationalism, 12, 96,
    201, 206n20, 206n22; *The Salt
    Eaters* and, 15, 147–50, 154–56,
    162–65; *The Sea Birds Are Still
    Alive* and, 10, 101, 103, 115; "A
    Tender Man" and, 132; *Those
    Bones Are Not My Child* and,
    178, 184–86; truth telling and,
    202; "Xmas Eve at Johnson's
    Drug Store" and, 139–45; youth
    and elders in Bambara's work
    and, 59, 61, 87, 90, 204n6
stasis, 5, 132, 135, 137, 138, 206n22

Stewart, James T., 7
Stewart, Maria, 10
Student Nonviolent Coordinating
    Committee (SNCC), 30, 34
suicide, 149–51, 154, 157

"the things behind the things," 19, 21,
    45, 49
Thorsson, Courtney, 13, 16, 200;
    Women's Work, 4–5
Those Bones Are Not My Child, 7, 11,
    16, 160, 166–91, 194, 196, 200;
    African roots, reattachment
    to, 149, 184, 190; African
    spirituality in, 169, 184–85;
    allegory in, 189; on Atlanta
    child murders, 40, 43–44,
    167–68, 173, 178, 209n28;
    Black church and religious
    philosophies in, 178, 187, 190;
    Black feminism in, 172, 182,
    190; Black Nationalism in,
    170, 182; call for activism in,
    48, 166–67, 181, 183, 188, 190,
    200; covenants with ancestors
    in, 16, 179, 188–89; failure to
    protect children in, 178, 184,
    187–88; family building in, 170,
    189, 190; gender equality in,
    182, 186; gospel music in, 165,
    181–84; healing of community
    in, 178–80, 183; healing of
    family in, 175–76, 186; inward
    reflection as path to truth and
    justice in, 153; liberation in,
    172, 178, 183–89; loss of faith
    and abandonment of history
    and traditions in, 16, 176–77;
    love in, 175, 186; mediums'
    role in, 179–81; narrator in,
    171–74, 180, 197; opening from
    Bambara's own journal notes,

Watts, Dan, 34

West, Dorothy, 193

White aesthetic, 205n13

White supremacy, 13, 173, 197; Anglo-Saxon tradition and, 28; correction of White-imposed social and cultural symbols, 205n13; eradication of, 8, 11; reaction to Black pride, 30–31

Williams, Shirley Anne, 213n4

Williams, Wayne, 40, 167, 168, 174

witches in African cosmology, 179, 211n8

womanhood: *The Sea Birds Are Still Alive* and, 98; "Xmas Eve at Johnson's Drug Store" and, 140–43. *See also* Black femininity

Womanism, 18, 20, 48, 207n28, 213n4; black womanism, 54

women: "bad woman" joining in "bad man" mythology, 135–37; Black church and, 184–85; in Black political movements, 185; as caretakers, 22, 120; civil rights struggle as part of women's equal rights struggle, 33; doing cultural work, 5, 13–14; marginality of Black women, 47, 199, 201, 206n22.

See also Black femininity; Black feminism; gender; male/female relationships

women's studies, 29

Women's Union, 36, 99–100

Wright, Michelle, 212n3 (Conclusion)

Wright, Richard, 112

Writers of the Black Chicago Renaissance, 4

writing networks, 39

Ya Salaam, Kalamu, 36, 45, 208n12, 210n4, 212n2 (Conclusion)

Yoruba beliefs, 141

youth and children: African adoration of, 87; Atlanta's failure to protect from serial child murders, 40, 43–44, 167–68, 178, 184, 187, 189–90, 209n28; "The Lesson" and, 48; protection needed by, 95; representing future possibilities, 32, 134, 173–74; spiritual wholeness and, 61, 116, 204n6; in struggle for liberation, 38; "Sweet Town" and, 55; transformation and renewal in stories of, 49. *See also* contracts and covenants; cross-generational alliances and conflicts

About the Author

Thabiti Lewis is professor of English and interim associate vice chancellor of academic affairs at Washington State University, Vancouver. He is also the editor of *Conversations with Toni Cade Bambara* and *Ballers of the New School: Race and Sports in America*. He writes about African American literature, masculinity, sports, and popular culture.

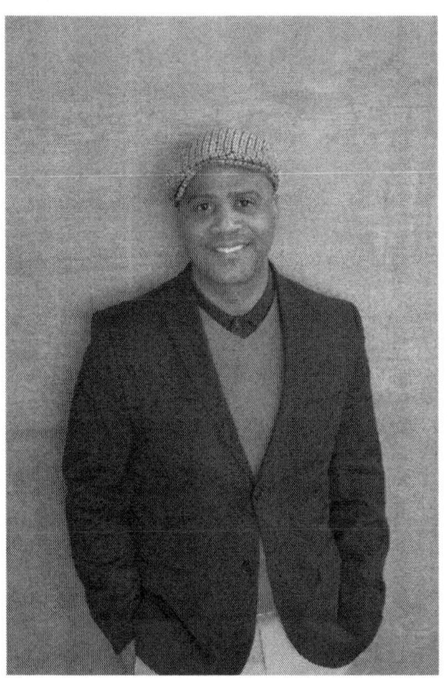